To Ken,

Around Ten Minutes After

Middle of the Kop

They Were Hot Off The Press

Best Wishes Bro

Peter Etherington

Published 2004 by the author, Peter Etherington.

British Library Cataloguing in Publication Data.
A Catalogue record for this book is available from the British Library.
ISBN 0 9548427 0 7

Printed by Flexipress, Ormskirk, Lancashire. L39 4QB

ACKNOWLEDGEMENTS

First and foremost, many ap-o-lo-gees for the delay in publication of this book. I had promised it for Christmas 2003. However, due to circumstances entirely beyond my control (as all the best excuses say) I had to stop writing for large chunks of 2003 and 2004. Never mind, here it is in all its power, pomp and glory. Thanks to everybody for being patient, sticking with me and pre-ordering what at one time looked likely not to happen.

Sales figures for both ONE BOY AND HIS KOP and MY YOUTH – MY KOP continue to be good so swelling the coffers of about 25 charities including the one that if not closest to the hearts of all Liverpudlians bloody well should be – the Hillsborough Justice Campaign. Thanks to all the good people involved in that campaign including Gerry, Sheila, Kenny, Robbie, John Mac and Peter at the shop for allowing me to sell my books there. For those who don't know, the new shop is situated right opposite the Albert and is a much smarter looking operation than the old place on Oakfield Road. Please pop in there before a match to say hello to the fine people I mentioned.

Gangs of tas to the editors of the various zines and message boards for their continuing support and encouragement. The likes of Peter Bromage, Dave White, Gareth, Bob Kurak, Gary Purvis, Tom Johnston, John Macken, John Pearman, Max Munton, Dave Usher and Administratos (only you know who you are) make selling this book so much easier

Big thanks but no hugs to Nicky Allt. Nicky kept me laughing and entertained in the summer of 2004 not only with his superb book, "Boys From The Mersey" but by actually coming to see me and sharing a few laughs. The writer's life can sometimes be a lonely, solitary one so it's good to get a friendly grid in your gaff sometimes. Thanks Tosh. Thanks also to another great Liverpool writer Dave Kirby for doing much the same as Nicky in the laughter stakes. If you haven't bought Nicky and Dave's book "Kop Stories" then do yourself a favour and buy it now. Look out also for Nicky and Dave's new play "Brick Up The Mersey Tunnels" coming to a theatre near you very soon.

I had the very greatest of pleasure this year, although it cost me an arm and a leg, in accompanying my eldest daughter up (or is it down?) the aisle and giving her hand in marriage. Thanks Evelyn for putting up with my moaning and groaning while I was trying to organise your nuptials and write this book at the same time. Thanks also to my other two wonderful children, Steven and Angela. Without my children this book wouldn't have happened.

To anybody I've left out who feel they should have been mentioned: I apologise but please, everybody who has bought any of my books I truly am very grateful and hope you enjoy reading them as much as I do writing them.

Evo.

~~~~~~~~~~~~~~~~~~~~~~~~~~~~
~~~~~~~~~~~~~~~~~~~~~~~~~~~~

This book is dedicated to Timmy and Jimmy.

Timmy and Jimmy were two Bootle lads and great Reds both taken to the Kop upstairs far too early.

TIMMY AND JIMMY YOU'LL NEVER WALK ALONE.

R.I.P.

CONTENTS

CHAPTER ONE

WIGAN WARRIORS

I was unfaithful to Big Ev in the Summer of '78. Well, nearly unfaithful. Deffo would have been if I could have got my hands (not to say my nether regions) on the object of my lust. I fell madly, hopelessly in love with a beautiful blonde. I was hopelessly devoted to her! Good job I could never get anywhere near her, never mind attain the pleasurable delights of her lissom young body. No, the nearest I would ever get to my new beloved was via the flickering cinema screen at the Focus in the Concourse. When she sang, "You're the one that I want!" I was convinced it was to me. No chance for me of course – John Travolta was boning her. No, come to think of it not even he was, although it was rumoured that Cliff had strayed from the path of the righteous and had a little dabble. Ah yeah, but they said that about Sue Barker too didn't they when I wanted to bone her a couple of years earlier? Chris Evert too had been the object of my lustful mid 70's. Considering I was married to the most beautiful dark haired lady in the world I did seem to have a penchant for blondes. But then again they have more fun don't they? Never did Rod the Mod any harm!

Come on Evo, stop waffling! Who is she?

Well surely if you're over the age of about ten you must know my carnal desires were being trained on Olivia Newton John (would have made a great half-back line) as the film "Grease" must be the most repeated film ever in the history of repeated films on television. I did love that film though. Strangely enough I hated the last ten minutes when Sandy Dee (ONJ to those still following this) turned from the lovely little innocent blonde girl into a leather clad raving sex siren. I tell yer, a psychiatrist would have a field day with me!

I'd just about finished pervin' at Olivia Neutron Bomb (it's not pervin'! A man admiring the attributes of a beautiful young lady is deffo not pervin'!), pity I couldn't have the tug I was dyin' for as Big Ev was watching Top of the Pops too, when it was time for a Thursday night out with the mates in the Derby Arms. I joined the merry all-star cast of Stu, Molly, Wooly and Ste already assembled in the Derby.

The other lads didn't join in my raucous rendition of Olly and Trav's number one hit preferring instead to warble the hits of the new punk sensations The Boomtown Rats. Sure, I was bang into the scruffy one's raunchy, unadulterated brand of rock but given a choice of getting a twinge over Olly and even thinking about Bob Geldof then the heavenly blonde won every time.

"Fancy goin' to Wigan lads?"

Ste's suggestion was met with great delight by the other lads even though it was now nearly closing time at the Derby. They'd all been thinking about it but nobody had yet had the bollocks to suggest it. I'd actually never been on a night out to Wigan. The nearest I'd been was when I'd been to Wigan market with Big Ev a couple of years previously and had a drink in Billy Boston's bar. There was though a very good reason why I'd never been and why I didn't fancy it on this occasion.

"Fuck that, we'll get fuckin' battered!"

I know I was a big shithouse, still am I suppose, but I'd heard too many horror stories of Skem lads going into Wigan for a night out and returning minus a few teeth, not to say broken noses. I'd had my conk bust too many times to be up for this. Sure, I didn't mind risking getting me hooter rearranged in the cause of LFC but not for a shitty night out in a shitty small town and then being set upon by shitty small-minded people. It wasn't that Wiganers hated Skem people in particular; they just hated everybody! Even Wiganers don't like Wiganers!

"Fuck off Evo yer shit'ouse, come on, let's go."

Wooly was speaking from a position of strength seeing as he was built like a brick shithouse.

"But it's fuckin' 'alf ten now! What time are we gonna get 'ome?"

"I don't fuckin' know, when the clubs shut I suppose; abarr two or three o'clock."

Stu had done this before and wasn't the slightest bit scared of his missus. I, through bitter experience on the other hand, was shit scared of mine should I get home at that time having had what was supposed to be after all just a few pints with my mates.

"Okay, 'ow are we gonna get there? Taxi?"

A reasonable assumption I thought seeing as the buses to Wigan had probably stopped running at this time.

"Fuck that! We'll rob a car."
That wasn't even a suggestion from Molly, it was a command!
"Yer fuckin' jokin' aren't yer? I'm the unluckiest bastard in the world; we're fuckin' bound to get caught!"
"Come on Evo yer big shit'ouse. We're wastin' valuable drinkin' time!"
"We're all fuckin' bladdered! Who's gonna drive?"
"I am!"
"Oh deep fuckin' joy Ste! You're the most bladdered of us all and the fuckin' maddest!"
"Ack, ack, ack, ack!"
That manic laugh meant there was no point in further objections to Ste. I was just gonna have to go along with it and resume my criminal career which had been put on hold for the past eight years or so.

"Ee arr, this one looks good."
"Nah, fuck that, it's only a Mark 2 Cortina!"
"What the fuck are yer goin' on about? I 'aven' got a fuckin' clue! A Mark 2 Cortina's no fuckin' different to a Mark 1 Jaguar as far as I'm concerned. If it gets yer from A to B that fuckin' does me!"
"Fuck off Evo yer Phyllosan!"
Molly meant a Philistine but he was always getting his worms muxed up so I knew what he meant.
"Come on, just let's get this fuckin' one and fuck off quick before we get sussed."
If I was gonna do this at all I liked Stu's suggestion best.
"Yer fuckin' tramp Stu! That's worse than the other fuckin' one! That's only a Mark 1!"
"Mark my arse! We're in. Come on, let's go an' crack a few woolybacks!"
Now robbin' a car was bad enough. Robbin' it when we were all pissed was worse. The certainty that we'd get caught compounded all that. Topping it all off though like a big dollop of Bird's Dream Topping on a load of blancmange was the fact that the loonies wanted to go and fight the Wiganers. As if we weren't gonna get enough ag off them! It was okay for them; they were all hard bastards. I was soft as shit with a nose to match so I was certain to get filled in and locked up. Not necessarily in that order!

So off we jolly well went in our little trundly Mark whatever whatsits.
"Right, let's get out 'ere!"
We were in the middle of Wigan right next to a high-rise block of flats. If we were gonna get filled in this is where it would happen. There were bound to be loads of lads hanging around here at this time of night looking for stray Scousers to crack.
"'Adn't we better 'ide it somewhere Ste so we can get 'ome in it?"
Ste looked at me like I'd just asked him had he ever shagged his Granny.
"Yer fuckin' knob'ead! No, are we fuck, we're gonna rob another one to get 'ome."
"Oh fuckin' marvellous! I'm just gonna go the cop shop now and give meself up. It might at least save me from a 'idin'!"
"Come on yer fuckin' girl, let's get back on the ale."
Four Wigan meat'eads approached us. This was it – kick off time! It was at times like this I was glad of Ste who was scared of no fucker.
"What the fuck d' you fuckin' lot want?"
"Nowt mert. We're just wertin' for taxi."
"Well there's yer fuckin' taxi. Now get in that and fuck off before yer get fuckin' 'urt!"
The meat'eads did as they were told, whether they wanted to or not, as the second lot of passengers in the stolen Mark thingy and headed for wherever they were heading for, probably some dark outpost of Wigan, with their wooly tales firmly clamped between their jellified legs.

The first club we hit, literally, was Tiffany's. Understandably at turned midnight on a Thursday night the place was not exactly jumping. A few shady looking Wiganers and assorted birds of varying states of ugliness were about to be invaded by five drunken Scousers up for a bit of anything that came their way. Things went okay for half-an-hour or so. The ale was flowing, everybody was having a laugh and I was strutting my stuff alone on the dance floor; not even the ugly ones would dance with me! Then it all kicked off. To be honest, it wasn't our fault. I mean, they call us Scousers thievin' bastards! A couple of Wiganers were attempting to exit the club with a couple of framed pictures off the wall, no doubt looking

to add these to their marvellous collection of Van Gogh's and Monet's.
"Eh yer fuckin' robbin' woolybacks twats! Put those fuckin pictures back!"
Now Ste wasn't the most conscientious of people and anywhere else wouldn't have given a fuck about a couple of pictures being lifted off a wall but a fight was a fight, especially with a couple of wools.
"Fuck off yer Scouse cunt!"
Wrong thing to say!
Ste flattened the two of them before you could say Peter Paul Ruebens.
"What the fuck's goin' on 'ere?"
The sole bouncer who was probably just supplementing his income from doing the door at Mothercare on a Saturday morning was looking not to sort this one out.
"Not us mate. This pair of robbin' twats we're tryin' to do a Hoffman with yer pictures!"
I was getting brave in my ale-induced sate and gave the errant art thieves a boot up the arse before the bouncer, aided by the rest of our motley crew, lashed the dastardly duo into the street.
"We'll be fuckin' back later with a team yer Scouse bastards!"
"What, the fuckin' Wigan rugby team? Ack, ack, ack, ack!"
"Yeah, fuck off yer fuckin' sheepshaggin' woolyback twats!"
Having saved the art collection of Tiffany's and surely bound to make the front page of the Sunday Mirror it was free ale for the five amigos for the next half-hour before we headed off for our next port of call.
"Let's go to 'Arry's."
Molly apparently knew this club quite well from previous dodgy dealings. 'Arry's actually turned out to be Aries but given that Molly was truly well pissed and that his worms were muxed right up his arse it wasn't a bad effort on his part. Aries went off quite peacefully. The nearest we came to a fight was when, sick of the world not getting the opportunity to revel in my dancing skills, I decided to share them with a girl (loosely speaking) just a shade prettier than a pig I'd seen on a school visit to a farm in Formby. Please bear with me while I digress. We were supposed to be going to the Formby pig farm to learn of how the country people lived and maybe to consider farming as a career. If the sight of the pigs didn't put you off then the smell of their two

shits a minute certainly would! "The fresh air will do you good!" Mr Breen, our Science teacher told us.
Err Mr Breen (the wankin' machine) we live in fuckin' Liverpool! The nearest place we're gonna get any fresh air is probably fuckin' Finland!
Anyway, back to the Wigan pig. In a certain light (the dark - "used that one before Evo." "I know but it's fuckin' good isn't it?") she looked a bit like ONJ. Well come on, I was pissed.
"You're the one that I want. The one I wanna die for, ooh, ooh, ooh!"
Oh fuckin' am I now baby. Right, 'ere I fuckin' come!
"I got tears they're multiplyin' and I'm losin' control, cos the power you're supplyin', it's electrifyin'!"
Who the fuck writes this shite?
"What the fuck d'yer think you're doin'? Go on, fuck off!"
"Oh fuckin' charmin'! Ee arr girl I was only tryin' to dance with yer!"
"Well, yer can fuck off! I'm not fuckin' easy yer know!"
"Ee arr I only wanna dance with yer I don't wanna fuckin' marry yer! I don't even wanna shag yer!"
"Fuck off, I'm not cheap!"
"I know, me mate over there said 'e's shagged yer and it cost him ten fuckin' bob!"
"As if I'd dance with you, yer fuckin' ugly fat bastard!"
"Fuck me, yer sound just like me missus! Which reminds me, the one I've got at 'ome is ten times the woman you are so fuckin' do one and go and get yer brother to shag yer!"
"Fuck off Friar Tuck!"
"Fuck off Miss Piggy!"
Had to have the last word didn't I!

The back streets of Wigan were no place to be at half-two in the morning much less looking for a car to rob around there.
"There's the Scouse bastards!"
The art thieves had caught up with us and brought a rugby team with them. Not the proper Wigan rugby team like but a shower of big bastards nonetheless. There was only one shithouse among us five intrepid lads. Guess which one. I was on my toes and halfway down a back jigger when I heard Wooly.
"Come on, stand an' fight."

Err, well, seein' as we're outnumbered two to one I'd rather run away (run away, run away!) if yer don't mind but I'll come back if yer insist. An' what's this fight? I can't fight anyway and trying to stand is beyond me after a dozen pints of Stella.

Our saviour was to be a daft Wiganer who thought Ste was an easy touch. As well as playing rugby it seemed the Wigan Art Collector's Society were also fans of hurling, hockey, shinty or some other of those daft sports played with a stick as they all had big fuck off pieces of wood in their hands. Never did get what people got out of twattin' a ball with a stick but each to their own I suppose. Back to the plot (if there ever was one): Daft Wiganer points at Ste and says to a fellow rugby/shinty player, "Mind 'im!"

"Mind me? Fuckin' mind this!"

Rugby/shinty man was spark out on the floor before the stick had even left his hand. Stu tried to demolish the rest of the Art Collectors by throwing a handily placed (for us) beer keg at them. Unfortunately Stu was not the best skittle player in the world. Instead of scoring a perfect strike of the ten sporting artists the keg only managed to crash with an enormous noise through the window of the Wigan Reporter office.

"Fuckin' leg it!"

Ah, now that's much more like it Molly!

There was actually no need to leg it as the big shower of pansies had shit themselves at the cheek of us twattin' them and throwing beer kegs at them and decided to go home to their sisters.

Was South-West Lancashire the graveyard for Mark 1 Cortinas in 1978? Certainly it was the exact same make of car (as If I knew or even cared) we robbed, from the block of flats we'd left the first one too, as the one that had got us to this God forsaken town in the first place. Had the lads from earlier on (seemed a million years ago now) accepted our invitation to use it as a taxi to deepest Winstanley and then actually brought it back in a previously unseen gesture of Scouse/Wigan goodwill? Who gave a shite anyway? I just wanted to get home. I was in fuckin' gangs of trouble with Big Ev as it was.

"Let's rob that ciggy shop."

Oh fuckin' great idea! As if robbin' two cars (or was it just the one?), twattin' wools and beer kegging the local Wigan paper's window

wasn't enough yer now wanna burgle, break and enter or whatever yer call it some poor fucker's (who's done no harm to us by the way) shop. Nah, fuck off, yer way outta order!
"Nah, we can't do that. Just let's fuckin' get 'ome!"
"Well ee arr Evo, you just keep Dixie. Stu, you keep the car revved ready to fuck off."
"Revved? That's a fuckin' laugh! I'd be better just putting me fuckin' feet through the floor and runnin' on the spot!"
"Fuck off Fred Frinton; just get it ready!"
We knew Molly meant Fred Flintstone.
"You two, shut the fuck up! We'll be in an' out with a loada ciggies in two minutes. We just rob the ciggies an' out. No 'arm done to anybody."
Except the poor fucker whose shop it is that is.
I really was genuinely concerned. We'd had a good run so far and not been caught. We'd had a couple of rucks and come out of them unscathed. It was more than a bit shady robbin' two cars (even if they were shite) but robbin' a shop was not only out of order and not good but went against everything I believed in i.e. things that people work hard for shouldn't be stolen from them. Not being moralistic – just telling it how it is, or how I feel it is.

I was properly shittin' meself in that stolen car keeping Dixie. Why did they call it that? Gotta find that out. I shit meself even more when I heard a scream which I recognised to be Ste's. Not that I'd ever heard Ste scream before (don't get the wrong idea) but you know what I mean.
"Come on! Let's fuckin' go!"
Blood was pissin' out of Ste's arm.
"What the fuck 'appened?"
"Soft arse slashed 'is fuckin' arm open tryin' to break the window with 'is bare 'and!"
"Just fuckin' drive Stu before I fill this cunt in!"
"Oh that's all we fuckin' need isn't it, fightin' between ourselves!"
A fight between Ste and Wooly would not have been a pretty sight!

Ner, ner, ner, ner! Yeah, yer've guessed it. Plod was on our tail. Fuckin' inevitable I suppose as I'd warned everybody all night but would they listen to me? Would they fuck! It was pointless trying to outrun them. We were fucked, well and truly! Plodcar pulled us into the side of the road and then proceeded to ask all the questions they knew the answers to. They must have had at least half-a-dozen reports about our shennanigans so knew full well that the stolen car they'd been following for a mile or so contained the Scouse miscreants.

"'Ow did yon mon cut 'is arm?"

"I was fightin' with some woolybacks and cut it on a glass in a club."

"Eh, less of the fuckin' woolybacks!"

Now there's a thought!

We were standing at the side of the road being questioned by these two uniformed plod who were about to call the meat wagon to take us in to the station. Not good!

"Come on Evo, do the Hoffman."

Stu could whisper across six fields

"Fuck off Stu, I can 'ardly stand up never mind run."

Like I was gonna make it across a big fuck off farmer's field leading to fuck knows where. I'd probably get shagged by a pig on the way across but then again I'd get the fresh air Mr. Breen (the wankin' machine) had always told me about. Any inkling of doing so was soon squashed though by big Plod.

"Tha' fuckin' moves anywhere from 'ere yon mon an' I'll shove fuckin' truncheon up th'arse!"

Well seein' as yer put it like that officer!

We were duly taken to Wigan bizzy shop, photographed, fingerprinted and lashed in separate cells to await interrogation by the C.I.D. I must have been the last to be questioned as I'd heard shouting and banging going on for about half-an-hour or so before two plain plod entered my cell. Ooh err missus! It was the classic good cop, bad cop scenario.

"Come on Peter. Just tell us everything and we'll get you off with a few things. Just tell us exactly what happened tonight."

"'Ow the fuck did yon shower of Scouse bastards get 'ere?"

We got the bus."

Smack!

"Yer lyin' twat. Tha' mates said tha' got a taxi."

"Oh that's right yeah, we did get a taxi."
Smack!
"What clubs 'as tha' bin to?"
"Arry's."
Smack!
"Tha' fuckin' knows it's not 'Arry's. It's Aries!"
Smack!
"Fuckin' 'ell then okay! Fuckin' Aries!"
Smack!
These smacks weren't hurting by the way. Soft arse who was crackin' me thought they did though as I was rolling all over the cell in fake pain. Did no harm to do that. Fact was, the snivelling little cunt who was slappin' me had the smallest hands ever in the memory of bizzies with small hands. Cunt! I'd been slapped harder by my Little Ev. As for Big Ev – fuckin' 'ell there was no contest! Which reminded me; if I was in deep shit here I was in even deeper shit when my beloved got hold of me.

Eventually Plod decided to charge us variously with stealing a motor vehicle, travelling as a passenger in a motor vehicle knowing or believing it to be stolen, travelling in a motor vehicle without insurance (like we were gonna go and seek insurance just before we robbed a car), criminal damage and burglary. I think they threw a few other things in too for good measure, just blaming things on us as it was convenient for them. There was a mountain of forensic evidence all over us including blood and glass. We were stripped of all our clothes which were then sent to the Forensic Science lab in Chorley. The nice policemen gave us blankets to wrap around us to preserve our modesty. Policemen were sent to our houses to inform our wives that we had been arrested and charged but were being bailed so they would need to come to Wigan police station with replacement clothes for us to travel home in. A full set remember as we had *everything* taken from us.

We breakfasted well at the Hotel Wigan Bizzy Shop on cardboard and rubber loosely disguised as toast and fried eggs.
"Right, tha' wives are 'ere. They've brought tha' clothes so once tha's dressed and got tha' charge papers tha' can fuck off 'ome."

A couple of minutes later a bizzy came into the cell and threw me a plassy bag. I wondered why he was pissin' 'imself laughin'. I soon found out!

"What the fuck?"

Ev, my darling beautiful Ev much as I loved her had, in her infinite wisdom, decided that a full set of replacement clothes consisted of a pair of skids and a pair of socks. That's it, socks and fuckin' undies! For fuck sake! I waddled out of the cell wrapped in the blanket. Mates and bizzies alike were all pissin' themselves at me.

"Look what she's fuckin' brought me!" I screamed as I whipped the blanket off me. I wouldn't mind but the skidunkers were of a particularly dodgy nylon variety bearing the legend something like, "Big Boy!"

I looked around at the other lads who were in various states of undress but nowhere near as bad as mine.

"She forgot me fuckin' shoes!"

Wooly was sock-clad.

"Mine forgot me fuckin' shirt!"

Molly was bare-chested.

No such problems though for Ste and Stu. Their birds had seen and done it all before so they were both kitted out fully.

"Look what she brought me! Skids an' fuckin' socks! Skids an' fuckin' socks! If my tart 'ad 'alf a fuckin' brain she'd be dangerous!"

That had everybody rolling around.

"There's an Oxfam shop round the corner. I'll go an' tell tha' wives to go an' get tha' some clothes."

"Fuckin' tell mine to get me a decent pair of grundies while she's there!"

Things went from bad to worse when the loony wives returned from their Oxfam shopping trip. Not for Wooly and Molly that is. No, they were kitted out in a pair of smart shoes and a boss shirt (well, bossish – about as boss as you can get from Oxfam) respectively. Bear in mind we hadn't seen our wives by this time by the way. They were in reception passing things through while we were still in the charge room waiting desperately to fuck off. The bizzy on the desk looked in my Oxfam bag, nearly fell off his chair laughing and then threw it to me. I took the bag back into the cell. Good reason for the laughing policeman.

"For fuck sake Ev, yer doin' me fuckin' 'ead in!"
I think they must have heard my screams in Marsh Lane police station never mind Wigan. Inside the bag was a pair of white pumps (and I do mean pumps, the sort me Ma used to get me for five bob from Brooksies when I was a kid and were expected to last me six months, not trainers), a shirt that was out of fashion in 1967 with the biggest fuckin' flyway collar you've ever seen and a pair of two-tone flares. I came out of the cell and back into the charge room looking like Coco the bastard Clown. That was too much for everybody. Bizzies and criminals alike united in uncontrolled mirth. The laughing policeman just about managed to officially give us our charge papers in between his peals of laughter. Now for the hard part – facing the women. No problem for Ste; his bird had fucked off as soon as she handed his clothes over. Not too much for Molly either; him and his bird went on the piss in Wigan. Wooly and Stu were getting the silent treatment off their birds but would no doubt get grief in spades when they got home despite their world-weary, "I've seen it all before" looks. Me? I was getting it with both fuckin' barrels!
"Yer fuckin' stupid twat! What the fuck are yer doin' gettin' into this trouble?
"Ev, I'll explain when we get 'ome, honest."
"Yer supposed to be a responsible married man with kids!"
Oh fuckin' sorry! Am I never to be allowed to make a mistake just because I'm married with kids?
"I know Ev. I was fuckin' stupid. Can yer leave me alone now 'til we get 'ome?"
"No, I fuckin' won't leave yer alone! What will yer Mam an' Dad think of yer?"
I got this every fuckin' bastard slow inch of the bus ride back to Skem. Wooly and Stu were both pissin' themselves at me but theirs was to come and they fuckin' knew it! Ste was the most raucous of all. He too would get shit but the difference was he just didn't give a fuck! This was all quite apart of course from the fact that I obviously hadn't turned in for work; a fact that would not be lost on Shift Supervisor Eddie Clarke who already had me on a final warning because of my absenteeism. In fact I was actually on my second final warning. I was the only person ever in the history of Grimwood's to hold such an "honour". The other Shift Supervisor Ted Eaton once told me that

I was worth my weight in gold (which would be a lot of fuckin' gold I tell you) when I was actually in work but I wasn't in often enough. The ten, jack, queen was inevitable as also was my dismissal from refereeing in the Skem League should Tommy Rogers get to hear about my misdemeanours. Who could blame any of them though eh? I had let down my wife and children but most of all I'd let down myself.

The final word (apart obviously from Big Ev who was gonna give me loads of words when she got me back in the house but only for that day; I would be getting the double whammy of grief for a day and the silent treatment, probably for a month) on this most horrendous night/day was left to Eddie Rocke. Eddie was going into the Derby Arms as me and Ev were getting off the bus there:
"Alright Pete. Goin' to a fancy dress party?"

CHAPTER TWO

GRASSES AND PASSES

Eddie was waiting for me at the clock when I turned in on Monday.
"Don't clock on Peter. Wait in my office."
Right, this is it; ten, jack, queen - see yer later. To be honest, because of the silently monastic weekend I'd had (Ev had even withdrew the old conjugal rights – she must have had a fuckin' big cob on) it would come as a blessed relief to get it over with, go home and tell Ev the news who would then surely fuck off and take the kids with her. Even the kids were a lot quieter than usual. Perhaps they sensed Dad had overstepped the mark properly this time. I'd have my refereeing badge taken off me for sure as people were bound to find out about the great Wigan incident once they heard I'd been sacked. The world was shit and I knew it. My own fuckin' fault though. What the fuck was I gonna do without a job? How was I gonna bring my kids up and support my beautiful family? Oh, I'd forgot, they were fuckin' off anyway. Marriage over, see the kids once every fuckin' cheesy moon. Tears weren't far from my eyes. With all this rollin' round my bonce I hadn't given a thought to making an excuse up to Eddie as to my whereabouts on Friday. Not that it fuckin' mattered; I was goin' anyway. Eddie left me stewing for half-an-hour while he did what Shift Supervisor's do at the start of shifts. Basically fuck all I suppose but they make it look good.
"Right then Peter, what happened on Friday?"
Fuckin' 'ell Evo lad, think fast. Make it a fuckin' good 'un too.
"I wasn't well Ed. I 'ad a really bad 'eadache."
Was that the fuckin' best I could come up with? Well what the fuck could you have come up with given the circs?
"Well what were you doin' in Wigan on Friday mornin'?"
Shit! Who the fuck from work saw me in Wigan?
"Ok then Ed, I'll tell yer the truth. Like fuck I will! I went to see a solicitor about a divorce."
This wasn't that far from the truth actually the way things were goin'.
"Okay then, what was yer wife doin' with yer?"
Shit! Whoever had clocked me had clocked me good and fuckin' proper! Twat! QUICK, FUCKIN' THINK YER STUPID FAT BASTARD!

"Well err, what it is err Ed is that yer both 'ave to go together at first to see err if yer can get back together err so there's err no need for a divorce. It's like an err pre-counsellin' err thing."

Where the fuck did THAT come from?

"Okay Peter. What d'yer want me to do? What are we gonna do with yer?"

Err, I suppose a pay rise is out of the question?

"I don' know Ed. I don' want the sack or anythin'"

"But yer already on two final warnin's Peter."

"I know Ed but I'll start getting' me act together I promise yer."

I actually fuckin' meant that too.

"Okay Peter but I don' wanna see yer in this office again, cos if I do it'll be the last time. Okay?"

Fuckin' 'ell I've fluked it!

"Thanks a lot Ed. I really appreciate it. Just tell me, who was it saw me in Wigan."

"Dicky."

I fuckin' knew it! Tricky fuckin' bastard cuntin' arse'ole Dicky ! Fuckin' Guy Fawkesed me again the twat! Done me like a fuckin' big kipper that's been well done! Why the fuck didn't 'e just leave me alone and let me get on with me fuckin' life? What the fuck was 'e doin' up on Friday mornin' anyway? 'E'd been on fuckin' nights on Thursday. Is 'e a fuckin' vampire or somethin? Yeah, 'e fuckin' is! Which reminds me; I must get a mallet and a wooden stake when I next go to Garner's.

"E's a case Dicky isn't 'e Ed."

"Yer could say that. Now get on the press and close the door after yer."

"Okay Ed, thanks mate."

"Peter."

"Yes Ed?"

"Don't call me mate."

"Okay mate.... I mean Ed!"

I finished my shift and debated with myself whether to go straight to the Cistercian monastery or call in at the Derby for a couple of pints on the way to continuing my monastic punishment. In enough trouble already; don't make it worse. In so much trouble it doesn't matter anyway. A rock and a hard place. Just as well in the end I chose the former.

Waiting for me on the table when I got to the abbey was a mountainous meal of sausage, peas, tomatoes and of course the ubiquitous chips; fuckin' big wagonloads of them too. All steaming hot as well. One of Ev's special meals meant one of two things - either I was in the biggest trouble in the history of big trouble or having been in trouble I was now absolved from all sins and was about to enjoy a sexual encounter as steamy as my dinner on the table. Trouble was, I never quite knew 'til it happened. I wanted it to be the latter obviously, not just because my hoover bag was about to burst but because I didn't wanna lose my darling wife. She could be a fuckin' nuisance at times but I truly did love her and I hated not talking to her. If I got away with it though it was surely gonna be my last chance. It was mad though; things I should have got royally fucked off for I got away with while I'd suffer badly and she'd disappear for days for the most innocuous "offence."
What was it to be?
Cue drum roll.
"What 'appened in work?"
"Got a bollockin'"
"I was expectin' yer 'ome early. Thought yer were gonna get sacked."
"Nah, I talked me way outta it."
"Ready for an early night?"
"Too fuckin' right!"
"So am I. 'Urry up and finish yer tea!"

"Awroit yoof. You're a ref aren't you m'duck."
Who the fuck's yoof? And why was this perm-haired fucker behind the bar in the Viking calling me a duck? Do I look like a fuckin' duck? Don't answer that! Cue Evo joke:
"Mam, there's a man at the door with a bill."
"Can't be. It must be a duck with an 'at on."
Coat!
Duckman, who sounded like, and looked not unlike with his mad perm, that Betty Turpin bint in Corry was waiting for an answer.
"Yeah, that's right mate, I am."

"I'm startin' a team up from 'ere. We've got a friendly on Sunday at Dunlop's. Do you wanna ref it?"
"Startin' a team up from 'ere? Fuckin' 'ell, you're a brave man aren't yer? Wouldn't like to go round collecting subs off this lot."
"You wanna fuckin' ref it or what?"
"Yeah, okay then. Keep yer fuckin' 'air on!"
"Right you are then m' duck. Ten o'clock at Dunny's field."
"What's yer name mate?"
"Dave Webster."
"Okay then Dave. Glad to meet yer. I'm Peter."
"I know m' duck; I've seen you reffin' at Blaguegate."
"Dave, I'll ref this game on one fuckin' condition."
"What's that m' duck?"
"Yer stop callin' me a fuckin' duck!"
"Owkay then m' duck."
"Who are yer playin'?"
"Roughwood."
"Roughwood from Kirkby?"
"Yeah."
"In a friendly?"
"Yeah. Why, what's the matter?"
"Teams from Kirkby don't play friendlies!"
"My lads can handle themselves don't worry!"
"Why, who yer got playin' for yer?"
"Joey Laycock, Geoff Barnett, Bobby Fury, John Humphreys, Steve Best, Jimmy Mahon, Billy Bins, Tommy Fallon, Bobby Currie. You know, all those lads."
"Fuckin' 'ell, why don't yer just give Shake'ands a game too and 'ave fuckin' done with it – cause a proper riot? Yer right though; your lads can 'andle themselves. That's not gonna be any friendly I can promise yer but yeah, I'll ref it. Yer gonna supply the shin pads?"
"Yeah m'duck. My team's fully kitted out."
"I don't mean for the players – I mean for me!"
"Fuck off m'duck, I've seen you reffin'; you give as good as you get!"
"I know. I'm shittin' meself 'alf the time but I can't let them see that. Where yer from Dave?"
"Derby."

"Ah, that explains everything!"
"Explains what?"
"Yer stupid fuckin' accent, yer mad perm and yer callin' me a fuckin' duck!"
"Fuck off, you're only jealous!"
He was right about me being jealous. Not about the accent like – that was shite – about the perm. I'd toyed with the idea for a while about having a Graeme Souness style perm but had decided against it on three counts: firstly it would cost too much – about seven squid; secondly I'd look a prize twat; thirdly and probably most importantly, I didn't really have enough hair left on my head to make into a perm. Evo – the baldiest perm'ead in Skem!
"Okay Dave, buy us a bevy now, it'll cost yer three squid on Sunday for me fee an' if yer call me a duck during the game I'll shove me whistle up yer arse!"

The game went off well. The trouble I'd expected from two such teams just didn't materialise. Two boss sides gave nor took no quarter and were slamming into each other like good 'uns but I think they were so shit scared of each other that it didn't kick off. The Viking won 1-0; quite a victory, even in a pre-season friendly as Roughwood were one of the best sides in Liverpool at the time. Highlight of that game was a pass I still remember to this day. The ball was knocked long out of defence to Steve Best who was around about the halfway line. Steve rose like an eagle, hovered in mid air and then passed, I swear to God passed, not flicked or glanced, the ball thirty yards out to Jimmy Mahon on the wing. A pass with his head! That is one of the most beautiful things I've ever seen on a football pitch. Sure, my mate Besty was a fuckin' loon but he couldn't half play football, which I suppose was true of most of that Viking side. Yeah, game went well, I got me three squid beer tokens and I didn't have to shove me whistle up Dave's arse! I got twelve more squid after that as I stayed on to ref another four games that day. Dunny's was the only pitch available in Skem to play pre-season friendlies so everybody turned up, without a ref of course, to get a game there. I didn't have to tout for business as everybody knew me and also knew that they would get their money's worth out of me in return for the beer tokens. Fifteen fuckin' squid! I was fuckin' loaded! I was fucked as well like but I'd have a boss time in the

Derby tonight. I was though burnt to a crisp as it was a murderously hot July day. No sane man would have spent seven-and-a-half hours sweating his bollocks off in that sun but I've never claimed to be sane! My head looked like an oversized big red beach ball and I had blisters not only on my feet but all over my undercarriage accompanied by massive nappy rash. Maybe Big Ev would ease my discomfort by rubbing in that zinc and castor oil shite she used for our Little Ev's bum. Nah, that was too kinky even for me! Cue Evo joke:
Bloke goes to prostitute:
"Ee arr, 'ere's a 'undred quid. Just go along with what I want yer to do."
"For a 'undred quid I'd do fuckin' anythin'!"
Bloke gets into the shower fully clothed.
"Right turn the shower on."
Prossy turns the shower on, thinking, "This one's a right fuckin' weirdo!"
Bloke's standing under the shower, "Ah, the rain, the rain! Leave the shower on an' bang on the wall with a bin lid."
Prossy, getting a bit concerned now, leaves the shower on and bangs on the wall with a bin lid.
"Ah, the thunder an' the rain! The thunder an' the rain! Leave the shower on, keep bangin' on the wall with a bin lid an' turn the light switch on and off!"
Prossy, shittin' 'erself now, leaves the shower on, keeps bangin' on the wall with a bin lid and turns the light switch on and off.
"Ah, the rain an' the thunder an' lightnin'! Ah, the rain an' the thunder an' the lightnin'!"
Prossy, sick of all this, says, "Ee arr soft arse, yer gonna shag me or what?"
Bloke says, "What, in this fuckin' weather? Yer think I'm a pervert or somethin'?"
Coat!
And no, it wasn't me!

"Where the fuck 'ave you been all day?"
Oh, I've been 'avin' a nice pleasant time at Buckingham Palace takin' tea with the Queen at a garden party in Buckingham Place Ev. 'Adn't I told yer I'd been invited? Oh, how remiss of me!
"I've been reffin'"

"'Til now? Yer left 'ere at nine o'clock this mornin' an' it's nearly seven o'clock now!"
Big Ev always could tell the time.
"Yeah, I reffed five games."
"Oh, at three quid a game that's fifteen quid isn't it?"
The beautiful one also knew her three times table!
"Err....yeah"
"Where is it then?"
Quick Peter, think on yer feet or she'll 'ave it off yer!
"Err....well...it *should* 'ave been fifteen squid but most of the tight twats fucked off without payin' me. Fuckin' mingebags!"
Big Ev wasn't soft and probably knew I was lyin' but as the dosh was secreted in my kit bag there was no way she'd find it. I'd take her the Derby Arms – that'd keep her sweet.
"Wanna come the Derby luv?"
"No, I'm gonna tidy the 'ouse."
Fuckin' 'ell, yer gonna tidy the 'ouse? Is the fuckin' Queen comin'?
"Okay luv. I'll go over there after I've 'ad a bath then. Some of me mates'll be over there."
"Not those fuckin' loons yer got into trouble in Wigan with?"
No luv, some other loons.
"Nah, these are sound Ev."
"Well don't be goin' to fuckin' Wigan then!"
Of course not my precious! Would I dare do such a thing? You can choose exactly where I go an' who I go with from now on
"I'll 'ave me dinner before I get a bath. Where is it?"
"In the oven. It's been there since three o'clock. It's burnt."
Oh, is me dinner burnt Ev? It's not is it? That is a surprise! 'Cos I've never 'ad a burnt dinner 'ave I?
"Ah, it doesn't matter luv. I'll eat it anyway; I'm 'Ank Marvin."
My beautiful darling wife for all her many qualities, not to mention her lovely looks, was no Cordon Bleu chef. She could do a lovely roast dinner when she'd a mind to but she wasn't joking about this one being burnt! Rock hard roasties as black as the night; charred, dry as a nun's minge, chicken; peas that could have been fired out of a cannon; a tree-like thing that slightly resembled cauliflower but could just as easily have been something from the garden that had blown in through the open kitchen window on to my plate and topping it all off Ev's speciality – black, and I mean *properly* black

cockroach gravy. Lovely grub! I ate it all though! Not to do so would have meant certain grief and probably pain. I wouldn't have cared anyway if Ev served me up dog shit on a plate – I would still have loved her. Besides, as I said – I was 'Ank.
"That was lovely Ev. It wasn't that burnt." Lying through my char blackened teeth
"Okay, go an' get yer bath and get out while I tidy up. An' don't be goin' to fuckin' Wigan!"
"I promise yer luv, I won't."
I did actually mean that promise too!

I met the aptly named Towers brothers, they were both about nine feet tall, Gary and Frankie in the Derby. Frankie's mate, Keith Braithwaite was there too. There have been many fine footballers played in Skem but few, if any, better than Keith. Keith had played football for some good pro and semi-pro clubs including Wigan Athletic and Northwich Victoria. I think Keith must have had his pro career cut short by injury as that was surely the only thing, with his massive talent, that would have stopped him. I was reffing a match once when Keith, playing for BOC, hit a ball full on the run, right on the meat, that screamed, I say screamed (do I sound like Fred Elliott? "No Evo – more like fuckin' Billy Elliott!) into the net and tore away the grips keeping the net in place. You might think I'm exaggerating but there were a lot of people watching that match who could confirm it. Stan Roughley, who must have watched a million games in Skem, still talks about it to this day. Keith used to tell a great story about when he was playing for Wigan in the old Northern Premier League. Wigan were playing Fleetwood. Playing out his days for Fleetwood after a good career at Everton and other clubs was none other than Sandy, yes good old "best own goal ever in the history of boss own goals" Sandy, Brown. Now Keith as well as being a great bloke and boss footballer was also king of the wind-up merchants. Sandy, for once actually connecting with something with his boot other than fresh air, was kicking lumps out of Keith. To rattle Sandy off his game Keith decided to wind him up. Wigan had a corner that was about to be aimed at Keith's head.
"I'll leave this one Sandy. You just head it in mate."
Sandy then proceeded to chase Keith all over the park causing a two minutes stoppage in the game. The wind-up worked though as Sandy

completely lost the plot, Keith scored and Wigan won the game. Used to crease me to fuck that tale. Keith's been in New Zealand for years now coaching in the NZ equivalent of the FA Premier League and I think even had a stint with the national team. Good Luck to him – he's a great lad.

Even though I was completely Stellatised when I returned home from the Derby It had failed to dull the pain of my face and head being on fire. I was also sore as fuck in the undercarriage region. I did what any grown man would have done in the circs – moaned about it. I think I even had a little cry too! Fuck all wrong with a grown man crying if he's in pain. Ev was in bed but awake.
"Why are yer walkin' like John Wayne?"
The hell I am!
"Because of this!"
I took off my kecks and grundifications, lay flat at the bottom of the bed, spread my legs wide and hoisted them up into the air. My arse looked like the beginning of Bonanza!
"Oohhh, that's 'orrible!"
Oh thanks for yer fuckin' sympathetic concern!
"I know. It's sore as fuck Ev. Any chance of yer rubbin' some of our Little Ev's zinc and castor oil into it?"
"Fuck off yer perv! 'Ere, rub this calamine lotion into yer 'ead and put this talc on yer arse, yer should be alright in the mornin'. Now get asleep, yer've got work in the mornin'."
Oh thanks so very fuckin' much for remindin' me!
"Okay, ta Ev. I suppose just a quick tug's outta the question?"
"Go asleep."

Ev was right about the calamine and talc though. I would have preferred the rubbing of the zinc and castor oil but things were a lot less fiery top and bottom the next morning. I looked like a big fuckin' pink and white blob like but at least I wasn't in as much pain. Calamine and talc – remember where yer 'eard it first!

Brougham Terrace sounds as if it should be a footy ground doesn't it? Possibly one in some far-flung outpost of Scotland with a capacity of about 2,000 and an average crowd of 18 plus 2 dogs. It was in fact the scene of the latest Evo wedding – the local registry office. After two years of trying to hook our John, Janet had finally landed the big fish. They had paid due deference to my wishes though and decided they would get married before the footy season started. Nice one! Star of the show though was our little Price. Just turned 11 and the most mischievous little bag of tricks you've ever met. Not that the uproar caused during the nuptials was entirely his fault though. The registrar doing the ceremony had this big, booming dead posh voice that was sending most of the assembled congregation into fits of barely controlled laughter anyway. Our John just couldn't help but send the whole thing up. As the registrar asked John to repeat after him the wedding vows John did so in a perfectly mimicked voice. The registrar shit himself and couldn't believe this bloke he was marrying (you know what I mean) was taking the piss out of such a solemn ceremony. Price had the giggles and nothing was going to stop him. As the registrar battled valiantly to get the service done John took the piss and Price giggled even more. Ma was giving John Lily Eyes but John I suppose was getting his own back for years of being tortured by those burning eyes and was taking absolutely no fuckin' notice! Ma was sitting next to Price and had cracked him over the head about half-a-dozen times. Now when me Ma cracked you, you stayed cracked! This wasn't stopping Price though who was made up to be the centre of attention.

"Take that little boy out now!"

I almost felt sorry for the registrar. He did the only thing he possibly could in the circs and stopped the service. Had this been a ploy by John to get out of the whole thing? If so he wasn't getting away from Janet's big hook that easily! The service restarted with John paying due respect to the wedding vows and Price in the corridor outside, his peals of laughter still very audible in the wedding room, or whatever it is you call it.

In the Evo way of doing weddings there was no grand reception, just a few sarnies and a bevy back at John and Janet's flat and then over to their local, The Turtle in Netherley. Now there was rough and rough but this gaff was fuckin' rough! John had ingratiated himself with the locals though so there was no ag. I fell in love (in a non-physical sort of way) with Janet's Dad. Eddie, or Gamer as everybody, including I think Janet's Mum, called him was a smashing little fella who deffo liked a drink!

"Me and Bobby Magee."
Gamer sang that song virtually non-stop and I couldn't get it out of my head for weeks. I'd never heard it before and I've never heard it since except for the odd occasion when I've had a bevy with Gamer again but that song is as much stuck in my brain as You'll Never Walk Alone.

It was back to John's to finish off the wedding day in the typical Evo style: beer, sarnies and dancing. It was though fairly difficult to boogie to our John's record collection. John Travolta wouldn't have got within a million miles of our John's stylus so it was boogie time to Bob Dylan, Leonard Cohen, John Lennon and Bob Marley. Still, it was a great day. It was good to see my kid bro so happy and settled. We'd had so many rucks when we were kids, the great programmes/bike battle of 1967 being particularly nasty (although it's funny to look back on) that to see us both settled down, me with a couple of kids and John surely ready to add a few more Evo's in the fullness of time, must have done Ma's heart good. Not that Ma appreciated it on the day mind as she was absolutely bladdered. There are still people in Netherley receiving counselling for the traumatic effects of seeing Lily's pink bloomers during another stirring rendition of Lily The Pink. Good on yer Ma! Pinking it in heaven. Love you.

CHAPTER THREE

ARGIES AND BARGIES

Come on Evo, where's the footy!
Okay. Take it fuckin' Nelson! It's comin' now!

The season started with a home game against QPR. Making his debut for us was Alan Kennedy. Alan had signed for us from Newcastle United in the close-season. In the Joey Jones mould of "run through two brick walls for yer" Alan would affectionately be known forever more as "Barney Rubble." He actually looked not unlike Fred Flintstone's mate. The Geordie public had obviously not cottoned on to that fact as when we sang, "Barney Rubble" Alan and his team-mates were doubled over laughing. Joey was still at the club but with Barney in as his replacement the mad one's days were numbered. Barney wasn't exactly sane either. When a barnstorming run by Barney down the left wing ended up with him falling over, Alan Hansen looked to the skies in dismay as we sang, "Oh Joey Joey. Joey, Joey, Joey, Joey, Joey Jones!"
This wasn't meant as we wanted Joey back in the team, just likening Barney to his slightly madder predecessor. As in the previous season Kenny scored our first goal of the League season. Bobby McGee...I mean Paul McGee (fuck off Gamer) equalised. Steve Heighway scored the winning goal to set us off to a good start. We'd played okay but had given no indication then of the greatness to come that season.

A midweek trip to Ipswich with the consequent two days off work required was out of the question for me which was a great pity as we demolished the FA Cup holders 3-0. This was much more like it! I would have been looking forward to going to the away game the following Saturday but for the fact it was against......Manchester City. Oh, fuckin' 'ell no! Do I 'ave to go through all fuckin' that again? Well, I didn't have to but I wanted to go. When I got on the train at UpHolland it was already chocker with loads of scalls who'd got on at Kirkby. Happy Days. I'd stick with these so should be okay. That was 'til they started talking about going "shopping" in Manchester. Err...no thanks, not for me. Awaiting trial for my part

in the great Wigan incident a few weeks earlier I could do without anything else to confirm my custodial sentence thankyou very much. I'd become quite familiar with the trip from Aytoun Street to Maine Road now so was able to blend in with the City lads without being sussed. Once in the Parkway though it was all Liverpool.
The talk in the Parkway was not so much about the forthcoming afternoon's game (that was going to be a piece of piss) but more about the draw for the first round of the European Cup. The draw, somewhat unkindly, had not pitted us against the usual minnows we drew at that early stage but against last season's Football League Champions Nottingham Forest. Forest had been unseeded in the draw due to the fact that the last time they'd played in Europe was when Robin Hood went over on a longship selling bows and arrows to the Froggies. Brian Clough had indeed assembled a fine side and it was going to be very tough over two legs against them. I still hadn't got over the trauma of the eventually two-legged League Cup Final against them the previous season. Still, we'd beaten better sides than Forest over the years. We cogitated on the possible ticket allocation for the away leg, which would be played first, and sort of settled on the fact we'd have to be content with about 6,000 tickets when we would probably have taken twice that many.

Ah, bollocks to all that anyway! One game at a time – the Liverpool way. I was once again in the Platt Lane stand behind the goal. I would have felt sorry for our loons having a right old battle heading the usual array of Moss Side bricks, bottles and iron bars if I thought they weren't enjoying it! It was mental watching it as the loons were actually waving to us in that double-armed way that had become commonplace between the Road End and Kopites as, at the same time, they were battling like fuck with the City lads. Why did the Road End sing, "Kopites are gobshites" and then wave to us after it? Did they like us or hate us? I was a confirmed Kopite – loved it in there but I would have loved to have gone in the Anny. Couldn't be goin' in the Road End though could I with all those loons when I was a well-respected local referee and husband and father to boot? Mind you, if things went against me, as I expected them to, in court over the Wigan fiasco then I'd be sent down and it wouldn't matter a fuckin' jot then when I got out whether I went in the Anny or the fuckin' Directors Box!

FUCKIN' 'ELL EVO – YER DON'T 'ALF DIGRESS!
I KNOW. FUCKIN' LEAVE ME ALONE ANWAY! IT'S MY FUCKIN' STORY AND I'LL DIGRESS AS MUCH AS I WANT!
"Oh, I went to Man United with a shotgun on my knee. We went to take the Scoreboard for the famous LFC. We are the Road End, the Pride of Merseyside! We do all the fightin' while the Kopites run and 'ide!"
Wasn't strictly true of course as there were plenty of Kopites always ready for a good old ding-dong should it come their way but the Road End weren't having that. Anyway, why let the truth get in the way of a good story? Did Everton's Park End boys sing the same sort of thing to their Gwladys (that's how you spell it Evertonians) Street counterparts? I don't know nor really care. The Road End were a law unto themselves.
"Oh we're the barmy Anny Road army na na na na na na!"
"We are the Kopites, we all went to Rome! We all went to West 'am while the Road End stayed at 'ome!"
Again, truth and good story spring to mind. Quite proud of the fact I made that one up myself many years later. Not that I went to Rome or West Ham mind. Read all about it in MYMK if you haven't already.
"We are the barmy Anny Road army, you make me 'appy when skies are grey. You'll never know just how much I love you so don't you take my Road End away."
The Road End would never have made Poet Laureates but I wasn't gonna tell them that!

Out on the pitch, away from all the fighting, singing and arm waving, Souness, Kennedy (R and A), Dalglish and co were doin' the biz and how! We won 4-1, taking sweet revenge for the abysmal defeat there the previous season. Where was that fuckin' cow with her bell now? Liverpool players and fans alike were loving it but it was okay for those actually out on the pitch wasn't it? After the game they'd have a nice shower, a bevy in the players bar, maybe sign a couple of autographs and then be escorted the fuck out of there on a boss luxury coach. Piece of piss that. Us? Run the fuckin' gauntlet again mate and pray you got home in one piece!

Did well so far in actually getting to Princess Road and mingling in

with the City loons waiting to get a bus back to Victoria. Doing okay that was until I heard a familiar voice. A voice I hadn't heard for years but still familiar nonetheless. How could I forget it?
"Alright Peter. "Ow yer doin? Great that wasn't it?"
Joey M was a Scouser and didn't give a fuck who knew it. That was okay for him. He had a knack of attracting trouble but then getting out of the way before it actually went off big time; after nearly pooin' his pants of course.
Oh no! Joey, nice to see yer again after all these years but why don't yer just fuck off and leave me alone! Every bastard season I come 'ere and nearly end up getting fucked every time. Today, you're gonna make sure it goes off and then disappear while I get a fuckin' good kickin' aren't yer? Today is the day Joey that I finally get the shit kicked out of me good and fuckin' proper at Man City. Oh fuckin' thanks Joey for bastard nothin'!
"Joey, fuckin' shut up will yer! We're gonna get fuckin' killed!" I managed to mumble under my breath between clenched teeth and equally clenched arse cheeks. Not easy that you know!
"Nah, we won't. It'll be okay."
"It fuckin' won't! Fuckin' look at them; they're all fuckin' loons!"
Clench, clench!
The bus arrived before the City lads got on to us. Joey was bound to ask the driver how much the fare was and then carry on a conversation with him. I was gonna have to pay his fare to get him outta the fuckin' way.
"I'll get yours Joey."
Clench, mumble, clench!
Don't get me wrong; Joey was a boss lad. I'd had many fine awaydays with him in the late sixties and early seventies but he was gonna get me fucked here. He continued his rabbit on the bus. The City lads must have been distracted talking about their battle plans for Victoria as they never got on to him. They must have wondered though why one bloke was talking to another bloke who was just totally fuckin' ignoring him! We were nearing Victoria when we passed our lads being escorted by the bizzies. What a mob! Even the City lads were impressed. Some foolhardies (are they related to Oliver Hardy and is he related to Imre Varadi?) wanted to jump off and have it but were persuaded by their mates that this perhaps wouldn't be such a good idea as there were probably 2,000 bona fide

(certificates to prove it) lunatics in that escort. I gave it half a think of jumping off the bus myself to join our mob and leave Joey to it, he would have fuckin' gabbed the City lads to death, but knowing my luck I would got battered by my own kind thinking I was City. When the bus got to Victoria the City lads just fucked off, probably put off by the size and stature of our mob. It was indeed a very impressive site. I bade my farewells and a promised lie to keep in touch, arse cheeks and teeth now unclenched, to Joey as he went for his train to Limey while I was to make my little old happy way to The Up of Holland and a celebratory bevy. Once again at City I'd got away with it. No fuckin' thanks to Joey though!

We went out of the League Cup at the first hurdle at Third Division Sheffield United. How mad was that after the start to the season we'd had?

Tottenham were up next. The Lillywhites had started their first season back in Division One with a 1-1 draw at Forest in a game refereed by a mate of mine – Ray Guy from Kirkby. They had still yet to win a game though even with the two Argentinian World Cup Winners, Ossie Ardiles and Ricky Villa, in their team as they'd lost at and drew at home to Aston Villa and Chelsea respectively. No thoughts of anything other than a resounding victory in this one and so it proved. What followed was what many believe to be Liverpool's greatest ever performance; certainly most people agree that one of the goals is the best ever scored at Anfield, and we've had some crackers!

Tottenham had brought a large loony following. I'd had first hand experience of them the previous season when I'd gone with a mate Mick Robins to watch Bolton's FA Cup replay against them. Mick's Dad, also Mick, was a Bolton fan and as I had fuck all else to do decided to tag along with them. Spurs fans were loons that night and no less so on this brilliantly sunny September day. It was all the bizzies could do to contain them outside the Anny as they tried to storm the gates. A ref in the Skem League, Tommy Clough, was a bizzy on duty at Anfield that day and got quite badly hurt in the mayhem. That was before the game! They weren't gonna be too happy once it started. The Road End lads weren't letting them have things all their own way though. Blackbeard must have been a busy (no pun intended) man that day!

Tottenham were pummelled and hopelessly outclassed from the first minute. Even the early loss through injury of Emlyn which caused a major reshuffle, I think we moved one player, bringing on Davey Johnno couldn't put us out of our stride. We were 3-0 up at half-time; Kenny netting two and Kennedy (R) the other. Kicking into the Anny in the second half we just carried on as the first half. With 15 minutes to go we were 6-0 up; Supersub Johnno had chipped in with two goals while Zico Neal had slotted with his usual aplomb from the penalty spot. Pity Phil couldn't play balls up the line in the same manner. He always seemed to find the same fella in the Kemlyn every game with those "up the line" balls. Then came the coup de grace; what I feel is the best goal I've ever seen at Anfield – maybe of all time. Spurs won what I think was their first corner of the match. The ball broke to Kenny, back helping out in defence, on the edge of our penalty area. Terry Mac started running. Kenny played nothing more than a two yard pass to Johnno. Johnno hit a magnificent 40 yard pass out to Stevie Heighway steaming along the left wing. Johnno, with commendable modesty, claims that he mishit the pass. Well, if he did it's the best misplaced pass, possibly even the best pass I've ever seen. Certainly the best pass Johnno had ever hit. Passing was not big on Johnno's quality list. It wasn't big on his "must do" list either as he was a bit of a greedy bastard when he had the ball. Johnno would either dribble the ball 'til he ran into a blind alley or shoot; didn't matter what the distance was. Anyway, on this ocassion the ball was placed perfectly just a few yards ahead of our Beep-Beep. Stevie, running at speed banged the ball towards the far post as soon as he reached it; no touch, no having to bring the ball under control. Steve knew exactly where the ball was going and who it was going to. Terry Mac's run from well inside his own penalty area had taken him the 80 odd yards or so to well inside the Spurs penalty area. The speed on the ball from Steve's cross made it perfect for Terry to bullet it with his head and into the Anny Road net for the most gloriously simple but brilliant goal ever. The goal was made up of no more than a short pass, two well hit first time long passes and a header but what a goal! Normally, a goal to put a team 7-0 up would be seen as just the icing on a particularly delicious cake; polite handshakes all round and maybe a hint of celebration on the terraces. Such was the quality of this goal though the place, players and fans alike, went fuckin' mental! Everybody present knew they had been privileged to witness something truly special.

I went to Birmingham on my "Billy no mates" special aboard Crown. I normally knew somebody or would get talking but this time was a quiet trip. A nice quiet entrance into the Tilton End too gave no hint whatsoever of the mayhem that would ensue inside the ground. "There's only one Tilton army!"
To the tune of Guantanamera – never heard a footy song put to that tune before. Sounded good though. Or would have sounded good if about 5,000 loons hadn't been singing it. Then came the bricks. I've no idea where the Brummie loons got their ammunition, a building site outside the ground maybe or perhaps the concrete slabs came from their own crumbling terraces but whatever, there was enough masonry flying around to comfortably build two houses. Of course we didn't keep what was being hurled at us to ourselves. They went back and with some interest. There were some terrible scenes. Fans from both sides of the fence but mainly ours were being led or carried out with horrific facial and head injuries. One lad, I'm not sure from which side, was being led away, arm up his back but blood pouring from his face, wearing a T-shirt bearing the legend, "Who coshed the driver?" This was a reference to a song by the Sex Pistols in praise of Great Train Robber Ronnie Biggs who had teamed up with the Pistols to make a record. Sick maybe? Of course it was but the sight of that lad being led away wearing that T-shirt was surreal indeed. Bricks, bottles, concrete (and the clay beneath my feet begin to crumble – Unit Four Plus 2 – No. 1 1965), stones and pebbles were going back and forth like mad. This all continued unabated even after the match started. The official police policy seemed to be to panic and just lob out as many people as possible to try stop it. There must have been near 100 people either taken out injured or thrown out but whatever, the police policy didn't work. The Anny Road darts team were out in force too; not sure though whether they scored the double top this time. It was horrible to be amongst all this though. This was possibly the most frightening hooligan experience I'd had so far. It really was life threatening. One of those bricks could easily have killed somebody. I think it was a minor miracle that nobody was

killed that day. Certainly there must have been people who came close to losing an eye. A brick hit me on the foot but I had my work steelies on so it didn't hurt ner ner ner ner ner! The next fuckin' one did! A fleton (knowledgeable about these things you see) thudded into my fingernail as I was holding on to a crush barrier. Hurt like fuck that did but was preferable to getting my bonce bricked. The match? Oh yeah the match! Well it seemed almost an irrelevance seeing as it could only be glimpsed in snatches in between looking out for where the next house brick was coming from. From the brief snatches I was able to get it seemed we were playing very well seeing as we won 3-0. I did though manage to get a very good view of the third goal – Barney's first for the club. The mad one must have been taught goal celebrations by Emlyn Hughes as he came racing over to us in the way that Emlyn did. Now this was all very well if we were at home or playing somebody like Derby away; you could celebrate like mad with Emlyn, or in this case Barney, and not worry about being killed by opposing fans. Barney's actions though only seemed to increase the Brummies desire to throw more houses at us.
"Fuck off Barney will yer, yer soft twat! Yer gonna get us all fuckin' killed!"
I don't think Barney gave a fuck though. If the Brummies had thrown a brick at him he would probably have just headed it straight back in amongst them and probably twatted one of them on the head with it too!
"There's only one Barney Rubble!"
We knew the Sandpipers song too!

After the Battle of St. Andrews the trip to Nottingham for the European Cup match would be a doddle. Not that the Forest hordes weren't capable of giving us a hard time. I had experience of that and still bore the scar of being twatted on the head with a light bulb there eight years earlier. Apart from a few minor skirmishes around the ground and a few objects (but no light bulbs) being lobbed in our direction in the ground things weren't going too badly off the pitch. On it was a different story. Forest had taken an early lead given to them by their young, raw centre-forward Gary Birtles. Birtles had been playing for somebody like Long Eaton a few months earlier and looked nothing like a First Division striker should. He was bloody effective though and took his goal well. Forest fans had caught on to

the Sandpipers tune too:
"There's only one Gary Birtles!"
That tune would very soon become part of every football club's fans songs to this day. It sounds great if the player you're singing about has a total of four syllables in his name but shite if you try to sing it about a player with more or less syllables than that. We didn't sing if for ages, preferring to stick to our own traditional songs rather than the mainstream terrace songs being churned out by every other cub's fans, and then totally fucked it when we did. Who can ever forget how shite this sounded:
"There's only one Paul Waaalsh!"
See, you can't put a syllable where a syllable won't go!
EVO, SHOVE YER DIGRESSION UP YER ARSE!
OKAY!
We remained one goal down 'til there were only about five minutes left to play. Some knob'ead then decided that we should remind Forest that a one-goal lead wouldn't really be sufficient for them to take to Anfield. Cue Boney M:
BONEY WHO EVO? THIS MORE OF YOUR DIGRESSION?
Well yeah I suppose it is. Boney M were a shite German group who, much because they were shite and German, had great success in the UK charts. They had released (or did it escape?) a song called Rivers of Babylon. The words German, shite and pop spring immediately to mind but it sold fuckin' loads of copies. So, having got that song to be bought by enough of the gullible great British record-buying public to reach No. 1 Boney M's record label Atlantic/Hansa decided, "Nah, we were only messin'. Rivers of Babylon wasn't really the A side. This is the A side! Brown Girl In The Ring."
Right on cue the aforementioned gullible great British record-buying public left their homes in their droves to go out and buy it, even though I suspect many of them had the fuckin' thing already! So it was that Brown Girl In The Ring by the shite German pop group Boney M became part of football terrace culture. I much preferred the words,"We're gonna win the League tra la la la la!" to what aforementioned knob'ead (remember him) chose that night at Forest:
"One goal's not enough tra la la la la!"
Oh well thanks very fuckin' much you knob'ead and all those joining in with you. Let's just fuckin' remind them of that fact shall we?

LET'S MAKE THEM GO ALL OUT FOR A SECOND GOAL SHALL WE?
Sure enough, Forest, and remember they were a very good side, got steamed up enough about this to throw everybody forward in search of the second goal that might well be enough to take back to Anfield. Sure fuckin' enough also they got it. Full-back, yes fuckin' full-back, that's how desperate they were to get that second goal after being reminded of the fact they needed it, Colin Barrett volleyed home a truly great goal to give Forest the cushion that would probably be enough. Fuckin' thanks lads! Fair do's to the Forest fans, they threw our song straight back at us:
"Two goals are enough tra la la la la!"
TWATS!

CHAPTER FOUR

THE TALE OF THE HAGGIS

We continued our 100% start to the season with a 1-0 home win over Coventry in front of another 50,000 crowd.

"Errrrr……fancy goin' to West Brom tomorrow Peter?"
"Would do Baz but I'm Bernie Flint."
"Errrr…so am I. We'll thumb it."
I quite fancied the idea. Hadn't used the thumb method to get to an otherwise unobtainable away for a couple of years so yeah, looked a goer.
"Yeah, why not. Giz a knock about 9 o'clock."
I'd been to a few matches with Baz and always enjoyed it. As well as being a boss laugh I could buzz off him and his mad sayings.

After struggling at first with a couple of short lifts we copped for one with a Cockney truck driver. Only problem was this bloke was a fuckin' screwball and a racist screwball to boot. He spouted his racist bile for the hour or so we were in the truck with him. Baz wasn't having any of his lunatic views and was arguing vehemently, as only Baz could, with the loon.
Baz, shut the fuck up will yer, we need the lift! Just agree with the soft twat 'til we get out the truck, then yer can tell 'im to fuck off.
Not that I disagreed with Baz giving the twat loads, of course I didn't. I just wanted to make sure we got to the promised service station, I think Hilton Park, Tommy Trucker was taking us to. Having got to our destination Baz told him exactly what he though of the arse'ole's mad views. We needed just one more good lift to get us to the Hawthorns. We got it from the Shrewsbury branch of the Supporters Club. Baz wasn't too keen on the growing out of town infiltration of our support but we gratefully accepted their offer of the lift. Good lads they were too. I know a few Reds now from around that neck of the woods. Not sure if any of them were on the coach that day but if they were – nice one lads.

"We're not fuckin' payin' to get in!"

"I've got no fuckin' intention of payin' Baz. It was a piece of piss bunkin' in last season. Can't see it bein' any different this time. Ee arr, come on. This is the turnstile I got in last season. Let's go for it."

I'm not sure if it was the same turnstile operator as the previous season or whether the operator this time just couldn't be arsed chasing us but the two of us were under the turnstile and up on to the terrace in much the same way as I had the previous season before you could say false teeth.

Why false teeth Evo?

Well, Baz had been in a fight at the ODVA club in Bootle some years previously, I think over footy. Apparently, as Baz told the story, he'd been bottled in the grid, resulting in him losing his two front teeth. Now Baz didn't like people knowing about these teeth, in fact I felt quite privileged to have been let in on his dark "secret." The fact that the rest of his pearly-whites were his pride and joy made him even more self-conscious about his two replica gnashers. Anyway, with twenty minutes to go we were 0-1 down and playing absolute shite, looking for all the world like we were about to lose our 100% record. There was no sign of the free-flowing football that had characterised our season so far and even less sign of a goal for us. We were packed in our usual half of the Smethwick End while our players were "attacking", if that was the correct phrase during this abysmal performance, the other end. West Brom goalkeeper Tony Godden received the ball from a back pass. Ah, those golden days when a goalkeeper could pick the ball up after it had been kicked to him by one of his own players. Swirly, misty clouds scud by. So there was Tony with the ball safely in his hands and about to boot it upfield towards the head probably of Cyrille Regis who would promptly head it into the net and put us all out of our misery. Nah, Kenny was lurking like a big lurker! Soft arse Tony dropped the ball. In a flash like the piece of shit off a shovel he was Kenny had the ball in the net. From our end nobody could quite tell what had happened and anyway most of our end was preoccupied with giving our Albion counterparts on the other side of the segregation fence loads. So when we did realise what had happened and we had actually scored from probably our only "shot" of the game pandemonium broke out.

"Goal!" Baz screamed.

As he shouted, Baz's two front gnashers, false remember if you're still following this, went flying out of his grid. I swear this all happened in a flash but it seemed frozen in time then. Baz's chompers were flying through the air and would surely fall to the terrace to be trampled on and smashed to little pieces by celebrating Reds therefore consigning my mate to the ultimate gummy embarrassment of having a big fuck off hole in his gob for the rest of his life, or at least until he could get to a dentist anyway. Baz, defying all forces of nature and gravity reached out his arm as his falsies were spiralling through the air. In a feat of never before known athleticism from Baz he caught the teeth (Graham Gooch would have been proud of that one – Baz actually looked not unlike Goochy) and had them back in his gob before anybody noticed they'd been out of his black hole in the first place! Fuckin' amazin' Baz! I suppose you had to know Baz, realise how self-conscious he was about his two false pearlies, and most importantly actually be there to have found it as funny as I did. Me? I couldn't celebrate for howling laughing. The last time I'd been like that after we'd scored was when Sandy did his biz at Goodison nine years earlier. Quality stuff Baz; I'll never forget that!

I was still laughing as we left the ground but this was really no laughing matter now. There were loads of angry Albion lads all over the place and we were stuck without a lift. We tried to get a lift back on one of our coaches but were royally fucked off by all of them. Getting scary. Then I noticed a lad I knew from Skem who played for Skem Legion, Mick Kenny, peering out from the back of a battered owld Ford Tranny.

"Mick, giz a lift! There's only two of us!"

"Come on then, fuckin' 'urry up an' close the fuckin' doors! If we get sussed 'ere we're dead!"

Albion did indeed seem to have far more loons out than they had in any other season. We closed the doors firmly behind us as we entered the Black Hole of Calcutta, or West Brom in this case. There must have been twenty lads in that van, all with Betty Swollocks on a scorching hot day but there was no fuckin' way we were gonna open the doors until we were safely on the motorway. Mick and co dropped us off safely, with all teeth intact in Kirkby and refused to take any dosh off us for the lift. Nice one lads. We bussed it back from Kirkby, the driver accepting half fare in exchange for no ticket from us but not before the usual argument I always seemed to have with bus drivers.

So the whole day had cost me and Baz 25p each. How's that for mingin' it? Class!

Our dream of emulating Real Madrid, Ajax and Bayern Munich in winning three successive European Cups went crashing to pieces against a virtual one-man wall. That wall was Peter Shilton. We were brilliant that night, throwing everything we had at the Forest defence and Shilton in particular but the Sherwood Foresters (they never like being called that), especially Shilton were equally as brilliant. We honestly could not have done any more to win that game by the requisite two or more goals but Forest defended as if their lives depended on it which they probably did knowing Brian Clough was their manager. One save by Shilton from Kenny had to be seen to be believed. It wasn't quite in the "Banks from Pele" class but it was indeed a stunning save. Kenny's thunderbolt had seemed destined to end up in the top right-hand corner of the Anny Road net but Shilton, on supposedly his weaker side although I don't believe he had a weakness, managed to claw the ball away. Forest looked about as intent on scoring as the Pope in a brothel (marvellous mental image) so the game almost inevitably finished goalless. Out of two Cups it was time to concentrate, even this early in the season, on achieving our first ever League/FA Cup Double. Believe me; we were good enough.

Two days after the Forest game Granada TV made a BIG boo boo! Granada's Friday night programme, KICK-OFF, reviewing and previewing games was avidly watched by anybody in the Northwest who had an interest in footy. The programme was presented by Gerald Sinstadt who, I think, mostly liked Liverpool. Certainly old muzzy features seemed to be mightily impressed when commentating on our matches, most noticeably the famous St. Etienne match and also the 7-0 mauling of Spurs. To be honest I think poor old Gerald was landed in it by the Producer/Director of the programme Paul Doherty. Doherty was also a sometime presenter and could come across a bit of a smug twat. So what we didn't need two days after going out of the European Cup to our then fierce rivals Forest was to have the piss taken out of us about it. Quite rightly the game was reviewed by Sinstadt in his usual calm, knowledgeable manner. What we didn't need was for the closing credits to feature a tearful, inconsolable Thommo and other players dejected by having our European Cup ripped from our grasp. To add insult to massive injury the song, "THE PARTY'S OVER" was played over those images. Somebody from Granada was gonna cop for it the next time they covered a game at Anfield. Of course with Sinstadt fronting the programme it was gonna be him and not old sly arse Doherty, whose idea it must have been, slinking away in the background. I hated Doherty then almost as much as I hated Tony Anthony H Twatface Wilson for laughing at tearful kids when Shanks resigned.

The game against Bolton turned out to be Jimmy Case day. I always felt sorry for Jimmy when Internationals came around. All the other first-teamers and even some of the reserves would be off to far-flung, inhospitable places like Wembley while Jimmy was left to train either on his own or with the likes of our youth team. Jimmy never complained though and just got on with things in the Liverpool way. I'm sure it must gall him now though (it does me) to see players with not half the ability he had picking up caps willy-nilly. It seems nowadays that you only have to string together three decent performances to "force" your way into the international reckoning. Howard Kendall too suffered the same fate as Jimmy of never having played for his country. Kendall was, and make no mistake about this, a brilliant player in an age when brilliance abounded. I'm not suggesting for one minute that Jimmy was as good a player as Howard - far from it - Jimmy's game was entirely different from Howard's based more on the work ethic than Kendall's silky skills but if Jimmy should have won 20 caps then Howard should have won 50. Howard's main problem of course though was that he had far too much skill to fit into an England side managed by Alf Ramsey. Not decrying Ramsey at all here – he picked teams for success and obviously got it. The likes of Howard Kendall wouldn't have fitted into Ramsey's way of playing in much the same way as Peter Thompson didn't but it remains one of the great mysteries not to say travesties of all time in the football world that Kendall never played for his country. Of course back in the good old days of the 60's and 70's England teams were picked and stuck to using only a couple of subs even in friendlies. Now England field two teams in one bloody match! How mad is that? I'm not really decrying players of today; if they can get picked for England because they can kick a ball straight then good bloody luck to them, it does tend to add another 10k a week to their wages when they next come to discuss a new contract two years before the one they've not long signed has expired, but they needn't think they are any better players than the likes of Jimmy Case or Howard Kendall just because they've got 20 caps under their money belt and about 50 – 60k a week in the bank because I can tell them categorically they are not! Poor Jimmy eh? If he'd been playing today he would be a millionaire with a stack of England caps to his credit. Anyway, back to the Bolton game. Jimmy's game was based on his ability to work dead hard like a dead hard working thing (never like using that Trojan word – the word Trojan frightens me to death in this computer age; PC buffs will know what I mean!) prodigious tackling and a cannonball shot. He was never a prolific goalscorer; his role in the great scheme of things in our teams wouldn't really allow him to be although he did chip in quite nicely with maybe 9 or 10 a season. Christ, that would get him a place alongside Michael Owen for England these days! Jimmy had scored a hat-tick a couple of years previously against Slask Wroclaw in a UEFA Cup tie but never remotely looked like repeating the feat in a League game – until this day that is. Jimmy scored all our goals in the 3-0 win. I wonder if he's still got the match ball? If he has it's probably still got the marks on it from when Jimmy hit it at about a million miles an hour; the ball didn't, on this occasion, go into the net but stuck in between the Anny Road railings. It was jammed solid for a good 20 seconds or so 'til it was punched out by a Road Ender (practice for after the match I suppose). How the ball didn't burst like a too hot haggis I'll never know.

Where does haggis come into it Evo?

Long story – you don't want to know – believe me, you don't want to know! You do? Oh okay then!

Ma and Da after 25 years of marriage and never having been on holiday (none of us had ever been on holiday even when the school sent poor kids on holiday to Loggerheads – we were too poor to go to Loggerheads) suddenly decided that as all the kids were grown-up (Price was only 11 but 41 in the head so able to be looked after by our Collette) they were going to live a little and take themselves off on holiday a few times a year, and bloody good luck to them – they deserved it for bringing us rabble up. Thing is they didn't really go for the tourist hotspots such as Magaluf and Torremilinos. Mam and Dad were quite happy going to the likes of Weston-Super-Mare (not that there's anything wrong with W-S-M you Weston-Super-Mareans), Devon and Pwhelli (no chance I've spelt that right). Digression for Welsh jokes:

I was down a back jigger with a Welsh girl once. She said, "If you can speaks Welsh boyo (they don't really say boyo do they?) you can shag me you can."

So I says, "Ee arr..Press dat in!"

Press dat in? Prestatyn? No? Never mind. Next one:

I was down a back jigger (always down them) once with a Welsh girl. I said to her, "I've got a Welsh place name tattooed on me cock."

Suitably impressed Welsh girl says, "Oooh, let's 'ave a look then (boyo)!"

So I whips me donga out.

"Oooh, you little liar. It only says LUDO!"

"Play with it a bit more and it says LLANDUDNO!"

Shit I know but eh – I never claimed to be Chubby Brown!

Anyway back to the haggis sketch:

The furthest afield Mam and Dad got on holiday was Germany but they didn't like it. This might have had something to do with the fact that Dad was nearly arrested for doing a John Cleese/Hitler/Freddie Starr impression and trying to take a gun off a German soldier when he was pissed – me Dad that is, not the German soldier. Ma moaned for years after at having to pay the equivalent of half-a-quid for a cup of coffee when the going rate over here in a similar café would have been about 20p. Ma never did get to grips with prices/wages ratios, currency fluctuations, inflation and all that. So it was decided that future John and Lily Evo holidays would be spent in England. So where did they go next? Edinburgh! That was Lily for you though. On holiday with our Collette once in Betws-Y-Coed, which I've never been to but I believe is a particularly beautiful part of Wales, Lily came out with the classic:

"It's lovely in this Wales isn't it? Yer'd never think yer were in England."

Top stuff Ma!

I made the mistake (as it turned out) of going to see Ma and Da on their return from Edinburgh to find out how their holiday had gone. I could smell this fuckin' evil thing as I walked along the entry going towards Ma's back door. It smelt like somebody had a Baby Burco on the go boiling shitty nappies, Ghandi's thundercrackers and JC's sandals all at that the same time. As I neared Ma's back door it became apparent that the noxious fumes were coming from her kitchen. Holding my nose and breath (nice trick if you can do it) I lifted the lid from the steaming cauldron that was Ma's saucepan. Inside was what looked like something gone wrong from the Quatermass Experiment – all boiling, bubbling and smelly and the size of Auntie Mo's arse (lovely woman Auntie Mo and I loved her dearly – still do – but she was rather broad of beam).

"Ma, what's that?"

"Oh, it's lovely Peter. We ate some lovely things in Scotland. We were eatin' that all the time – it's called 'aggis!"

"Yeah, I've 'eard o' that Ma. Never 'ad it like but I'm sure it's not supposed to smell like that."

"Oh, it is Peter. It's lovely."

"What's in it Mam?"

I shouldn't have asked; not knowing, as I did, what Ma ate for normal meals anyway. Ma's belly must have been made of steel as it was forced to accept such culinary delights as pig's feet, pig's belly, tripe (yuk and double yuk!) whelks, eels and possibly worst of all those fuckin' horrible kewin shellfish things which you had to get out of the shell with a needle and looked like a bit of snot with a crow attached you'd just picked out of your nose! I can't quite remember what Ma said was in this haggis shit but it was something like sheep's head, dog's brains, bull's balls, cow's udders and lamb's foreskin all wrapped and bound together inside the skin from a goat's scrotum. The fuckin' thing had probably been on the boil since last Pancake Tuesday too knowing Ma's philosophy on cooking anything, " Boil the arse off it – it'll do yer good!"

Ma once boiled me two eggs before I left for an away match at Wolverhampton. The eggs were entirely inedible, rock hard as they were, but were perfect for lobbing at the opposition loons. Must have been a couple of sore heads in the Wolves end that day!

"We're 'avin' the 'aggis for tea Peter. Why don't yer stay son?"

Dad shot me a glance from his armchair as if to say, "Yer fuckin' mad if yer do!"

I swear to you what happened next is the absolute truth. Ma took

Auntie Mo's arse out of the pan, nice trick doing it without hiring a JCB, and lowered it gently, well me Ma's idea of gently anyway, onto a plate. It was like a scene from Alien as the bag of shite steamed, bubbled, squeaked, farted, spluttered and hissed on the plate until even the goat's scrotum skin gave up the ghost after being boiled to fuck. Auntie Mo's arse split with a loud pop depositing the evil shite all over my best Adidas t-shirt leaving me looking like that priest from The Exorcist after the devilgirl has spewed up all over his vestments. Nice one Regan!

I was Hank Marvin though so decided to risk eating what me Ma scooped out of Billy goat's scrotum skin. Bad decision! The smell and the look of it were as nothing to the taste. Mixed in with all the other shite Ma told me was in there was I'm sure a ton of sawdust. I don't wish to upset any of my Jock readers here, I have some boss Scottish friends, but that shite is fuckin' disgusting! All Jocks should get together and formulate a plan of how to infiltrate haggis into normal meals. I tell you – Jocks would rule the world if they could force-feed that shite to people. Osama Bin Laden and Saddam Hussein wouldn't stand a fuckin' chance! Al Qaeeda? My arse! Mind you, the aforementioned international terrorists don't scare me now half as much as me Ma did then. Yer didn't mess with Lily! I still have the scars to prove it.

"What was that like son?"

"Ah, it was lovely Mam. Thanks."

I was doing a sterling job of keeping the contents of various animals' bellies inside my own belly at the moment. Couldn't spew it back. That would have offended Ma and couldn't possibly do that; at 25, married with two kids, I still wasn't too old or too grown up to be getting a crack or worse still, Lily elbow.

Ma, you're a star and long may your memory live on but I've never touched that haggis shite since. Those poor fuckers in heaven were expecting manna and nectar; instead they're getting Lily's boiled to fuck haggis shite!

Class Ma!

CHAPTER FIVE

SMOKEY AND THE BANDITS

It had to happen! After the equivalent of nearly two full seasons of refereeing I had my first sending off. I don't know how professional referees in the higher echelons of the game feel when they send somebody off but for me and I'm sure most other refs involved in amateur football it is a real gut-wrenching experience. It is the ultimate punishment. Not only does that player miss the rest of that game but as punishments at amateur level are far more severe than they are in the pro game a player can miss a couple of months of football for not half as bad an offence as a professional player will miss one game. Referees at Sunday League level don't want to stop anybody playing football, I mean it's what we all look forward to all week, but if there's no other way round it that's the way it has to be. So it was that Joey Smith of St. Joseph's FC became the first victim of the Evo red card. My stomach really was in knots when I realised I would have to send Joey off. Joey was a solid, wholehearted player who could dish the dirt but also take it. Having had to book him in the first-half though for three fouls in the space of about fifteen minutes he then went and repeated the feat in the second half.

"Can I have your name please?"

"Yer know me name ref yer got it in the first 'alf."

"What's your name please?"

"Joey Smith."

"Mr. Smith, this is an official caution for persistently infringing the laws of the game. As I have already had ocassion to officially caution you this is now your second caution. I am dismissing you from the field of play for persisting in misconduct after having received a caution."

I hated all this formal shit but that's the way I was trained to do it. Surely Joey was now gonna lamp me. Not having done it before I didn't know how players reacted when they were sent off.

"Okay ref."

As easy as that! Most players do just accept their punishment when they know they've been out of order but I can assure you it's not always that easy. I felt sorry for Joey as he slowly trudged of the pitch. St Joseph's lost the match to Point Six 3-1 and there would be no more footy for Joey for a month but hey, that's the referee's life!

Once again I had to miss out on the trip to Norwich. I'd never been to Norwich and still haven't to this day. Must just be one of those grounds I'm destined not to go to. Stopping me on this ocassion was the fact that it was Little Ste's 7th birthday the day after. How those seven years had flown. Ste was doing very well at school and had a reading age of 43 or something like that so his teacher's told me and Big Ev. He wasn't a particularly big child for his age but he seemed all grown-up if you know what I mean. Not kids for long are they? Pity I know but that's life – you can't hold the youngsters back for your own selfish ends. Making up for Ste's growing up rather too quickly for his Mum and Dad's liking though was the cute little bundle of blonde-haired fun otherwise known as Little Ev. Little Ev really was like a little doll being the tiny little thing she was. Anyway, there was a party for Little Ste on his birthday to which all his friends (and no doubt some of his enemies) had been invited so money dictated that the party went ahead rather than me frittering it away on a trip to East Anglia. Fair enough, the little fella deserved a party, good lad that he was but I was still pissed off at having to miss our 4-1 win. Never mind – next away game was the Goodison derby so I'd be able to go to that and of course we were gonna piss it. In the meantime we had home games against Derby County and Chelsea.

The 5-0 win against Derby was, apart from the demolition of Spurs, our best performance of the season so far. In five home games so far we had scored 18 goals bringing the cry from the Kop of, "We want a scoreboard!" Strange that Anfield had never had a scoreboard even when it had various facelifts over the years. This was the first Anfield match Granada TV had covered since the infamous "THE PARTY'S OVER". As expected poor old Gerald Sinstadt copped for all the flak. "Sinstadt is a wanker" was one of the milder chants. The one I liked best though was, "The party's only starting!" Fuckin' right it was! Watching the game the following day the "Party's only starting chant" came through loud and clear although they obviously cut out the bits where we accused Mr. Sinstadt of being rather partial to fondling his private parts. But then what man isn't? Fondling their own private parts I mean, not Gerald's. I did genuinely feel sorry for Sinstadt. He had been a very good commentator for many years and was the voice of Granada TV footy coverage throughout the seventies. He wasn't quite in the same commentary league as the likes of Wolstenholme, Coleman, Brain Moore or Motty but he certainly was very good and came out with some classic sound bites. Again, not in the class of "they think it's all over" but some good 'uns nonetheless. It's my opinion that he was totally embarrassed by "The party's over." It just wasn't like him to slag off Liverpool Football Club. It wasn't his fault that Doherty had that crass idea; it was just Gerald's misfortune that he had to actually front the programme while that bag of shite was going on. It would have been great if Gerald had interrupted his commentary on the match by screaming into his mike, "It wasn't fuckin' me! Blame that twat Doherty!"

We eased off a bit the following week against Chelsea, winning by just the couple of goals. No need for a scoreboard this time but we were playing the best football I'd ever seen from a Liverpool team. Everybody in the team was playing their part and in top form apart for some strange reason from Phil Neal who had looked strangely out of sorts for a few weeks now. Kenny had scored nine goals in the first eleven League games and with the likes of Johnno and Razor chipping in regularly we were well set for the Derby having dropped only one point in those eleven League games. The fact that Everton hadn't beaten us for seven years was also filling us full of confidence despite the Blues themselves making an excellent start being unbeaten so far winning six and drawing five. The Blues though weren't prolific scorers having netted just 14 times in those eleven games compared to our 35. Their success so far this season had been built on a sound defence and work ethic under their dour, but no doubt good and tactically astute, manager Gordon Lee. For once it was us giving the Bluenoses loads in the build-up to the match over what we were gonna do to them. All the jokes came out too:
"My dog sings and dances whenever we beat Everton"
"Oh aye, what does it do when Everton beat us?"
"I don't know – I've only 'ad it seven years."
Bring 'em on!

Shit happens doesn't it? Big shit happened this day! Outplayed, outfought, outthought and finally, deservedly, beaten by a wonder goal from Andy King. King later said he actually mis-hit it and it came off his shin. Well all I can say is it was one fuckin' hell of a mis-hit. Bastard! I felt sick to the pit of my fuckin' stomach as I was right behind the ball in the Park End watching it swerve and dip at about a million miles an hour over the despairing hands of Clem. Honestly, there wasn't a Brazilian who could have hit a ball better, sweeter or with as much power as King that day. It was a great goal. Which leads me on and back to the fact that Andy King was another one of those players who never got a chance for England although he definitely deserved it. Deffo would have got a game these days. One player missing from the Everton line-up that day who would have enjoyed the victory more than anybody was Mike Lyons. Lyons was another of those non-England players although there is a good trivia question about him concerning England: Which player was on the substitute's bench for England 'B' for the match in West Germany in 1978 and the following night was also on the substitute's bench for the full international against West Germany but didn't play at all in either match? Yes, you've guessed it – good old Micky! Shame that as Mike was a good player – better at centre-half than centre-forward and Everton through and through. I've met Mike a couple of times and can tell you he's one of the nicest blokes you could come across and always willing to talk footy, not just Everton; unlike so many of today's players who when you see them out or at an airport somewhere wouldn't give you the steam off their own shite let alone the time of day. It's like *we owe them* something!

Still hanging over me like a big hangyover thing was the impending court case for my Wigan indiscretions a few months ago. Apart from a few interviews conducted by Ploddy Small Hands we'd heard nothing since being charged. Apparently it was taking quite a while to sort all the forensic evidence out. For fuck sake, we'd only smashed a window, robbed a couple of cars, had a few fights and generally just been knobs! We hadn't murdered anybody! It was still looking like clink though should we be found guilty. Ste decided that it was high time we got ourselves a decent brief. We were gonna use his regular solicitor in Liverpool. Not a problem I suppose; we could go on the Monday morning and I'd still be back in time for my

afternoon shift. Ste knew exactly what he was doing but it was a whole new world to me: depositions; statements, committals. Anyway with all the business done by 11.30am it left plenty of time to get the bus home and get ready for work.
"Come on lads, let's go an' 'ave a bevy."
Ste's suggestion was eagerly seized upon by everybody except me as I was the only one due in work that afternoon.
"Can't Ste. I'm on afternoons."
"Come on, it's fuckin' early yet. Yer'll be back in time for work."
"Yeah, come on Evo. Yer'll enjoy where we're goin'"
Out of this mad fuckin' lot Stu was probably about the most sensible so I thought we'd be okay and that I could get back home in time for my shift.
"Okay, just one or two though. Where we goin'?"
"The Bier Keller."
"Never 'eard of it Wooly."
"Well, yer'll fuckin' remember it once yer've been there."
HE WASN'T FUCKIN' JOKIN' EITHER!

We arrived at the Bier Keller just on noon. The place was absolutely fuckin' heaving! Jam-packed solid.
"Fuckin' 'ell what's goin' on 'ere?"
"Never mind what's goin' on, just get the fuckin' ale in soft arse!"
I did as I was bid by Ste. Not much point in arguing with him.
"Five pints o' lager please mate."
"We don't serve pints, only litres."
"Okay, five fuckin' litres then."
I hadn't realised before just what a litre of ale looked like. Fuck me, I was gonna have trouble holding this never mind drinking it.
"Ee arr lads, table over there by the stage."
Ste, as ever, had taken charge. Once sat down, everybody in the place it seemed was singing and banging their glasses (their ale glasses soft arse, not their specs) on the table.
"Fuckin' 'ell it's brilliant this! Is it always like this?"
"Is on a Monday Evo. The act comes on soon."
Ste was a seasoned Bier Keller man it seemed.
"Oh right, they 'ave a band or somethin' on do they?"
The table rocked then not just because of people banging on it but with raucous laughter.

"This ale's good too. Never tasted anything this strong."

Strong it might have been but it was flyin' down my neck like a good 'un!

"Yeah, it's proper German lager not like the Grunhalle shit you drink in the Derby."

I actually thought Grunhalle was quite nice, even if it was brewed in Warrington with a German name but I couldn't lose face and let the lads know that. Wasn't as good as my lovely Stella though! Molly's round next. By the time I'd polished off the bevy he'd bought me while the rest of the lads were still on their first (I was Billy the Fish) I was well on my way to being walloped.

"Fuckin' 'ell it's nearly one o'clock! We'll 'ave to go or I'll be late for work."

"Fuck work! Giz the number an' I'll ring in for yer."

"No Ste, I'll 'ave to go. Go on, just one more, then we'll 'ave to get a taxi or somethin'"

Twenty minutes later (I was slowing down now) and I was in no fit state to go the shops never mind work.

"Ste, phone work for me."

"Good lad! What d'yer want me to say?"

"I don't fuckin' know! Make somethin' up."

"Okay Evo, leave it to me."

"Where's this fuckin' act anyway?"

"'Ere it comes now Evo lad!"

"Jee-sus!"

There, strutting along the stage was a bird about six feet tall wearing not much at all. It was fairly obvious that what little she did have on wasn't gonna stay on for very long. Not only were her skimps not gonna stay on but she was about to do the most amazing things with the private parts of her voluptuous body. Twenty minutes of doing her stuff on stage and the glass was being passed around for Betty Beef to do her "special" act. This time she left the stage and walked along the long tables with about 200 men in the Bier Keller egging her on. Betty stopped at Ste.

"Giz a drag o' yer ciggy mate."

Nothing wrong with that; the girl probably just needed a quick puff on a Woody before she carried on her act. Only she didn't smoke the ciggy with her mouth did she? My eyes nearly popped out of their sockets when she lay on the table right there before us and with the ciggy in the old Auntie Annie puffed on it for all she was worth. It truly was the most fuckin' amazing sight I'd ever seen, and I've seen some I can tell you! I've seen it since but that first time had me both in stitches and strangely turned on.

How does your fuckin' mind work Evo?

I don't know – 'aven' gorra fuckin' clue. I mean how can yer get turned on by a flaming fanny? It bloody worked too as plumes of smoke emanated from where I would have liked to shove my dick. Not that by this time I was capable of shoving my dick anywhere. It was all I could do to get the old chap back in me kecks after having a piss. That girl was deffo gonna get cancer of the flaps if she wasn't careful. Another couple of girls came on doing similar tricks, one of them was a dead-shot at firing ping-pong balls into a glass (use yer fuckin' imagination), until by chucking out time we were all totally, utterly and completely bladdered. Good stuff that German lager! Or was it German lager? Maybe they just told us it was German and by the power of autosuggestion because we were in a German type environment we thought it was German and stronger than it was. One thing was for certain – I was definitely pissed. Actually there were another two things for certain: the first one was that I was in for mountains of grief from Big Ev; the second was that I was gonna be sacked the next day.

"Ste, what did you say to work?"

"I don't fuckin' know! I can't remember. Somethin' abarr yer Granny I think."

"Yeah, that'll do. Fuck them anyway! If they're gonna sack me they're gonna sack me. Fuck all I can do now."

No suggestions this time of robbing a car to get us home, anyway it was still only early evening; not even these loons would rob a car in broad daylight – I THINK!

The excuse for work was sorted – somethin' abarr me Granny Ste had said, at least I think that's what he said, could've been anything now. Beer was still seeping into my already addled brain befuddling it even more so it was all I could do to remember my name. Fame – we're gonna live forever! Sorry, digression there. What the fuck was I gonna tell Big Ev though? I needed an excuse not only for not coming back from the brief's in Liverpool in time for work (fuckin' murder for missing work – can't be missing work – crime of the fuckin' century – you make sure you get to work an' bring 'ome the

money an' I'll sit 'ere an' count it) but also for the fact I was raging fuckin' drunk. Oh shit! No sign of life as I entered the house – I'd been given my own key by this time. That's nice isn't it? Fuck, I hoped she hadn't done a runner yet again. My luck was in for once. There was a note written on the back of a Sovereign packet on the couch:
"Peter, I've gone to our Linda's with the kids. Haven't saw her for ages. Be back tomorrow. There's soup in the flask for you I love you. Ev."
An' I fuckin' love you too! Fuckin' yippee! Haven't seen her for ages Ev. Haven't seen. Not, haven't saw. I have seen. We have seen. They have seen. I saw. We saw. They saw. Not 'appy that me tea's in the flask like but I suppose a lucky man can't 'ave everythin'. Soup, Corry and bed seemed to be the best bet and just hope she didn't come home before I left for work the next day. If she did I'd deffo be sussed as being on the ale all day as I was bound to have the stinkiest of stinky ale breath and the most massive of massive hangovers.

I continued to ride my luck as my darling and my beautiful children hadn't arrived home before I left for work. I did hope Big Ev would be home tonight though as I was twinged up to fuck after watching the great smoking fanny. Must've been a trick that! Yer can't get smoking pussies. Or can yer? Or did I dream it? Nah, it was only abarr six inches away from my face so I couldn't have done. Well, it wasn't six inches away 'til I put my face six inches away. Had to have a proper look at that! Shit, what was I gonna tell Eddie? I'd completely forgotten what excuse Ste had given to him. Didn't matter anyway I suppose; he was just gonna sack me anyway. Stay lucky Evo!
"Sorry to hear about your Grandmother Peter."
Phew! Ted was on shift not Eddie so I had a chance. What the fuck was he on abarr me Granny though?
"Oh err…yeah Ted."
WHAT THE FUCK ARE YER ON ABARR?
"Yes, your brother rang and said she'd died very suddenly."
Fuckin' 'ell, is that what Ste said? The cheeky twat! Sayin' me Granny had died is one thing but pretending to be me bro is another! Not sure what me Granny Martha would say to all this though.

Probably twat me over the 'ead with 'er 'igh 'eels!
"Yeah Ted, terrible it was. I'm sorry I was off but I 'ad to be there."
"I understand Peter. Just make your hours up today and tomorrow."
Oh thanks fuckin' very much Ted. I've got a bastard blindin' 'eadache 'ere an' you want me to work twelve fuckin' hours today and fuckin' tofuckinmorrow as well! An' at single fuckin' pay too when I probably would've worked overtime tomorrow anyway! Yer not as fuckin' green as yer cabbage lookin' are yer?
Is that a particularly Scouse thing where we split words up with a swear word?
"Ah thanks a lot Ted, I appreciate that."
"When's the funeral?"
"Next Monday Ted. Can I 'ave the day off?"
"Yes, as long as you make your hours up through the week."
Quick thinkin' there Evo lad. Back down to the Bier Keller next Monday to see Smokey again. Fuckin' yes!

My beautiful darling wife had indeed arrived back from her sister's when I got home from work. Having waited up for me my darling was, even at three o'clock in the morning, looking particularly attractive, even more so than usual, which was pretty damn attractive anyway.
"'Ow'd yer gerron at the solicitor's?"
"Oh, alright yer know. Just 'ad to make these deposition things an' statements an' that. Ste did most of the talkin'."
"'E usually does!"
"We've gorra go back next Monday for more statements an' stuff. I've cleared the day off with Ted. 'E said I can make me hours up through the week."
"Did yer get back in time for work yesterday?"
"Yeah."
"'Ave yer missed me?"
"Course I've missed yer love."
"Yer didn't 'ave yer tea last night."
"Tea? What tea"
"The tomato soup in the flask. Yer didn't touch it. It's still there."
"Oh right. Oh, I don't know. I must've just been dead tired after work. I worked four hours overtime so it was nearly three o'clock this mornin' before I got to bed anyway."

I AM ONE LYIN' BASTARD!

" An' yer worked overtime tonight as well? Ah God, yer musta been knackered."

Is that a tired Arab?

"Yeah, I'm working overtime tomorrow night too,"

"Oh good! Three nights overtime on the run. Yer a good worker. We'll be loaded next week won't we?"

Well no actually we won't but I'll cross that particular bridge when I come to it. Anyway, whaddya mean we'll be loaded? I won't be – you will! I only work for the money remember!

" Yeah love, I suppose we will be. What's for tea now anyway?"

"Yer can 'ave that soup. I'll take it outta the flask and warm it back up for yer."

Oh thanks very fuckin' much! Fuckin' soup in a flask woulda been fuckin' bad enough anyway but fuckin' day an' a 'alf old warmed soup at three o' bastard clock in the mornin' is fuckin' shit!

"Okay, ta love."

"Nah, I'm only messin'! Yer tea's in the oven. I'll get it now."

Fuckin' go 'ead! Big fat dinner! A *full* Fray Bentos steak and kidney plate pie all to myself with loads of veggies. I truly did love this woman. After walloping my most marvellous repast my nether regions told me it was time for bed.

"Come on Ev, are we goin' to bed? I 'aven' 'alf missed yer."

"Alright, I'll just finish this ciggy."

Hmmm….! Could she? Would she? Nah, don't even think abarr it Evo!

After our traumatic Derby defeat we faced Leeds at home in what appeared would be a fairly comfortable game for us. Leeds weren't doing too well so far this season. I suppose we should have known better though. Any Liverpool v Leeds game was going to be tough, even if Leeds were well past their pomp. A first-half Arthur Graham goal, flying winger of the tubby belly – bit like Forest's John Robertson, was only equalised by a late Terry Mac penalty. Phil Neal was bloody awful in this game, continuing his early season poor form, but didn't deserve the abuse he was getting from the patrons of the Paddock and Main Stand. Us Kopites soon sorted that out though. Even though we too thought he was having a stinker and weren't happy about it ourselves we weren't having one of our players being given stick by our own supporters. We started chanting his name as a great show of support. I don't think Phil Neal ever looked back after that. Nice one Phil and nice one Kop!

It was nice to have a sleep-in on the Monday morning due to having to attend "my Granny's funeral" rather than go to work. The Monday Club duly arrived at my door at 10:30 am – plenty of time to get good seats in the Bier Keller for another luscious view of Smokey Sally and Ping-Pong Po. Young ladies taking their clothes off, doing marvellous tricks with their Top Hats and loadsa strong German lager – fuckin' marvellous! I wondered how many more of these Mondays off I could swing, making my hours up through the week without it becoming a pain in the arse. Not many, probably not any, I decided so I was gonna have to make the most of this one.

We did indeed get prime specs in the Bier Keller. I think only Smokey Sally's gynaecologist could have got any closer to her doctor's syringe than I did. Strangely though it wasn't turning me on as much as it did last week – I mean, once yer've seen one smoking Roger yer've seen 'em all 'aven' yer? It was still fuckin' funny though. No, it was Ping-Pong Po's turn for the Evo donga to stand to attention this week. That girl was fuckin' brilliant! Ping-Pong balls were flying in all directions. She could fire one of those little plassy things into a glass from ten yards away. Fuckin' amazing! Then, with the "special act" glass full to bursting came the sight of all sights – Sally and Po getting it on together! Fuck me, I thought I'd died and gone to heaven! Okay, maybe an act and all simulated stuff but fuck me it was horn-inducing. There was gonna have to be a big tank-emptying exercise when I got home. Well, it was good while it lasted but as with all good things it had to come to an end. Couldn't possibly drink that lager every Monday anyway but once in a while after that would be good – and it was!

"Did you get anythin' sorted out at the solicitor's?"
"Err....yeah Ev. We like err....just 'ad to tell 'im exactly what 'appened an' that."
"Where've yer been anyway?"
That was fast becoming Big Ev's favourite question.
"I told yer, the solicitor's."

"I mean after that smart arse, yer bladdered."
"Oh, we…errr…just 'ad a little bevy in town."
"Whereabout?
Fuckin' 'ell, what is this – The Spanish bastard Inquisition or what?
"Don't know Ev. Just a few bars and that. The 'Anover and that I think. Not sure."
"Yer can't go any fuckin' where without a drink you can yer?"
D'yer really want me to answer that?
"Ah, it was only a little drink Ev. Not doin' any 'arm."
"We'd 'ave a lot more money if you didn't drink so much."
Yeah, and we'd 'ave a lot more if you didn't fuckin' smoke so much but I'm not fuckin' moaning at you am I? You just stay at 'ome eh an' smoke an' I'll go out to work but you just fuckin' stand there and moan at me about drinkin' won't yer. Yeah, that's fuckin' fair isn't it?
"Look Ev, I've 'ad a drink. Not the end of the fuckin' world is it? I 'aven' raped anybody an' I 'aven' murdered anybody. Giz a fuckin' break will yer."
"Well when this court case comes up yer might go to jail anyway."
"Yeah, I just fuckin' might! Sounds like you *want* me to go to jail."
"I don't but yer might do."
"Yeah, well if I do I won't get as much fuckin' grief as I get 'ere!"
That was a bit unfair but I was fuckin' riled now. What fuckin' harm had I done? I suppose though in a way I deserved the grief I was getting now having got away with it last week. God, if there is one, always has a way of paying you back doesn't he? I expected the silent treatment for the next six weeks or so but, unpredictable as ever, Big Ev had mellowed out by bedtime.
"Ev."
"What?"
"'As our Ste still got those table-tennis balls?"
"I don't think so. Why?"
"Nothin', it doesn't matter. Come on, let's go to bed."

CHAPTER SIX

A WINTER'S TALE

We got back on track with wins at QPR and at home to Manchester City. The win against City was only courtesy of a very late Phil Neal penalty. Phil had recovered from his poor early-season form and now looked every inch the attacking full-back. Not quite in the Chris Lawler mode as Phil didn't score anything like the number of goals as Chris did from open play but there weren't many better penalty takers around than Phil. Phil didn't celebrate like Chris either. Phil was in the Emlyn mode for animated celebrations. Even after scoring penalties Phil would be legging it round Anfield like Joey on speed. Christ, that doesn't even bear thinking about does it?

A scoreless draw at Tottenham was followed by a 2-0 win at home to Middlesbrough; Graeme Souness scoring against his old club adding to Terry Mac's earlier strike. What a buy Souness had proved. There was no better midfielder in the country and there were some very good ones. The Flying Dutchmen at Ipswich – Frans Thyssen and Arnold Muhren were doing brilliantly but Souness was taking the eye in almost every game. It's not often you get a player blessed with sublime skill allied to rock-hardness, a will to win and leader of men. Souness was all of that and more.

Arsenal inflicted upon us only our second League defeat of the season as we went down 0-1 at Highbury. David Price, surely the hairiest-chested player ever in the memory of hairy-chested footballers (he had mounds of it sticking out over his shirt), scored the only goal.

Next up was the visit of our old friends from Robin Hood country. Now there were all kinds of reasons for wanting to win this one! Revenge for our undeserved League Cup Final replay defeat. Revenge for them knocking us, deservedly, out of the European Cup. Most of all though was the fact that they were unbeaten so far this season in 18 games and added to their unbeaten run of 24 games in the second part of the previous season they had set a Football League record of 42 unbeaten games. Now that doesn't happen if you are not a VERY good side. Forest were of course just that. That really is a remarkable statistic when you think about it – the equivalent of a full League season (yes, youngsters – there used to be 42 matches in a League season) unbeaten. So you can imagine the size of the task we had on our hands. Forest's critics said they weren't pretty to watch and maybe they weren't but they were bloody effective and goes without saying, although I'm saying it anyway, hard to beat – bloody near impossible to beat in fact! We approached the game and Forest's unbeaten record in exactly the way we should have done i.e. bollocks to them! Our up and 'em style I think caught Forest somewhat unawares as they were expecting the normal game between the two teams over the past season and a half – cagey with few openings. We blew all that apart with an all out assault on Shilton's goal. Shilton was again in outstanding form. Even the great man had to crack eventually though and he was finally beaten by a Terry Mac penalty on the half-hour. Terry added to that goal three minutes into the second-half and that was more or less that. We could have scored further goals but Forest offered little of their normally doughty resistance after that. Although there was great excitement around the ground at having beaten our closest rivals for the title and therefore ended their brilliant unbeaten run events on the pitch stuttered tamely to our winning climax.

Forest came to Anfield. Cloughy all smarm and guile.
He thought they were invincible. They hadn't lost for a while.
Their forty-two match unbeaten run came crashing to an end.
Terry Mac scored twice and the Kop went round the bend!

A very unlikely defeat occurred in the next game as we lost 0-1 at Bristol City. Guess who scored too? Old fuckin' big 'ead – head the size of a rhino – Joe Royle. Once round Joe's 'ead twice round Birkenhead!

We were back in European action at Anfield three days later. We won the second-leg of the European Super Cup Competition beating Anderlecht 2-1 with goals from Dalglish and Hughes but the Belgians won the Cup due to the fact they'd resoundly beaten us 3-1 in Brussels a fortnight earlier. I'd love to be able to tell you what

Kenny's and Crazy Horse's goals were like but I can't as I didn't see them.

Why Evo – didn't you go?

Of course I bloody went but the game was played in thick fog and should never have got underway. I had trouble seeing the bloke in front of me never mind what was happening out on the park!

The trip to Old Trafford on Boxing Day was once again relatively quiet (before the game anyway) as the Crown's coach I was on dropped us off virtually inside the Scoreboard End. We had the usual tea and piss thrown at us from above but during these times I actually preferred (for lack of trouble that was) to go to Old Trafford rather than Maine Road. Mind you it might have been a case of that you knew what you were gonna get from the City boys. They'd front you and be quite open that they wanted to beat you up. Now you could handle that whatever way you liked. I, mostly, got out the fuckin' way as I was normally either on my own or with just one or two others. If you wanted the battle with them though you got it! No quarter asked or given either! The United lads on the other hand were a right shower of snidey twats. It was okay for them being above us in K stand to throw all kinds of shite down at us but apart from the odd skirmish outside you hardly ever saw them after the match. Until that is you were queuing to get the train at Warwick Road station when they'd once again be pelting you from the higher ground. Very rarely did they ever want a big front. This day was to be no exception. We'd completely played them off the park; Razor, Jimmy Case and Davy Fairclough scoring in an embarrassingly easy 3-0 win on a freezing cold day. Not many problems getting away from the ground until we passed under a bridge. The snides were waiting with their ammunition. There weren't many windows left unbroken on the coach and it was a miracle nobody was badly hurt or cut. Fuckin' freezin' on the way home too. TWATS!

A long, cold winter kicked in and our next game wasn't played until January 10th when the previously postponed FA Cup 3rd Round tie at Southend United's Roots Hall in front of their record crowd of 31,033 finished scoreless. The Shrimpers did quite well in the replay, holding out for 38 minutes until Jimmy Case put us ahead. An

amazing miss by Davy Fairclough after an hour should have put us two up. The ball came to Davy from the right. Running in at speed and only about a yard from goal Davy somehow, a near impossible feat from where he was, managed to lift the ball up and over the bar without another player in sight! I looked at the spot in the Kop goalmouth from where Davy had struck the ball for fully two minutes, scarcely able to believe what my eyes had just witnessed. Southend took heart from this (from Davy's miss that is, not me looking at the Kop goalmouth) and came close to scoring on a number of occasions. The game was put beyond their reach with 15 minutes to go after a marvellous decision by referee, Keith Hackett. I really admired Mr. Hackett for his tough, no nonsense approach. He got respect from players and fans alike for looking like he actually enjoyed refereeing, having a laugh and a joke with the players whilst at the same time keeping a firm hand on the game. I did try to model my refereeing on Mr. Hackett, especially his use of advantage. It was this part of Mr. Hackett's game that contributed directly to our second goal. Jimmy Case, for once on the wrong end of a bone-crunching challenge, was left writhing in agony on the frozen pitch. Mr. Hackett, instead of blowing immediately for the free-kick had a quick look to see where the ball would land. It could not have landed in a better place as far as we were concerned as the whole ground could hear the shout of Mr. Hackett, "Play advantage!"
Ray Kennedy's left foot guided the ball unerringly to Kenny who deftly lobbed the goalkeeper to give us the 2-0 lead. It really was a piece of top class reffing from Mr. Hackett and it was nice to see Ray Kennedy go over and congratulate him on the decision before Southend restarted play. Razor himself wrapped things up ten minutes later to give us the 3-0 win – a scoreline that was slightly harsh on Southend.

With the freezing winter seeing games postponed left, right and centre it was nearly a fortnight before our next game – another FA Cup tie at Anfield, this time against Blackburn Rovers. Rovers did even better than Southend had in the previous round. The game looked to be heading for an Ewood Park replay until Kenny put us into the fifth round with a goal eight minutes from time.

We finally got back to League action with a game, and what a game, against West Brom at Anfield. West Brom were a fine side and had become our running rivals for the League. West Brom, having lost just twice were top with 34 points. We were a point and a place behind, with a game in hand. Everton, on the same points as us but with a vastly inferior goal difference, were third and had also played a game more than us. Albion were managed by Ron Atkinson in his first stint as a top-flight Manager, having previously managed Oxford United. No matter what you say about Big Ron, and everybody has an opinion on him, he always produced good footballing teams. This Albion side were no exception. They had beaten Man U 5-3 at Old Trafford the game after we'd stuffed United there. It was such a pity that this was in pre mass televising of live games days. The highlights of Albion's win at Old Trafford were breathtaking as were some of the goals, not least the hat-trick by Cyrille Regis, fast becoming the best English striker in the country. Cyrille was another one of those players who should have had a great international career but was largely bypassed. Cyrille won only five England caps in his career and didn't score a goal. The fact he didn't win many more might have been down to the fact that he was somewhat Emile Heskeyish in style in that while he had the physique to be knocking people all over the place he very rarely did, being too laid back for his own good. Cyrille was one of three black players in that very good Albion side; the others being Brendan Batson and the late Laurie Cunningham. Black players were just coming into prominence in the Football League with Forest's Viv Anderson becoming the first black player to represent England in a full international in the game against Czechoslovakia at Wembley a couple of months earlier. Among the less hostile nicknames the West Brom trio earned was "The Three Degrees" after the black all-girl Philadelphia singing group. In the main though black players at that time, including Regis, Batson and Cunningham suffered, by today's standards, the vilest racial abuse. Not making any kind of excuses but at the time fans really didn't consider it racist to sing, "There's only one team of niggers" or "There's only one All Blacks."

Make your own mind up if that was racist – I'm not really sure. Of course it would be considered racist today but this was in pre politically correct days. I'd like to think that the Kop did these things with a little more humour than most other crowds but I have to ask the question: were we all as non-racist pre John Barnes as we would like ourselves to believe? Worth thinking about for readers of this who were about at the time. Anyway, back to the footy: The gates were locked on this one well over an hour before kick off. I had a season ticket so no rush for me although it was only just turned two o'clock when I was walking towards the ground seeing streams of people, including a lot of Albion fans (why come all that way and not set off early enough to make sure you get in?) coming back the other way having failed to get in, such was the lure of this game. Baz had set off early to make sure he got in the Anny Road. He and the rest of the Anny knew that Albion would be bringing a big support, possibly for the first time at Anfield, and there would be fun to be had. So it proved as some of the thousands of Albion fans spilled over from their designated area of the segregated Anny only to be summarily booted back by the Road End. I couldn't spot Baz from my vantage point in the Kop but I knew he would be having a whale of a time. I also knew that Blackbeard and his merry plod would be earning their dosh today! Kenny put us ahead after 20 minutes and despite a ding-dong battle with Albion playing a full part the score stayed that way 'til half-time. Ally Brown became only the third visiting player to score at Anfield this season when he equalised early in the second half. That didn't last long though as a peach of a ball from Kenny was met by Davy to put us ahead once again. The scoreline remained the same to give us a vital victory.

Liverpool, Liverpool top o' the League! Liverpool, top o' the League!

In many other seasons our brilliant form would have had us miles ahead of the rest by now but it was credit to West Brom, that they were pushing us so close.

"Peter, yer 'ear Everton got beat one nil at Wolves?"

"Yeah, fuckin' great stuff Baz! 'Ow d'yer get on in the Anny? I saw youse all battlin'."

"Yeah, fuckin' boss! Yer wanna start coming in the Anny with us yer know Peter. It's fuckin' great in there! Better atmosphere than in the Kop."

"Yeah Baz, but 'ow much of the fuckin' game d'yer actually see? They're all fuckin' fightin' an' backwards an' forwards all the fuckin' time an' dodgin' fuckin' Blackbeard an' 'is twats. 'Ow the fuck can yer concentrate on the game with all that goin' on?"

I must confess I was a bit envious. I had considered, but not for long, trying to swap my Kop Season Ticket for a Road End one. I loved all the tales of what they got up to but I was happy to be in the Kop. We weren't the gobshites the Road End made us out to be and the atmosphere in there was a lot better than the Barmy Anny Road End would have you believe. Nah, a Kopite I was and a Kopite I was gonna stay!

WE ARE THE FAMOUS, THE FAMOUS KOPITES!

The season was being madly disrupted because of all the postponements due to the freezing cold weather. It was the worst winter on record since 1962 –'63 and it fuckin' felt like it too! For instance our 1-0 win home win over Birmingham played on February 13th had been due to be played on January 13th! Mad shit, it really was. The way the fixtures were falling though due to the bollock-freezing weather was being kind to us in that when we faced Norwich City on February 21st it was our third home game in a row. We were that good we didn't actually need any God-given advantages but we were gonna take whatever came our way anyway! Despite taking an early lead through Kenny there was little hint of what was to come in the second half as the scoreline stayed at 1-0 'til half-time. Then we absolutely went berserk. We battered Norwich in much the same way as we had when we mauled Spurs by seven goals earlier in the season. Johnno scored twice inside the first five minutes of the second half with one from Kenny sandwiched in between and then it was party time! All the tricks came out including one from Jocky Hansen where he came forward, dragged the ball under his foot, went one way and sent a hapless Norwich defender the other. It was that good Jocky even sent the crowd swerving one way as he went the other!

"We all agree, Jocky is better than Kenny!"

He actually wasn't far off either. This young lad in his first full season as a regular first-teamer was not just a very good centre-half; he could also play a bit of football too. He even had his own Kop chant by now – the old Alun Evans one:

Na, na, na, na, na, na, na, na hey, hey, hey Alan Hansen!

Then came something never before seen at Anfield. Well, okay

Barney had only been with us six months but we'd never seen him use his right foot. Apparently he did use it at home to kick the cat when it had pissed on the carpet but that was only so he wouldn't hurt it. I'd like to say that Barney's first ever right foot shot screamed into the net but it was actually a cross meant for the head of nobody in particular; even Barney didn't know! Norwich goalkeeper Kevin Keelan, who seemingly had kept goal for them for ever, was so surprised at Barney actually even using his right foot that he could only watch helplessly as the ball floated gently over him and nestled nicely in the top corner of the net. Barney was off and running all over Anfield with fellow loons Phil Neal and Emlyn in hot pursuit! Boy, could those boys celebrate a goal! None of this choreographed modern-day dancing like a twat shit. This was just sheer, unbounded joy. Meanwhile, us in (not on) the Kop were pissin' ourselves not only at Barney's right foot but his antics afterwards. It was left to the other Kennedy – R, to wrap things up right on full time with one of his specials. We'd made the most of our three successive home games: six points, nine goals and only one against – not bad eh?

Now, much as I enjoyed that 6-0 win my joy was tempered by what I had to face the following morning: the court case. Oh, fuckin' deep unbounded bastard joy. We all trooped off to Wigan Magistrates Court. If it hadn't been for the fact that this fuckin' thing had dragged on for long enough as it was – seven months – I would have asked for the trial to be stopped. Sitting there on the bench was the full time Area Officer of the Trade Union I was a member of at the time. Now, I won't go into too much detail as to who this man was; suffice to say that I was surprised to see a man of supposed Socialist principles sitting as a beak (an attitude I have somewhat moderated now) although if I knew he was to be a Knight of the Realm 25 years or so later I wouldn't have been!
"Stu, look who's on the bench."
Have you ever tried whispering out of the corner of your mouth? Fuckin' hard it is!
"I know! Dickie's Meadow!"
We'd given the erstwhile beak this nickname some years earlier as all he ever seemed to say when he met Grimwood's workforce after attending pay negotiations was, "If we don't accept what the

company have offered we'll all be in Dickie's Meadow."
Now nobody knew what, much less where, Dickie's Meadow was but we guessed it was some sort of Wiganese for, "We're in the shit!"
So maybe Dickie's Meadow meant shit. I don't fuckin' know; I'm just a plain-talking Scouser or as Stan the Skemmer in work once described us: "Scousers are only Irishmon (no he wasn't Scottish – just that Skemmers pronounce man or men as mon too) wi' brains kicked art!"
Anyway, all that aside we truly were in the shit – or Dickie's Meadow. He didn't recognise us anyway. Why the fuck should he? He didn't give a fuck about the people he met in a 100+ workforce much less recognise them. It just wasn't worth stopping the trial. A bit of argie and bargie between defence and prosecution came to the conclusion that only the motoring offences would be dealt with today. The other stuff would have to go to Crown Court as, if found guilty they could carry prison sentences of more than six months. The motoring offences on the other hand carried a maximum sentence of six months. Oh that's fuckin' alright then isn't it? We might only get six months today but we could get more than that in our appearance at the Crown. Oh, I'm fuckin' made up about that!
"Have you anything to say for yourselves?"
"Yes Sir. Very sorry. Nothing like this will happen again Sir."
Ste had to do it his way though didn't he?
"Yes Sir. I'm very sorry too but I'm taking up a position as a PT Instructor in Saudi Arabia in a fortnight Sir."
Ste was doing his best to stay out of jail; we all were but none of us had thought of that ruse. Nice one Ste. That might just sway Dickie's Meadow and co into not banging us into clink and fining us instead. 'Ang on though; the nearest you're ever gonna get to Saudi fuckin' Arabia is Southport beach!

After due consideration we were all fined a total of £110 each. Doesn't sound much now but it was a fuckin' fortune back then. Travelling in a motor vehicle knowing it to be stolen - yeah, I was throwing my hands up on that one – deserved to be fined £50 plus £5 costs for that. I was a bit miffed though about being fined £50 plus £5 costs for travelling in a motor vehicle knowing that the driver was not insured to drive it. Fuck me, I wasn't gonna ask the soft twat who robbed it was he insured was I? Fuckin' mad that! Mind you, we'd avoided the Big House. Maybe the beaks, having took pity on Ste, not wanting him to miss his opportunity of gainful employment with the Arabs, had decided to fine him and to be fair to the rest of his miscreant friends had also decided we should not be banged up either but pay our debt to society in hard cash. Yeah, nice one Ste. Did well there mate!

"How do you all propose to pay these fines?"

"We'd like time to pay Sir."

Mutter, mutter. Mumble, mumble. Rhubarb, rhubarb.

"The Magistrates have considered your request for time to pay these fines. You should all pay ten pounds per week into the Court Office adjacent to this building."

Well, a bit steep that is, I'll 'ave to stay off the ale for a bit and Smokey and Ping-Pong Po will 'ave to do without me for a while but mustn't grumble I suppose.

"Except, that is, for you Best. I am going to do you a favour."

Fuck me, yer not lettin' 'im off completely are yer?

"Not wishing to deprive you of the opportunity of taking up your position as a PT Instructor in Saudi Arabia and also not wishing you to have this fine hanging over your head while you are there I am going to give you two weeks to pay this fine."

I couldn't help it – I just fuckin' burst out laughin'!

"You, Etherington! If you continue to laugh I will find you in contempt of court and order you to be taken to the cells to await punishment for such!"

Now, anybody who knows me will tell you that once I start I can't stop and become a cross between Stuart Hall and Ted Heath. Watch them laughing and you'll know what I mean. I was almost, literally, pissin' myself in an effort to control the laughter. The others weren't doing much better either: Stu in particular looking properly pained trying not to laugh. Ah, my God, that was funny! The Magistrates had royally taken the piss out of Ste for trying to take the piss out of them!

"Sir, can I just say one more thing?"

"Yes Best, go ahead."

"Can you do me another favour please?"

"Yes Best, if I can."

"Don't do me any more favours."

Ah, fuckin' 'ell, it was so funny! How the beak didn't jail Ste for contempt of court I'll never fuckin' know. Maybe he was just so pissed off with this bunch of scallies he wanted us out of his court and away. Maybe he had a hot date with Ping-Pong Po or more likely the blow-up version of Ping-Pong Po; I just don't know but no matter what he let us all go.

"You are all free to leave."

I tell you I couldn't get outta that court quick enough! I was still doubled over when we hit the first alehouse in King Street.

"Fuckin' 'ell Ste, yer a cheeky twat. What was all that about Saudi?"

"Fuckin' sarcastic twat, "I'll give you a fortnight to pay". Fuck 'im and 'is fine. I'm fuckin' off to Jersey tomorrow. Ack, ack, ack, ack!"

And he did!

CHAPTER SEVEN

ARSES AND ARSE'OLES

I went on the special the following week to Derby County. I think I was probably the only Kopite on it and the Road End took the opportunity to let me know it!
"We'll look after you today!"
I loved being with them, it was good crack, but I wasn't having them singing that shit at me.
"Fuck off, I can look after myself!"
"We are the Road End, the pride of Merseyside, we do all the fightin' while the Kopites run an' 'ide!"
I was fighting a losing battle seeing as I was on my own so decided to become a Road Ender for the day. Good it was too. I was though gonna have to be prepared to get stuck in like the rest of them should we get any shit from the sheepshaggers - and we probably would. Not before or during the match that is. There were never any of them around before the game and during it we used to take their side (must be shit having a side rather than an end) but there always plenty of snides hanging around after the game. Leicester were a bit like that too.

The match itself was a piece of piss. This team was just getting better and better. Kenny scored a brilliant goal to give us the lead holding off with his arse, as only Kenny could, a challenge from a defender and rifling in an unstoppable shot. What an arse Kenny had! I don't mean that in any sort of gay way I hasten to add; just that Kenny's arse was as much a part of his footballing armoury as his legs. He used that arse to such great effect over the years. Defenders just couldn't get near him as he'd arse them off and then turn them in the blink of an eye giving himself that yard of space that is so vital. Of course Kenny wasn't the quickest around so had to make up for that lack of pace (although he wasn't actually a slouch) whichever way he could including quickness of thought and a boss arse. Oh okay then, there, I've said it – KENNY'S GOT A BOSS ARSE!
Kenny's goal would have been a candidate for the BBC Goal of the Season until Ray Kennedy scored what was to turn out to be the winner of that award. An eight man passing movement ended with

the ball at Razor's feet. Razor just calmly, no fuss, slipped the ball under the goalkeeper and that was it – game over! It wasn't the most spectacular goal you'll ever see, not like say a thunderous 30-yard volley but I could see why it won Goal of the Season. That was the way this team was playing their football now; great passing, hardly ever losing the ball, minimum of fuss, win the game, no problem. The game was virtually won with twenty minutes left so it was time to take the piss – and nobody could do it better than us – players and fans! I'm not sure why but Derby full-back, Steve Buckley, became the main butt of our mirth. It might have been the fact that he was a bit chub of chop but he was mercilessly ragged, to the point of actually being cheered by us, every time he touched the ball and sometimes when he didn't. In that twenty minutes Steve Buckley became almost a cult hero to the travelling Liverpudlians. Buckley, the rest of the Derby players and the 23,000 or so Derby fans inside the Baseball Ground must have wondered what the fuck was going on. Great fun!

It was always mad getting out of Derby's ground. You had to walk along the side we were in (the Leyside), get on the track, up on to the Osmaston Road terrace behind the goal and then use the gates at the back of that terrace to get out. Quite why there was never any more lumber than actually occurred at the Baseball Ground, with opposing fans mixing, I'll never know. Once outside, the bizzies were directing us down a road towards the station. Plod had the side streets cordoned off with flimsy wooden barriers. The Derby lads, snides remember, must have thought they'd be safe throwing bricks and bottles from behind these barriers. A load of Road End crashed through, under and over the barriers to teach the sheepshaggers a short, sharp, painful lesson that it wasn't very nice to do stuff like that! I was thankful that I didn't have to get involved, they didn't need me anyway, but it was fun watching the lads.

I'm not sure where all the ale and butties came from on the train home, maybe somebody had robbed an offy before we got back on, but I was glad of them Remember they used to have a buffet car on the specials? Must have been fuckin' mad to put that on! Wouldn't have liked to be the stock taker on that. I don't think they ever took more than two bob on any buffet car in all the years the specials were

running.
"We looked after you today!"
Well fair enough they did I suppose. Good lads and a great day.

Talk of the elusive Double intensified as we easily disposed of Burnley 3-0 in the FA Cup 5th Round tie at Anfield. This was followed by two goalless away draws at Chelsea and Coventry. Games were coming thick and fast now as the backlog of postponements was beginning to be cleared.

I was taking no chances for the trip to Ipswich for the FA Cup 6th Round tie. My only previous visit there ten years earlier had been a nightmare twenty-four hour round trip on Lawrenson's. I was going on the special for this one. That still necessitated an early start but staying at Ma's on the Friday night would make sure I was at Platform 9 Limey in good time. Three hours or so drinking in the Viking with Stu was NOT good preparation for the last bus from the Conny to the Black Bull journey.
"Black Bull please mate."
"Not goin' the Black Bull, only as far as Aintree Garage."
Yeah, just to be fuckin' awkward aren't yer?
"Okay mate, that'll do."
I shouldn't have had that last pint in the Viking as by now I was bursting for a piss. I wasn't sure that my overfilled bladder could hold out even as far as Aintree Garage.
Sure enough, by the time the "all round the world" bus had reached The Stanley Gate at Bickerstaffe piss was virtually leaking from me. I went downstairs to ask the driver if he could stop while I had a piss. Like he was going to!
"Can't do that ace. Behind schedule now. Gorra be at the garage for 'alf-eleven."
"Well don't spare the fuckin' 'orses then. I'm fuckin' burstin' ere!"
To his credit, despite the fact that all bus drivers in the world hated me he did just that. Even his breakneck speed couldn't keep up with my bladder though so there was fuck all else for it – piss on the floor of the top deck it was gonna have to be. I know it was dirty and I felt like a twat but I really couldn't do anything else. A bit of luck – an empty lemo bottle on one of the seats. Nice one! Even the lemo bottle couldn't take my cascading golden shower though.

STOP IT EVO – YOU'RE TURNING ME ON!

Shit! Well, no, rather piss, was all over the top deck floor and flowing like some great pissy Niagara Falls down the stairs. If the driver clocks this he's gonna lash me off but not before beating me up. I was frantically trying to mop up Niagara Falls with my Echo but it hardly stemmed the tide. The rainbow that was sure to follow would be my undoing. Bollocks to it – I'll sleep the rest of the journey and ask Dave the Driver to take pity on me as I'd pissed myself. I was woken by Dave's shouts as the bus was still in motion.

"Eh mate! Eh, you upstairs!"

Shit, he'd sussed the piss and was gonna beat me up as soon as he could stop the bus!

"Yeah, what d'yer want?"

"Eee arr, we're nearly at the garage. I'll take yer the Black Bull. I'm up on me time now."

What a guy! See, they're not all pricks.

"Ah, thanks a lot mate, yer a star."

It was me who was the prick for pissin' on his bus but what could I do?

"Couldn't take us down to the Windsor could yer mate so I can catch the chippy before it closes?"

"Yeah, no problem."

WHAT A TWAT I AM!

A night spent in my old bed at 21 Grogan Square was conducive to neither a good night's sleep nor a long day ahead of me tomorrow. Or rather today as it was now by the time I got to Ma's having walloped one lot of fish and chips from the chippy by the Windsor Castle and then hit another one on Moss Lane for Sweet and Sour Chicken with rice and a portion of chips. I really was becoming a fat bastard! That bed – fuckin''ell – must have been at least thirty-five years old! I'd certainly been sleeping in it since I was about five and I think it was already a hand-me-down from my Granny Martha. An owld iron thing it was with not so much lumps in the bed as a bed in the lump. I was grateful for it though and even more grateful to see Mam and Dad as I hadn't seen them for a while. Dad kept me up 'til about three in the morning regaling me with tales of his adventures in the Navy during the war. Dirty old goat! Good job Ma had already taken herself off to bed. Once Johnny Evo was done with his tales of derring-do in the Navy he got on to exploits at away games. I always loved those; the Portsmouth one with his mate and bro-in-law Jimmy Boyle (read all about it in OBAHK) just after the war being my favourite. Happy days!

Correct me if I'm wrong here anybody and if the old memory cells are fuzzed up but wasn't it the case that train and match tickets were sold together for this match and you couldn't buy one without the other? Seemed that way anyway as Limey was chocker and I got on one of the first of I think ten specials to leave Platform 9. The four-and-a-half-hour train journey was spent mostly sleeping. This was much better than the twelve-hour overnight coach journey to Portman Road in 1969.

Now there are knobs and there are knobs, some knobs are bigger than others and some people can't help being knobs but you tell me if this wasn't the biggest knob in Christendom! We had been warned via the Echo that there would be a huge police presence at Ipswich because of the sheer volume, not to say the reputation, of our travelling support and that said huge plod would be meeting us off the trains at Ipswich station. Now those of you who have been by train to Ipswich will know that it's possibly the shortest journey from station to ground there is in the country. So, shall we just get off the train, ignore the big plod, saying fuck all in case we get nicked and just go straight in the ground?
Well, yeah, Evo sounds a good idea.
No, 'ere comes Nobby Knob – straight off the train remember and into the arms of the waiting bizzies.
"Let's give the Ipswich a little bit o' knuckle!"
Nobby had spent about three seconds on Ipswich territory. Now what was the fuckin' point of that? Cost of train ticket, cost of match ticket, four-and-a-half hour journey just to get nicked. Fuck me; words almost fail me!

Ipswich were a good side in the process of becoming a very good side. With players of the calibre of the aforementioned Thijssen and Muhren together with Mariner, Gates, Wark and twin giant centre-halves Butcher and Osman Bobby Robson's team were no mugs. Only we had Kenny though didn't we? The King could make a mug

out of any player in the world. Early in the second half Kenny arsed off Butcher making him look a big galoot which he most certainly wasn't and curled a King Kenny special into the top corner of the net with goalkeeper Cooper flapping at thin air. The 5,000 or so of us (was there really that many) at the other end went ballistic. It was all hands to the pump after that as Ipswich laid a blue siege to our goal. The team ethic came into this one as even Kenny was defending to the hilt. Standing out above all others though like a big shining beacon was Phil Thompson. At the final whistle Thommo came right up to us and was almost dragged into the crowd by celebrating Reds. Portman Road had, a few years earlier, been the scene of one of Emlyn's greatest ever goals – and he scored a few crackers. Crazy Horse's mad celebration of that goal though was as nothing compared to his celebrations of this victory. What a team! When we needed to attack we were the best at that. When we needed to defend EVERYBODY defended to make us the best at that too.
DOUBLE HERE WE COME!

We started a run of four successive home League games with the visit of our lovely blue neighbours. Kenny scored to give us the lead after a quarter-of-an-hour but Andy King was to prove the player to be our undoing again. King's equaliser gave Everton three points out of four against us that season and how the Blues celebrated. Thing is though, which I took great joy in reminding my bluenose mates about as they were singing at me, "Three points outta four tra la la la la" is that three points out of four in a season against ANYBODY doesn't win you any medals – unless you win the League. 'Nough said?

The next two games in that run both resulted in 2-0 wins against Wolves and Ipswich. Next up was the little matter of an FA Cup semi-final against Manchester United at Maine Road. NOW THAT WAS MAD! It seemed as if the whole of Manchester had turned out to do battle with us. I'm not sure whether City had teamed up with United, I couldn't really see it, but I'd never seen Man U have such a mob that large before. I'd twisted ligaments in my ankle the week before so it was all I could do to hobble along never mind get involved in the agro. The lads I went with though, Alan and Larry, were doing their best to make up for my lack of activity and were quite looking after me. Loved those Road Enders! It was fuckin' mayhem! There were running battles everywhere before the game and even once inside, the flimsy segregation barriers at the back of the Kippax weren't enough to keep the mobs getting at each other. The match itself was a classic - one of the greatest ever FA Cup semi-finals. Both teams had to change colours so it was the first time we ever wore that shitty all yellow kit I so hated. We just didn't even look like Liverpool in that poncey kit. Kenny gave us the lead with another of his wonder goals. The King had the Manc defence turning this way and that like a rabid dog with worms before, tired of taking the piss out of them, he put them out of their misery and shot past Bailey. Joe Jordan equalised before half-time so it was game on. Greenhoff B (not the jammy bastard one) put them ahead. What the fuck Jocky Hansen was doing in the opposition's penalty area with only eight minutes remaining nobody knew but we were glad he was as he volleyed in an equaliser that had been looking increasingly unlikely.

The replay at Goodison four days later was equally as violent, off the pitch, as the first game had been. It was going on, or off, whichever way you want to look at it, all day in town, continuing in Stanley Park and the pubs around Goodison. We had to save our worst performance of the season for that game didn't we? Not taking anything away from United, they deserved to win it but we never looked like scoring apart from Ray Kennedy hitting the post late in the game. We were beaten by a goal from Greenhoff J (the jammy bastard one) and that was our hopes for the Double gone yet again for another season. It remains a mystery why our big players like Dalglish and Souness didn't perform on that night but then they couldn't be expected to do it in *every* game. Tears tripped me as I waited for the bus on County Road. I could hear the battles going on all around Goodison and could even hear the commotion coming from the direction of Stanley Park. I just wanted to get 'ome and get me fuckin' 'ead down.

FUCKIN' SHOWER OF MANC TWATS!

Sadly, that defeat was the last appearance in a Liverpool shirt for Emlyn Hughes. Emlyn had been struggling a bit with injuries this season and whereas in his previous 12 seasons he rarely missed a match he had made only 16 League and 11 Cup appearances this time around. Thommo and Jocky had started to forge a formidable centre-back partnership as had Thommo and Emlyn before them. Emlyn had been shunted between centre-back and left-back in order for Bob to accommodate him when fit but Bob knew what his preferred back four was now. Emlyn had remained captain of the team when selected and also captain of the Club. I know that since leaving Liverpool he hasn't always been everybody's cup of cocoa but for me he was Liverpool's greatest ever captain. Bob had decided that after a total of 657 games and 48 goals Crazy Horse's Liverpool career was no more. Emlyn's testimonial against our old German foes Borussia Moenchengladbach had been played a few days before the first Man U semi and drew a crowd in excess of 30,000 – a richly deserved reward for a player whose commitment to the Liverpool Football Club cause was never bettered. The money though from that testimonial would have meant nothing to Emlyn compared to the great times, great memories and host of honours he won with us.

There was great conjecture as to who would take over from Emlyn as Captain. Phil Thompson was officially vice-captain of the Club but Kenny had also done the job to good effect earlier in the season when Emlyn was injured for a lengthy spell. I'm sure it was the proudest moment of Thommo's life when he led the team out at Anfield for the game against Arsenal. Not that we were ever worried for one moment that Phil wouldn't make a success of this role but we soon saw the level of Phil's commitment and his leadership qualities. Thommo had always been a shouter and organiser on the pitch so he was in his element captaining the Club he loved so much. The Man U hangover was blown right away by a sterling performance as we romped to a 3-0 victory. A rare Alan Hansen goal gave us victory against Wolves at Molineux three days later.

Going into the Easter programme we were six points ahead of West Brom and while they had two games in hand we had the better option of points in the bag. The 2-0 home win over Man U on Easter Saturday was hardly revenge for the gut-wrenching Semi-Final defeat at their hands but it was sweet enough and easy enough anyway. The trip to mid-table Aston Villa two days later didn't look the hardest proposition in the world but we were in for a rude awakening. Villa hit us with everything in much the same way as they did when we

were humiliated there 5-1 two-and-a-half years earlier. It wasn't as bad this time as we only went in at half-time 0-2 down through goals from John Deehan and Brian Little. David Johnson pulled one back for us a quarter-of-an-hour into the second half. We gave it voice to urge the lads on but coming loud and clear from the Holte End was this song getting, as far as I am aware, it's very first hearing:
"You only sing when you're winnin'!"
Err...well. We're not actually winnin' but I know what youse mean. We weren't exactly raising the new Witton Road end roof, and very nice it looks too I might add – nice new terracing on the bottom replacing that shed of an end you used to have with that shitty shale terracing and a brand spanking new stand above it. Not sure about these fuckin' daft shiny new executive box thingies in between though with their Perspex Tommy Trinders cos if that twat in the one behind me doesn't stop giving us shit and flickin' the V's at me I'm gonna fuckin' smash through that shitty Perspex and strangle the bastard! OK? I had a cob on you see. I had even more of a cob soon after when Deehan scored again to wrap up the points for Villa and inflict upon us only our fourth League defeat of the season. Deffo wasn't 'appy, feelin' really pissed off, red hot and just wanted to get the fuck outta there so these Brummie twats couldn't give us any more shit. I really was a terrible loser. I felt like the world had come to an end whenever Liverpool lost. Wasn't often I know but it still hurt like fuck, maybe more because *I wasn't* used to it, when it did happen.

Ever been dipped? Well if you have you'll know that you know fuck all about it when it happens but when you realise you have been you remember that sudden movement of your pocket that you just dismissed as somebody brushing against you and the stomach-churning realisation some horrible, shitty bastard has had you off. Fuckin' Freddy the bastard Fish had done me like a fuckin' big kipper. Had me right off! He'd got the fuckin' lot as well – about an ill octopus (six squid – gerrit?) I was saving for the bus home from Skelhorne Street plus a fuckin' good bevy to drown my sorrows with when I got home and probably more importantly my fuckin' train ticket. Bastard! 'Ow was I gonna get 'ome? I gave it a think about trying to get on a coach but too many Villa around outside to be mingling round in the hope of getting a lift. Got away with too much stuff like that at too many places for my luck to hold out forever. Nothing else for it; I was gonna have to get on the train and try blag it. Not that I would have been blaggin' it, I was actually a genuine case, but I'm sure no guard on earth was gonna believe that. I would be able at least to get on the train anyway and see how I got on from there as tickets were never checked before you got on the train so that would be okay.

"Show all yow tickets please!"

Fuckin' 'ell, I don't believe this! I wasn't smart enough or quick enough to be able to dodge the assorted bizzies, guards and Railway Plod checking every single bastard ticket on the platform so I was gonna have to throw myself at their mercy.

"I 'aven' gorra ticket mate. I was dipped in the ground."

"Roight, gow over there and tell that policeman."

Fuck off yer Brummy twat!

"Okay mate, ta."

The guard clearly hadn't believed me and had displayed not one flicker of emotion or sympathy for my plight. The bizzy was similarly disbelieving but at least took some details and gave me a chance.

"Gow in the guard's van there and a Railway policeman will be along to interview yow."

"Thanks officer."

I meant it too. I'd probably be lashed off in the middle of nowhere (that song again – ah what memories!) but at least it was a start to getting home. Much preferable to dodging Villa all over the place or worse still having to go to New Street and dodge not only Villa but probably West Brom and Birmingham on the way back from wherever they'd been playing.

"Roight, yow the kid who's 'ad 'is ticket nicked?"

Well I'm 'ardly a kid soft fuckin' shite! I'm twenty fuckin' five years of age, married with two kids me fuckin' self but yeah, if yow, I mean you, wanna call me a kid then I'm a fuckin' kid. Just get me back to Limey for fuck sake!

"Yeah, that's me officer. Fuckin' twats aren't they? Yer own fuckin' fans dip yer. Bastards! Fuckin' arse'oles!"

"If yow doesn't stop swearing I'll nick yow now for obscene language!"

OOOHHHHH! Shades of PC Shaw – Hillsborough 1969. Yeah okay

I might be swearin' but I'm not mimiwaukin' yer am I?
"Yeah, sorry officer. I'm just wound up."
To give Ronnie the Railway Plod his due though he took every detail imaginable, checked it all out including me telling him exactly where and why we stopped on the way down due to the engine overheating (or was it leaves on the line? No couldn't 'ave been that – it only 'appens in Autumn that. Doesn't it?), and let me continue my journey back to Limey.
"Yow'll 'ave to stop in 'ere thow!"
"Yeah, no problem officer. Thanks."
There was still the major problem, given my run-ins with bus drivers over the years of trying to bunk some kind of a bus. It would either have to be the L3 to Linacre Lane, go to Ma's and bum the money for the bus home from the Black Bull off her or just take the chance of bunking the 305 at Skelhorne Street and risk not getting sussed all the way home. I couldn't make my mind up and was hovering between the Crosby and Skem stops.
"Hiya Peter. Been to Villa?"
It was Wilko, the Stan Harvey twatter, Road Ender and my fellow great West Brom bunker-inner.
"Yeah Gary. You there too?"
"Yeah, didn't see yer."
"Nah, I was in the fuckin' guard's van all the way 'ome. Some fuckin' twat dipped me. Got all me money and me train ticket. Gonna 'ave to bunk the bus 'ome."
"Ee arr, 'ere's a quid. Giz it back at the footy next week."
Mental note: must let Gary off with two bookings – 'alf a quid each. Nice one, enough for not only the bus 'ome but also my entrance fee to the Derby Arms – I could borrow some more dosh when I got in there. Laughin'!
"Ta Gary."
"Shit game wasn't it. We won't win the League yer know if we don't buck up. We'll fuckin' let West Brom in for it."
'E always was a moanin' fucker Gary.
"Yeah, ee arr Gary, let's get on before 'e fucks off without us."
Good lad Wilko. Shit footballer but great guy!

CHAPTER EIGHT

HORSES FOR COURSES

Bristol City were beaten 1-0 at Anfield before we embarked on another run of three successive away matches. The midweek 1-1 draw at Southampton was good enough and if we could get at least a similar result at Forest on the Saturday it would set us up nicely for the run in. A Bedford van full, well over full actually – there must have been ten of us in there, of Road Enders from Skem plus me on a special invite made the trip to Nottingham. We parked quite a bit away from the ground and were getting well and truly sussed on the way up by Forest lads but they didn't dare come near this bunch of loons. I mean, I *knew* the likes of Ashy and Gilly and even *I* was scared of them so imagine what Robin Hood's merry twats made of them! We were in that shitty side again, scene of so much shite thrown at us on previous visits. The good news was that the fuckin' yard was being pulled down in the close-season to make way for a new all-seater super-dooper stand. Oh fuckin' yippee! They'd probably make us stand on that equally shitty open end next season. The game was largely uneventful apart from Terry Mac hitting the post. Both sides seemed happy to settle for the 0-0 draw; Forest because they had the previous midweek reached the European Cup Final where they would play the Swedish team Malmo and ourselves because it was a good result for us in our bid to regain the title we'd lent Forest for a year. Forest themselves were more or less out of contention so a draw was happy days all round. Things were fairly quiet off the park too, we didn't even have any light bulbs thrown at us; the real fun was to happen on the way home! Apart from a massive battle on the bridge (about 500 a side) by the station we managed to make it back to the Beddy with not much fuss

I didn't know Uttoxeter from a hole in the ground. Well, there was one thing I knew about it – it had a racecourse and the Midlands Grand National was run there. Whoopy do! I also, in a vague way, associated it with luncheon meat. Why? Cos a firm called UNOX used to make luncheon meat.

Uttoxeter – UNOX – Luncheon meat? What *are* you on Evo?

I know, it's just the way my somewhat twisted mind works. Anyway, I'm sure it was a very nice place if not exactly where I'd choose to spend a Saturday night out. The driver of our RoadEndmobile, Billy Ash, decided that the good people of Uttoxeter were going to "enjoy" the company of our bunch of scally twats this fine Spring Saturday evening. For a couple of hours at least that is 'til we'd had our fill of ale. Harry the Horse, the landlord of the local hostelry gave us a look of disdain when we piled in to his previously near empty boozer.
"Neigh lads! You're not comin' in 'ere!"
Nah, he didn't say that. I just made it up. The few locals in there also gave us the Slaughtered Lamb treatment. I think there might have only been the one pub in the town. A one horse town – eh that's good isn't it? I can't remember the name of the pub – probably something very horsey. Right, I'm gonna make one up – THE HORSE'S COCK – yeah, that's what it was called. Whaddya mean I can't call it that? It's my fuckin' story and if I'm gonna make a pub name up with a horsey connection I'm gonna make it a good 'un. Fuck all this BAY HORSE/ HORSE AND JOCKEY shit. What kind of names are they? Fuckin' poncey names that's what! I mean, d'yer think when the writer of "An American Werewolf in London" was thinking up a name for the pub in that film he thought of THE SILENT LAMB or THE MEEK AND MILD LAMB or even worse still just THE LAMB? No, he went for the bollocks so to speak and came up with THE SLAUGHTERED LAMB. So if he's having THE SLAUGHTERED LAMB I'm having THE HORSES COCK!
And bloody welcome you are to it too Evo!
Thankyou!
THE HORSE'S COCK it is then! How far is the HORSE'S COCK INN? I've got a video like that! Anyway, I've got the design for the pub sign in mind: there's a farmer in a farmyard and he's leading his horse around on that strap thing. The horse has a piece of string tied to it's neck and at the end of that is a cockerel, you know like you sometimes see with a dog attached to the horse 'cos it's the horse's mate. So the cockerel is the horse's mate see? So: THE HORSE'S COCK. Where's the harm in that? THE HORSE'S COCK started filling up when the racing fraternity, bores to a fuckin' man, started coming in. Oh, fuckin' Harry couldn't do enough for them! Within five minutes there was horse shit everywhere.

"Oh I had three thousand pounds on a 9-4."

"Yes, I had twenty-eight thousand million pounds on the 500-1 outsider in the last race."

"I had a Yankee up!"

Well so did me fuckin' Granny during the war but she never went round braggin' abarr it! Fuck off yer fuckin' shower o' borin' twats. Do yer fuckin''ead in these gamblers don't they? I don't mean the likes of us who throw the odd flim, cock and hen or score on the gee gees – I mean these pricks who because they wear flash coats and daft fuckin 'ats think they're so much fuckin' better than us. Ever been the races an' seen them fuckin' poncin' around? 'As to be seen to be fuckin' believed I can tell yer. An' the men are no better! Funny 'ow these wankers are always full of themselves when they win, tellin' us 'ow much they've done on this day an' 'ow much last fuckin' week when they took their private jet down to Ascot. Never tell yer 'ow much they've lost when they lose big do they? Anyway, we were just sitting there, doing nobody any harm, having a quiet bevy (well, as quiet as this load of loons could be) and laughing at the day's proceedings when we heard this almighty fuckin' roar and saw a load of lads who we recognised to be Road End swarming towards the pub. Harry fair shit 'imself I can tell yer. Half an hour after having just Bert and Fred, the local horse wankers (I know a great story about that - good evening) in his pub he now had about fifty Road End in there – not good. Not that Harry knew they were Road End – he was probably less knowledgeable about the Road End than I was about Uttoxeter prior to my inaugural visit. Once they were there though he knew he had them! Ale, scallies, tales of nasties and battles of the bridge with Forest all mixed together with horse shit was a lethal combination. Harry didn't know whether he was coming or going. As he was pulling a pint for one lad another would be helping himself at the Guinness pump which was only a diversion anyway as another lad rifled the crisps and nuts.

"What's the Archie Moore 'ere anyway lads? Where've yer all come from?"

"The train broke down 'cos we kept pullin' the cord. They're sendin' another one out. They said it'll be abarr an hour."

"The special?"

"No, we were on the ordinary."

"All youse were on the ordinary?"
"Yeah, there's a load of others too gone into the town on the rob."
"Didn't think they 'ad a town!"
I was staying exactly where I fuckin' was. I was in enough shit already with the impending Manchester Crown Court case for the Wigan shenanigans. There was a very good chance of me going to jail anyway – a spot of raping and pillaging would deffo see me go down. Anyway, for all THE HORSE'S COCK was a shit pub frequented by a load of horse wankers (that really is a funny story – might tell you it in book 6) the ale was good, in fact perfect – Stella! So, the Road End indulged in looting, raping and pillaging. They raped the men and pillaged the women.
Don't you mean the other way round Evo?
No, this was the Road End – the Road End did it their way and who are we to argue with them?

A few of the local lads – Stoke supporters it turned out – came to THE HORSE'S COCK to see what all the fuss was about. After giving a bit of mouth, to which they received a slap or two, they did the most sensible thing they could have done with all these loons around and fucked off back to ostle their horses. They might have even been horse wankers. By the time THE HORSES'S COCK emptied (ooh err missus!) there were bizzies everywhere. Apparently a jeweller's shop window had been smashed and a load of gear robbed. They were on the lookout for anybody with cuts to their hands. Gilly had a cut hand.
"'Ow d'yer cut yer 'and son?"
"On our van officer."
Gilly was actually telling the truth. He'd cut his hand getting out of the van on a sharp edge of a part of the rust bucket that should have contained a light.
"Show me."
We took Horse the Plod to the van and showed him exactly where Gilly had cut himself. I hoped to fuck they weren't gonna take the van away for forensics 'cos if plod kept hold of it as long as they'd kept hold of my gear after the great Wigan incident we'd never get home! Freddy Forensic still had all our gear from that night nine months later. Fuck knows what they were looking for. We were in

luck as Plod instantly believed Gilly's true story which is downright fuckin' amazing if you ask me! I mean plod believing a true story? Whatever next? Apparently the bizzies got on the train at Crewe and recovered most of the stolen jewellery. We made our way home with the League Championship in our sights and merrily pissed but not so much that we couldn't manage a few in the Viking when we got home to regale the regulars with tales of THE HORSE'S COCK.

It snowed on May Day. I'm fuckin' telling you it did! Those of us at Burnden Park that night, and their massive Railway Embankment End was full of Reds plus a few in the Manchester Road terrace so there must have been a good 10,000 or so, know full well it snowed and snowed hard! There had been no sign of it during the day as it was warm and sunny. By the time we'd got to Bolton and on that big open terrace though it was like a scene from a Christmas card. Some people had been caught out badly, going the match in shirtsleeves, that was honestly how quickly it changed, and had to be treated for exposure. No, not INDECENT exposure yer tit! Wasn't too cold though for the Road Enders in the Manchester Road terrace to be involved in a bit of cuffs of fist.

Right, that's the weather report, now on to the politics. We were facing a General Election two days after the match. The Tories were expected to win it by a landslide due to the soon to be deposed Labour Government, especially poor old PM Jim Callaghan, being so helplessly out of touch with the Unions that a damaging, far-reaching Winter of Discontent had been suffered last Winter. Well it would be Winter wouldn't it being a Winter of Discontent. Still, a Labour Government, no matter how bad, was infinitely preferable to a Conservative Government. Too many people though were taken in by Maggie Thatcher – the housewives friend. My arse! **Oh yeah, she knows 'ow much a bag of shoppin' costs – let's vote for 'er!** Mind you, it couldn't have just been women who were taken in by her; the huge victory must have meant that plenty of blokes voted for her too. The housewives friend had within a month of getting her smelly feet into Number Ten increased the price of petrol from 84 pence to £1:18. Yeah, friend of the motorist too wasn't she? Okay, wasn't all her doing; there was an oil crisis going on in the Middle

East but The Iron Lady knew what she was doing alright! She'd promised everybody jobs too! Yeah, she was gonna reduce the dole queues and get everybody back to work. Good owld Maggie! Funny standing on that open end at Bolton, freezin' cold with the snow turning us all into Father Christmas as a particularly renowned Skem doleite, whose name I shall keep to myself to for fear of blowin' him up to the Soash (is that how you spell it? You know, that word that's short for Social Security) turned to me and said, "Fuckin' 'ell Evo, I 'ope that Maggie Thatcher one doesn't get in. She's said she's gonna get us all jobs. I'm fucked if I'm workin' in this!"

He never did get a job and as far as I know, 24 years later is still out of work. Maggie reigned supreme for eleven years as PM and the Tories were still in power for another seven years after that. How gullible are some people? Six months after Maggie came to power you couldn't find anybody, man or woman, who would own up to voting Tory at that election. You'd still be hard pushed now to find anybody who voted Tory at the subsequent General Elections either! That's all for the weather and politics; now on to football. Do I sound like Trevor Macdonald?

No Evo, more like Ronald Macdonald. Fuckin' gerron with it!

Right, the match - piece of piss, absolute piece of piss! By the time Graeme Souness had put the ball into his own net late in the game it didn't matter as that made the score 4-1 to us with goals from Johnno, Kenny and a brace by Man of the Match Kennedy R. Well, when I say Souey's oggie didn't matter I mean it didn't matter to us or I'm sure anybody else, except Clem who was fuming at his clean sheet being sullied (he was funny like that) but I'm equally sure it mattered a lot to Souness who was fuckin' blazin' and looking to blame anybody but himself. Bolton's Frank Worthington had scored a wonder goal in their previous home match against Ipswich. I'm sure you've all seen it by now as it's been replayed on telly about a million times. Frank had his back to goal just outside the Ipswich penalty-area with defenders Butcher and Osman behind him. Frank took the ball on his thigh, let it drop down on to his right foot, flicked it up, then flicked it again over the heads of himself, Butcher and Osman with his right foot spinning past the two centre-backs and into the penalty-area all in one sublime movement then hit the ball on the volley with his left foot into the net. A truly brilliant goal; one of the

best I've ever seen. The then Ipswich Manager Bobby Robson (that was before he was a Sir) still says it's the best goal he's ever seen and he knows a little bit about footy! So what did the massed Reds start singing as soon as Souey's goal went in?
"We all agree, Souey is better than Worthy!"
Shower of piss-taking bastards aren't we?

After having been to register my vote, for what it was worth but you have to vote don't you, I was off to referee a Skem League Cup quarter-final in the Skem League – British Legion v UHWMC. Playing for the Legion was Billy Bins. Billy's real name wasn't Bins it was just that he was never seen without his specs – even when he was playing. I had reason to book Billy during the match for dangerous play i.e. his foot was nearly wrapped around an opponent's head.
"Fuckin''ell ref, I've only got pumps on!"
"I know Billy but I have warned yer before and that was just far too high."
"But what fuckin' 'arm am I gonna do with fuckin' pumps on!"
"Well Billy it was dangerous play, I've warned yer before so I'm issuin' you with an official caution for persistently infringin' the laws of the game."
Knew all the terminology I did. I must have been right 'cos even the Legion's Manager John Kenny didn't moan about it and he most definitely would have done if he thought I was even one iota wrong. Great guy John but he couldn't half moan.

I was in the Viking the following night having my usual Friday bevy with Stu. The Viking footy team had played in the Wigan Amateur Saturday League Cup Final that night at Springfield Park but weren't expected to win it. They all piled in at about nine o'clock cock-a-hoop as they actually had won. Billy Bins played for the Viking. Oh shit! I wasn't gonna try to avoid him – I'd done fuck all wrong but at the same time I didn't want any confrontation over the previous night's carry on. I was on my way to the bog. Billy was playing the bandit. I hoped to skirt past him without him noticing. No chance!
"Eh you! You booked me last night."
"Yeah I know Billy but I 'ad no choice."

"I was only wearin' fuckin' pumps."

"Yeah, I know, you told me that last night but it was till a bad tackle an' it wasn't yer first."

Billy grabbed me by the scruff of the neck and lifted me up with my back against the fruit machine. If I hadn't been shittin' meself I would have found it funny to have me two little legs dangling helplessly about a foot off the floor. If I could have turned my head I would have looked round at Stu for help.

Ah, there he is! E'll be over now to 'elp me.

Stu probably couldn't see what was goin' on but wouldn't have got himself off his arse anyway. Besides, he was having a pint! This one was not gonna develop into any John Wayne. Billy was a big lad and one smack from him would be enough to do me in. I've seen some boss John Wayne's in the Viking over the years. Not many mind but when it goes off in there it goes off proper! The cavalry arrived in the shape of Joey Laycock. Joey was captain and I think Manager of Viking FC.

"Eh Billy, fuckin' leave 'im alone!"

"Joey, 'e fuckin' booked me last night an' I was only wearin' fuckin' pumps!"

Billy, will yer shut the fuck up about those pumps!

"Billy, just put 'im down will yer. 'E's only in 'ere with 'is mate 'avin' a quiet pint. Now let 'im gerron with it."

Yeah, put me down yer big fucker!

Billy did as he was bid. You didn't argue with Joey. Sound lad Joey; always had a lot of time for him. Not just because he saved me from a crack then but despite giving me down the banks on the pitch on many occasions the hand was there to shake even before I'd finished the third long blast on my whistle to signal the end of the game. Billy's sound too; boss snooker player to boot. Lost his rag on one occasion but don't we all do that. Ap-o-lo-gees were made and accepted. End of.

"What the fuck was goin' on over there Peter."

"Nothin' Stu, just a misunderstandin'."

"Oh, I thought Billy Bins was gonna crack yer."

Yeah, an' like you were flyin' over to 'elp me!

Mind you I couldn't blame him. As I say, good lad Billy but you wouldn't wanna tangle with him – unless your name was Laycock.

Phil Neal scored both goals in the win against Southampton taking us on to 62 points meaning we could clinch the title with a point against Villa in our last home game of the season three days later. There was never much doubt that we were gonna get the two points with a resounding win in this match never mind one, we were doing things in style this season, in the league at least, and so it proved. Barney opened the scoring in the very first minute to put us well on the way to Championship Number 11. Kenny added a second before half-time and Terry Mac's stunning volley gift-wrapped our trophy with more than half-an-hour left to play. All that remained now was to go for two wins in our remaining games at Middlesbrough and Leeds to give us a maximum points total of 68 beating Leeds United's League Championship winning record of 67 in the 1968-69 season. It was a tall order to get those maximum points but certainly not beyond us – nothing was for this fabulous team.

I went to Boro with Paul and Les from work. Les, who was driving, was a cracking bloke quite a bit older than me and Paul. He'd seen service in the Army during the war and never tired of telling us about it. It was funny though when he was telling us for the millionth time of a match he played in for the Army against the Navy during the war. Les was also second only to Baz as the Scousest man alive.

"Right, I don't know wedder I've told yer about dis lads so stop me if I already 'ave."

"Okay Les we will."

Oh no, not the story about the penalty again!

"Well we were playin' de Navy an' it was absolutely pissin' down with rain. We were playin' with one of those owld caseys. Remember them Peter?"

"Yeah Les."

"They used to 'ave these great big laces in dem an' dee were made o' pure leather, not like yer get now. When the rain got to dem it all soaked in so the ball weighed a ton."

Slight exaggeration there Les but carry on.

"Well our left-winger crossed it into de area an' I ran for the ball an 'eaded it, right der on me forrid. De ball was dat 'eavy an' dat 'ard it knocked me out. When I came round me mates told me I'd scored an' yer shoulda seen me forrid! I 'ad the imprint o' de ball an' a great big lace mark right across me forrid!"

Les for fuck sake keep yer fuckin' 'ands on the wheel and yer eyes on the road will yer!

Les would have been dumb without his hands.

"So anyway, dat was de equaliser an' der was only a minute to go. De ref was about to blow 'is whistle an' der centre-'alf fouled me in the area. So I picked meself up to take de penalty 'cos I was our penalty-taker yer see."

Oh right Les yeah, that makes sense.

We were building up now to this dramatic climax I'd heard so many times before. To be honest though I never tired of hearing Les tell this tale. He was a great story-teller and it was very funny anyway, if scary, to see him with his hands flying everywhere, ciggy in one, can of ale in the other. It was really a great feat of ingenuity too to be able to do all this with his hands, turn his head to tell me, sitting in the back seat, the story and drive at the same time.

"I picked de ball up. It musta weighed two ton!"

It was only one ton before Les.

Isn't that a soup yer gerrina Chinese restaurant Evo?

Shut the fuck up, it's my story or rather Les's story!

"I walked back to de edge of de area to start me run up."

Cue drum roll.

"I ran an' I 'it de ball as 'ard as I could, gave it everythin' I did!"

Come on Les for fuck sake will yer, it's not what 'appened next on Question o' Sport. We all know what fuckin' appened next, just finish it will yer, we're nearly at Boro now an' I wanna bit o' time to start shittin' meself.

"It flew in de net so we won de Forces Cup!"

Nice one Les. Fuckin' made up for yer.

"Oh, great story that Les. Wasn't it Paul? Paul?"

Jammy bastard Paul was asleep in the front or at least he was *pretending* to be asleep.

"VISITING SUPPORTERS ONLY."

It clearly said that above the turnstiles so what were all these Boro loons, and they were **proper** loons believe me, queuing up to get in? These cheeky twats weren't even *trying* to hide the fact they were

going in our end. Would have been nice if they'd been a bit cagey about it and not took the piss like this. That was a strange end at Ayresome Park. In the middle of that end was a stand with a small piece of terracing below it. Either side of it, in each of the corners, there was a sort of triangular piece of terracing. The left-hand side as you stood behind the goal was supposed to be reserved for visiting supporters as the sign above the turnstiles said. The right hand side was for Boro supporters only so ideal segregation you would have thought; keep the respective loons about eighty yards apart with a stand in between them. Of course this was pay at the gate days, years before all-ticket for every game, so as long as you weren't sussed you could really go on any terrace you wanted. The game though in these still fairly early days of crowd segregation was that if a terrace was *definitely* designated as for home or visiting supporters only then you stuck to that. The bizzies would also be on the gates making sure opposing factions, as far as possible, didn't mix. If we knew these were Boro supporters going in our end, and remember they weren't even bothering trying to hide that fact, then surely plod knew. Maybe they did know and decided to deal with it once everybody was in there but I wouldn't have thought it was the ideal way. Whatever, there were some very frightened Scousers outside the ground.
"Les, what're we gonna do? We can't go in 'ere we'll get fuckin' killed!"
"We'll 'ave to. It's gonna be as bad anywhere else isn't it?"
"Ah, we'll be okay. Don't worry abarr it."
"For fuck sake Paul, keep quiet. We're whisperin' 'ere so we won't get sussed."

Having got safely inside without being filled in we headed for the nearest copper. I don't mind admitting I was properly shittin' meself. The Boro lads were everywhere in groups of up to about 50. There were only a few Reds dotted around but as it was quite early I was hoping "our" end would fill up pretty quickly and we'd be okay. It filled up alright – with Boro. Christ, this was mad! This terrace was meant for us! The bizzy we were standing by moved away. We got sussed.
"Where's all your lads then? Not many here is there."
It was pointless trying to put a Middlesboro accent on. I can't even

write the accent never mind speak it!
"Oh, they'll all be 'ere soon. The trains mustn't be 'ere yet."
There were about twenty behind us three now. Paul's earlier bravado had gone. Les was bad but I was a bloody nervous wreck.
"How many's comin'?"
"About five thousand."
I lied, we probably wouldn't have much more than a thousand, but if Billy Boro thought we had numbers maybe he'd think twice about him and his mates filling us in.
"'Ow come yer all in 'ere anyway? I thought this was our end."
It was all I could do to speak as my mouth was that dry and it wasn't too easy to get my words out anyway seeing as my guts were in my mouth.
"We do this all the time. You shoulda seen us against Leeds."
Oh nice to know it's not just us then. Very soon yer gonna kick our fuckin' 'eads in aren't yer?
We were saved by the fact a good few more Reds had just come in and we're next to the fence by the Paddock. Billy and his buddies fucked off down there to do battle – at least the numbers would be more equal down there and the Reds had a chance but if they'd have kicked off on us we'd have been mincemeat.
"Come on, let's fuck off over there before they get back."
Keeping outta of the way of the agro though was virtually impossible as it was going off in little bursts all over the place. The specials arrived about half-an-hour before kick-off and then it really did go mental. There were running battles all over the terraces and both sets of lads were chasing each other up and down the stairs leading to the bogs and the snack bars. The bizzies then decided it was time for action – at fuckin' last - and moved a load of bodies in to that end which was nice as Boro temporarily forgot about us and started fightin plod. MAD! Honestly was fuckin' crazy. This was one match I'd be glad to see over and outta the fuckin' way. The Reds on that terrace were by now split into groups I would say of no more than ten. There was certainly no singing. Everybody was keeping it firmly schtum! Johnno scored. Yes. Little clench of the fist. Quick look and a glimmer of a smile at Les.
"Fuckin' go 'ead. Go ead Johnno! Fuckin' great goal!"
WHAT THE FUCK'RE YER DOIN?

Paul was fuckin' bouncin' up and down. I tried as far as the fairly tightly packed crowd would allow to get away from him. No chance – I was stuck with him. All the other Reds had the same idea as me so there wasn't much kick-off after the goal but if it wasn't for the bizzies in there I'm sure Paul would have got us beaten to a pulp. There were still thirty-five minutes to play. I just couldn't see us putting up with this for another half-an-hour or more. Les had the best idea five minutes from time.

"Come on lads, let's go. Ders gonna be murder outside after this."

That was the first and so far only time I've EVER left a match before the final whistle. It was the only sensible thing to do. Trouble was, a load of other Reds had the same idea so there was Les's predicted "murder" going on all over the road. We managed to get back to Les's car grateful for the 1-0 win and the fact we were still all in one piece. SCARY GROUND!

Trips to Elland Road could be scary too but anything we got there was gonna be nothing compared to Boro. I wish the 3,000 or so Reds at Leeds had been at Boro; maybe it wouldn't have been as scary but no matter. The Boro 3 plus Peter Whitty made the trip in Les's car to Leeds. Paul wised up and sat in the back seat with me while it was Peter who pretended to be asleep in the front as Les went through the tale of the penalty – you know, the one he'd never told us before.

As well as Leeds' record of 67 points we also had one other target to aim for in this match. A national "newspaper", the one we all hate now and whose name I even refuse to mention – hang on, can I digress here?

Digress to yer 'earts content Evo lad – just surprised yer asked!

If I ever become rich and enormously famous from writing these books I'd love this national "newspaper" to come to me and offer me a load of dosh for an interview or an advert, something like that. I'd give them the same answer as Ricky Tomlinson did when they offered him £40,000 for an advert:

SHOVE IT RIGHT UP YER FUCKIN' ARSE!

Anyway, this national "newspaper" had for a few years been offering a prize of £10,000 to the next team that scored 100 goals in a First Division season. Having conceded that was now virtually impossible to do they then revised that figure to 84 goals i.e. an average of 2 per game. We needed two goals in this match to achieve that target and therefore grab the dosh. Johnno reduced that target by one after twenty minutes. Twenty minutes later and the dosh was ours! Jimmy Case netted and the players as well as the fans went berserk. Jimmy and Johnno celebrated by both rubbing their fingers as if to say," We're in the money." How the players deserved it too. They had been brilliant all season. We could forgive the odd lapse in Cup games. Leeds fans were urged to up the volume by a message relayed to them in that naff American way via the electronic scoreboard. The Leeds fans duly did start encouraging their team. We had the answer though:

"You only sing when yer told to!"

Class!

Johnno scored our 85th and last goal of the season to give us a 3-0 victory and yet another clean sheet. We really had finished off the season in style winning all of our last five games, scoring 13 and conceding only one (Souey!). As far as I and many other Reds believe this was the best Liverpool team ever, certainly just League-wise. We proved we were the greatest Football League Champions ever with 68 points, 85 goals for and only 16 against. Quite simply – we were the very best!

CHAPTER NINE

RETURN TO WIGAN PLEASE!

I was about to walk away from Blaguegate in disappointment. The match I was supposed to referee couldn't be played as one of the teams, because there was nothing to play for in their last game of the season, failed to turn up. I'd needed the dosh for my ale money in the Viking too as I was Bernie Flint. Shit!
"Ref, haven't you got a game?"
"No mate. Team didn't turn up."
"I'm Mick Waite, secretary of the Ormskirk Saturday League. We've got a final over on Liverpool Road but one of the linesmen hasn't turned up. Do you want to do it?"
Too right I wanna do it mate! No ale otherwise.
"Yeah okay Mick."
"Okay, do you want a fee of three pounds or a trophy?"
I didn't even need to think about that one. You didn't get a choice in the Skem League; it was a trophy or nothing. Nice to have the choice for this one but, as I say, I didn't really have to make a choice.
"I'll take the trophy please Mick."
Yeah, I was gaggin' for a bevy and all that but there was nothin' like a trophy on the mantelpiece or wherever for a job done. It was a Cup Final after all and Cup Finals are about doing the job for the love of it, nice trophy at the end of it like, not the dosh.
"I thought you'd say that. We haven't actually got the trophies with us but we'll post yours out to you."
"No problem Mick."
Eddie Pope, good referee, was in charge of the Agricultural Cup Final between Aughton Men's' Club and Murex (bit too close to Durex for my liking but then I suppose that's just my twisted mind). It was a good game with Murex running out narrow, but deserved, winners.
"Thanks Peter. You did well there. Fancy reffing in the Ormskirk Saturday League next season?"
"Yeah okay Mick but I won't be available every week. I go to all Liverpool home games and a few aways, so I'll ref on the days I can't get to the aways. That ok?"
"Yes, that's fine Peter. Just let me know the dates you're available when the fixtures come out."

I liked this man. I was half expecting him to tell me there was no chance, it was every week or not at all. I might have to sacrifice a few aways I might normally go to but as dosh was getting tighter and tighter I probably wouldn't have been able to go to as many as I would have liked anyway, so at least I'd have some bevy money to make up for that. I thought I'd get cheeky.
"Do us a favour though Mick. I was bankin' on me fee from that match I was supposed to ref for me ale money tonight. I don't want money for doin' that line. I want the trophy but can yer lend's three quid an' I'll give yer it back when I ref me first match for yer next season?"
"Yes, no problem Peter."
RE-SULT-AMUNDO! Trophy and ale money! Lenzyerodz returns!

I used my three squid, well Mick Waite's three squid (I did give him it back – honest) to go the Derby Arms. My mate, fellow Grimwooder and fellow Red, Mick Robins was in there with his highly delectable bird Jeanette. Mick and Jeanette were about to be wed (well, not that night but you know what I mean) and a very nice couple they made too!
"Peter, comin' on me stag night?"
Too fuckin' right I was goin' on Mick's stag night! I loved stag nights. I liked Mick. As I say he was a fellow Red and one of me bezzy mates in Grimwood's, even though he'd only been there a couple of years or so. He was away soon anyway to go working for Mr. Kellogg in Mancland so it'd be a farewell bevy too. He was still gonna live in Skem and played for Newgate in the Sunday League so I'd still see him around plenty but it was a good excuse anyway, if excuse were needed, for a bevy.
"Yeah, sound Mick. When is it?"
"Seventh of July."
Seventh of July? Seventh of July? Why did that date ring a bell? Ah, that's right, yeah; it was the seventh of July last year that I got up to my Wigan misdemeanours. A year to the day. Brought back painful memories with the very real threat of nick still hanging over me like that Roman fella's sword. Mick wouldn't be goin' to Wigan for his stag do anyway. Nah, he'd be goin' to Ormskirk or into town not Wigan. Mick wasn't a Wigan type person.

"Where are we goin' Mick?"
"Wigan."
Oh fuckin' brilliant!
A year to the day was just too bad an omen. I was gonna be in more bother wasn't I? *Please don't go to Wigan Mick.*
"Nice one Mick. Look forward to it."
Jeanette, as I have previously intimated, was quite a fit young lady and blonde to boot. Now you know how I feel about blondes! I'd only just got over my fixation with Debbie Harry; surely the sexiest blonde ever lived! Remember that picture of her in the Daily Mirror in her schooly uniform and her legs open? My God, did some bashin' to that!
Eh Evo, fuckin be'ave! Go an' get a cold shower!
Jeanette used to wear these leather kecks that showed off her very nice bum quite lovely. She actually looked not unlike, with her blonde hair, leather kecks and bum, Olivia Newton John who you know from previous chapters I was hopelessly devoted to a year or so earlier. We were having a good bevy, a laugh and generally enjoying our Friday night out 'til this bloke took quite a fancy to Jeanette, her leather kecks and her bum. Not much wrong with that I suppose – you can't help looking at a pretty young filly can you? Only trouble was, where you would normally keep your thoughts to yourself about another bloke's bird, this bloke made his quite plain. I'm not sure that this bloke knew at first that Jeanette was Mick's bird anyway but Mick, I suppose quite rightly, took exception to his comments. This bloke, by the way, was also called Mick but I don't wanna keep calling him Mick in case I get you confused.
Yer fuckin' jokin' aren't yer Evo? Yer've been confusin' us for years with these fuckin' books. No fuckers got a clue what yer on abarr!
Okay, Mick me mate is now Robbo, with two b's. Bloke who fancies Jeanette is Mick. He's a taxi driver by the way. Also, Mick the taxi driver is big as fuck – about six feet four and seventeen stone. Mick me mate, sorry Robbo? He's about 5feet 10ish and as thin as yer like. Ten stone fully clothed in his duffel coat and steelies.
Jeanette was on her way to the toilet. I've gotta admit, even I was clockin' her bum but I wouldn't have been so coarse as to make lewd comments about her.

Oh, saint fuckin' Evo or what?
"The arse on 'er. That's one lovely bum!"
"Ee arr mate, d'yer mind, she's me bird."
"Yeah, so?"
"Well yer know like she's me bird. Stop lookin' at 'er."
"No."
"Well, stop sayin' stuff."
"No."
"Look mate, I don't want any trouble but yer know, fuckin' pack it in."
"No, you look, I'm clockin' yer bird an' whether yer want trouble or not if yer don't shut the fuck up yer gonna get it."
"Ah, come on you two fuckin' pack it in."
I was impressed with Robbo standing his ground but Mick, as I say, was a big fucker, a bit of a nark, and wouldn't have thought twice about lamping Robbo. Mick was well out of order for what he was saying but sometimes you just have to swallow it don't you and get on with it, especially if you're faced with a big fucker.
"Okay, but don't be fuckin' 'asslin' me."
Fuckin' 'ell Henry Evo Kissinger or what?
By the time Jeanette got back from the toilet all the fuss had died down and she knew nothing about it. By that time also, Mick the taxi driver had gone up to the Alex, probably to ogle some other guy's bird, which was a good thing all round methinks – Mick going up the Alex that is, not ogling some other guy's bird.
Moral of the story Robbo: If some big fucker about six feet four and seventeen stone fancies yer bird, let him get on with it.

Mick's stag do was superb. I'm safe to call him Mick now aren't I? I don't have to keep calling him Robbo do I?
No, you carry on Evo. Yer doin' well son!
Well anyway, the stag do was superb. We did the rounds of the clubs and bars and kept pretty much out of trouble. I did though avoid somebody's suggestion to go to Aries 'Ad enough of that fuckin' place! Tiffany's had this massive video screen. Not that I knew it was a video screen when I first saw it of course. I'd hardly ever seen a video so seeing last night's Top of the Pops replayed with Gary Numan and the Tubeway Army (the Anny Road Army woulda

battered them) giving it the big one with their Number One, "Are 'Friends' Electric" on this massive video screen was really something to behold. "Ring My Bell" was next on. Funny watching Mick on the dance floor. His bird might have been Olivia Newton John but he was certainly no John Travolta! That is 'til Mick had a bellyful of ale. Strange to see that; four or five pints and he was like Bambi on ice. Seven or eight pints plus a few shorts and he was struttin' his funky stuff man all over the dance floor! He was the only man I knew who danced better the drunker he got. We eventually got thrown out of Tiffany's when Mick insisted on belting out his favourite song "London Lady" from the Stranglers Rattus Norvegicus LP right there, on his own, on a table. One of the great sights in Skem in the late '70's was Mick and Gilly bringing the house down in the Viking doing "London Lady" on a table but everybody in the Viking knew they were nutters anyway; they just blended in with the other nutters. Nobody in the Viking gave it a second thought that it was mad but it didn't go down too well with the bouncers in Tiffs. The nearest anybody came to a bit of bother was near the end of night when I temporarily lost the other lads and encountered a few Wiganers. It was my fault 'cos I'd had too much to drink and was giving these lads, who to be fair to them had said fuck all to me and were doing nobody any harm, a load of mouth. I was saved from a good hiding when the Twinnies turned up. Well at least I think it was the Twinnies. It might have just been one of them and I was seeing double 'cos I was totally bladdered. There was absolutely no way of telling those two apart. I don't think even their parents could tell them apart. Must have been some fun with their birds!

Winning the Charity Shield was an easy affair for us. I was expecting a much harder game from Arsenal but we beat them easily 3-1 with two Terry Mac specials and one of those arse-turn, spin away from defender and slot past helpless keeper efforts from Kenny. The overall performance boded very well for the forthcoming season.

I'm not really sure why we didn't play on the opening day of the 1979-80 League season. I think it might have been that we were due to play Wolves away but as rebuilding work was still ongoing at Molineux the game had to be postponed – something like that.

Whatever, it meant that our opening game would be at home to Bolton on Tuesday 21st August. Having led the field a few years earlier in the sponsorship of matches Liverpool Football Club were the innovators in this country of shirt sponsorship. Liverpool Football Club received £10,000 (whoopy do!) from electrical firm Hitachi to have their name emblazoned on our shirts for the season, and very smart it looked too! It was though the only smart thing about the match as it ground to a boring 0-0 draw. The following Saturday was much better as Johnno with two goals and Terry Mac gave us a 3-1 win at home to West Brom.

The first day of a Sunday League season is always very exciting. Everybody's up for it and dead keen. All the new kits are on show too. I was reffing Brewers Arms V Broseley Athletic. Brewers, from Croxteth, were a new team in the League. Broseley had a nice new kit, yellow and black, very smart. Brewers…what the fuck is that? Brewers were kitted out in full Manchester United away strip; right down to those shitty red and black stripes they had down one side of the shirt. Man U had worn this kit when they beat us in the semi the previous season and traumatic memories were still fresh. Well these are getting fuck all off me! The players even looked like Man U players. The tall number nine with the blonde hair looked like either of the Greenhoff bros. The number 11 looked not unlike Lou Macari.

"Captains, come to the middle for the toss please."

The Broseley Captain was the first to approach the middle.

"Good morning Captain, have a good game."

"You too ref."

The Brewers Captain ambled towards the middle.

Fuck, Greenhoff's the Captain!

"Alright ref."

Fuck off Greenhoff! Fuck off Greenhoff! Fuck off Greenhoff!

"Good mornin' Captain. 'Ave a good game mate."

"You're a Liverpudlian aren't yer ref? Yer go the match don't yer?"

Yeah Greenhoff so fuckin' what! Wanna make somethin' of it? Yer fuckin' Manc twat! Not enough beatin' us in the semi-final last season yer wanna fuckin' rub it in by spoiling me Sunday mornin'!

"Yeah I do mate. D'yer go?"

"Yeah, I've seen yer at the match."

"Oh nice one, I'll say 'ello next time I see yer. What's yer name?"

"Gordon Broadfoot."

Pleasantries exchanged and the toss done I let the Broseley Captain go for his pre-match pep talk with his players. I kept Greenhoff back for a minute.

"Okay skipper, Broseley 'ave been in the League for a couple of years now so they know what to expect from me. As youse are new to the League I'll give yer the rundown on what yer can and cannot get away with when I'm reffin.'"

"Okay ref, fire away."

"If yer wanna take quick free-kicks without waitin' for the whistle yer can but don't moan at me about their players not bein' ten yards away if it fucks up. If I tell yer to wait for the whistle that means yer *can't* take the quick free-kick an' yer *must* wait for the whistle. If I tell yer to wait for the whistle, yer don't, take it an' score I'll disallow the goal an' make yer take it again. If yer don't wait for the whistle, take it and it cocks up I'll play on an' yer won't get the chance to take it again. A bad tackle in the first minute will be punished as equally as a bad tackle in the last minute, so watch yer tackles. If there's somethin' I think I might need to 'ave a word with a player about rather than get the book out I will but I won't do it twice; the second time yer'll be booked. If yer swear at yer own players, that's okay. I don't want yer swearin' at opposin' players and I certainly don't want yer swearin' at me. If yer let the odd fuck go I'll take that but if yer actually swear at me or call me something yer'll be at least booked. One thing that'll deffo make yer walk is if yer call me a cheat. Apart from that yer can do what yer want."

"Okay ref fair enough. I'll tell the players and keep them in order."

I was beginning to like Greenhoff.

"Just one more thing Gordon."

"What's that ref?"

"What the fuck are a team from Crocky doin' wearin' the Man United kit?"

"It was that daft fucker's fault! 'Im there, Paul Crowley. We sent 'im to Jack Sharp's an' 'e fuckin' comes back with that 'cos it was dead cheap, abarr fifteen fuckin' quid or somethin'! It's shit isn't it? 'Ow d'yer think we feel wearin' it? Most of us are Liverpudlians. Don't be givin' any fuckin' dodgy penalties against us though just 'cos we look like Man U."

Fuckin' 'ell, the Lou Macari look-alike stitched yer up good and proper there!

"I won't Gordon – promise yer."
To be fair, Brewers were a good side that played the game in the correct manner and some excellent football to boot. A very good game ended in a 2-2 draw with not a booking or dodgy penalty in sight. Good start from the Crocky lads but they were gonna have to bin that kit!

A 2-3 defeat at Southampton was followed by a 4-0 win at home to Coventry. Much more like it! Sandwiched in between those games was the Football League Cup 2nd Round 2nd leg against Tranmere which we won 4-0 having drawn the first game at Prenton Park 0-0.

Quiz question: Which Liverpool player won two full International caps whilst at Anfield but never appeared in a competitive first team game for us? No? Wanna clue? He's Scottish. Still nothing? Okay, I can't blame you not having heard of him, it was Frank McGarvey. Frank arrived from St. Mirren with a big reputation and an even bigger fee; three hundred grand of Liverpool Football Club dosh went to the Paisley club. For whatever reason Frank just didn't make it at Anfield. Maybe he fell out with Uncle Bob, who knows, but he certainly didn't get a sniff of first team action. The nearest Frank came was on two occasions when he was an unused sub. We took a 25k loss later in the season to offload Frank to Celtic. One of the great mysteries that one but certainly if Frank had been brought in to shake up Johnno with the obvious threat of replacing him then it worked. Johnno was in fine form, his two goals against Coventry putting him on five from the first four games. Another pre-season signing was Israeli international Avi Cohen from Maccabi Tel Aviv. A journalist pointed out to Uncle Bob that as Avi was of the Jewish faith he wouldn't be able to play on Saturdays, the Jewish Sabbath. Bob's reply was almost Shanklyesque, "There's a few other international players here can't get a game for us on a Saturday so he won't be on his own!"
I'm not sure how Liverpool Football Club and Avi Cohen got round that one but they did. Not that it happened very often though as Avi fared only slightly better with us than Frank apart from one glorious moment but more of that later.

Terry Mac's goal saw us take a point at Elland Road. Leeds United Football Club had in their wisdom decided to move visiting fans further to the right of the Lowfield Road Terrace (did hate those fuckin' sides) meaning that we had loons to the right and just nutters above us. Hot tea, Bovril, ball bearings and fuckin' ollies of all things rained down at us from the side and above. I was glad to get outta there that day. For a change there was no trouble getting back to the coaches but I did have a big fuck off coggie behind my ear from being hit with a oncer.

Our 100th European match saw us face opponents from the Soviet Union for the first time. Georgian side Dynamo Tblisi were virtually unknown but certainly made their mark at Anfield. David Johnson gave us the lead in the first half but Dynamo, inspired by their midfield general David Kipiani, made and missed three good chances before sweeper Chivadze gave them an equaliser and more importantly a precious away goal. A Jimmy Case special blockbuster of a free-kick restored our lead before half-time. Goalkeeper Gabelia ensured that's how the scoreline stayed with a faultlessly brilliant display. Taking that slender lead to Tblisi was precarious enough but 80,000 screaming Georgians would make it even tougher for us.
Teams must have been getting the hang, a la Bolton, this season of if they'd been twatted at Anfield the season before than they would come and put eleven men behind the ball this time round to frustrate us. So it proved with Norwich as, like Bolton, they bored their way to a goalless point.

Chesterfield were dispatched 3-1 at Anfield in the next round of the League Cup but not without putting up a spirited performance.

The mini bus to Forest (we were going in style this time, not by Ashy Tours) was chocker block with Grimwooders and the Hughes brothers. The Hughes brothers were Robbo's wife Jeanette's siblings. Christ there were about twenty-eight of them! They were all mad Reds but for them the added attraction of going to Forest was that they could visit their brother Michael who had a flat in Nottingham. Their Mum, Norma, was going to put on a bit of a spread at the flat after the match so Mrs. Hughes instantly became a friend of Evo's!

Feed me and you've got a friend for life. Jimmy Hughes got the unlucky seat next to Les.
"Jimmy, 'ave I ever told yer abarr this penalty I scored when I was playin' for de Army against de Navy?"
Well, poor Jimmy wasn't to know was he? I suppose us shower of twats could have warned him before we set off couldn't we? No!
"No Les."
By the time we arrived in Nottingham Jimmy's ears were cauliflowers, having been battered incessantly by Les's penalty and associated tales. One particular Grimwooder, John Guy, had never been to a football match in his life but wanted to come anyway for the ride and the scran no doubt – John liked his scoff too! Forest had indeed built their super-dooper new stand and very nice it looked too. We had, as I'd feared, been shoved up from the old shitty side where the new stand now stood (why do they call them stands when they've got seats?) into a tiny corner of their equally shitty open end. Good job it was a nice day! The match was shit. David Fairclough was absolutely dreadful and getting a fair bit of stick from his own fans. Both sets of supporters were subdued until we struck up with a rather half-hearted You'll Never walk Alone. This woke up the Forest fans who, loud as you like, replied with, "Can you hear the Scousers sing? No, no. Can you hear the Scousers sing? No. no. Can you hear the Scousers sing? I can't hear a fuckin' thing! Woah, woah, oh, oh!"
John said, "Oh, that was very musical wasn't it? Yeah, it was nice that. I like the way they sing that."
As we were losing 0-1 at the time it didn't go down too well with any of us regular footy goers.
"Peter, shall I kick 'im down the steps first or do you want to?"
"Nah Mick, yer okay. You 'ave a bash mate. I'll get 'im after the game."
"Ee arr…wake Peter Whitty up and let 'im do it."
Refereeing question: If a player scores against the opposing team directly, without any other player touching the ball, from an indirect free-kick is the goal allowed and if not how is the game restarted? Answer: Goal is not allowed. Play is restarted with a goal-kick. Of course whilst things like this make great refereeing questions (you ought to see some of them that are thought up at referees quizzes!) they very rarely happen. It happened in this match! I'd like to say

that Clem knew the Laws of the Game and was quite content to let Viv Anderson's indirect free-kick float over his head and into the net safe in the knowledge that the goal, as such, would be disallowed. I think the truth is though Clem was beaten by the flight of the ball. It was a good job for us that referee Derek Civil was on his mettle and alert to the situation. Mr. Civil of course disallowed the goal. Not that it mattered anyway to neither Forest nor us as Gary Birtles' goal (that twat again) gave Forest victory.

Me, Mick, Steve Hughes and Jimmy were standing beside the mini bus waiting for the others to come back. There were six or seven Forest lads on the other side of the road obviously weighing up their chances of getting into us without too much harm coming to themselves.
"I think they're gonna 'ave a go 'ere Peter. What d'yer reckon?"
"Nah Mick, if they were goin' to they woulda been over by now. Let's just see what 'appens when the others get back. If they don't get any more of their mob we should be okay. Anyway, when John gets back we'll ask them to sing a song to 'im. That should make them fuck off."
The Forest lads got off. About a minute later one of them, probably aged about no more than fifteen, ran past, twatted Steve and carried on running all in one, it must be said, rather graceful movement. It was pointless chasing after Nijinsky as we didn't know how many more troops had been rounded up and were waiting to ambush us round the corner. We couldn't have chased them anyway, even if we'd wanted to, as we were all on the floor with the injured (his pride that is more than his grid) Steve rolling around pissin' ourselves laughin'! Okay, it's not really funny, or shouldn't be anyway, seeing one of your mates getting twatted at the match but sorry Steve that was fuckin' hilarious.

Michael's flat was above or very close to a shopping centre. Us twelve Scousers got some strange looks as we walked through the shopping centre but apart from the odd "Scouse bastard" (shit, never been called that before!) we came through unscathed. The Robin Hooders must have been taken aback at the sight of a little fat bastard, yes me, staring lovingly at this huge water clock that was the centrepiece of the shopping centre. It really was the most beautiful thing. I think that was the start of my fascination with clocks. At present I have 61 tick-tocks in my flat. Some people think I'm mad, I probably am, and my kids think their old Pop is slightly eccentric but each to their own eh.

"Ooh, Steven, what's happened to your face?"
"I just banged it on the mini bus Mum."
Yeah okay Ste.
I was 'Ank Marvin and looking for the buffet I'd been told Mrs. Hughes had prepared. I thought maybe it would be on a little table in the kitchen somewhere. There was a table covering nearly a full wall with a massive sheet over it. Couldn't be under there. That sheet was like a bloody big sail. Mrs. Hughes took away the sail to unveil a spread the like of which I've never seen before or since.
"Christ Norma the size of that!"
Mick's incredulity at his Mother-in-Law's superb buffet was matched by mine.
"Well I knew you'd all be hungry."
"We'll never eat all that Mum."
Oh yes we will!
"It's like the Last Supper!"
"Nah, more like the Marriage Feast of Canaan."
"What did yer start off with Mum, five loaves and two fishes?"
All these religious connotations were quite appropriate as the Pope was on the goggle box being wheeled around in that golf cart thingy as he was making a visit to Britain.
"Mrs. Hughes, I do assure you that *none* of it will go to waste. If me and Big Ev ever split up an' you an' Mr Hughes go the same way, neither of which I hope happens, will you marry me?"
A couple of hours later with our bellies full of the food Mrs. Hughes had made for us as well as the beer she'd also supplied we were on our way home. We planned a slight detour so we could have a bevy in…Uttoxeter! Happy days!

Harry the Horse shit 'imself as we walked into THE HORSE'S COCK!
"No, no, no! You can't come in here. We had trouble with you lot last season!"

"Ee arr mate, I was in 'ere last season. It was just that the train with the scalls on broke down and they all came into the town. We're the only ones likely to come this time. Lightnin' doesn't strike twice does it? Just let us 'ave a few bevies an' we'll be'ave ourselves."
Whether Harry took this as a threat that if he didn't let us 'ave a few bevies then we would cause trouble I'm not sure but his mood definitely became more conciliatory.
"Okay, just don't be upsetting my regulars."
Fuck off will yer 'Arry! They're a shower o' stuck up toffee-nosed twats with all their talk of 'ow much fuckin' money they've got 'cos they've just got a 98 'orse accumulator up an' I wouldn't piss on the bastards if they were on fire but yeah, just giz a bevy an' we'll be quiet an' after we've gone they can give us shit be'ind our backs about bein' thievin' bastard robbin' Scouse twats an' then they can go 'ome and wank their 'orses! Now giz a fuckin' bevy will yer, yer 'orse 'eaded twat!
"Okay, no problem 'Arry."
"How did you know my name's Harry?"
"I didn't! Is it?"
What a guess!

"D'yer know what, I've 'ad a brilliant day. That was me first time but I'll 'ave to go the match again. I really enjoyed it."
"Yeah, it was a good day John, apart from the result."
"Oh I'm not bothered by the result, it was just a good day."
He shouldn't have been saying that in front of the massed ranks of the Hughes brothers, all Reds to the core, me and the others. Nobody was gonna argue with him though as he had a dart in his hand. Don't be stupid soft arse he hadn't, on his virginity-breaking match, been enrolled into the Anny Road darts team! John, no mean darts player, was having the showdown at THE HORSE'S COCK with fellow decent player Les.
"Come on lads let's fuck off from this shite'ole and get lazzies in the Alex."
"Yer kiddin' aren't yer Peter? We could leave 'ere at three o'clock tomorrow mornin' and still get lazzies in the Alex. In fact we'd probably get 'alf a dozen!"
"Arry, thanks for yer marvellous 'ospitality mate. Really enjoyed it."

"Yes, you were all really well behaved. So much better than the ruffians you brought in last season.
Fuck off yer 'orse wanker!
"Okay thanks 'Arry. Ta ra mate."
Above everything else in the singy songy on the way home was John's Pavarotti version of, "Can you hear the Scousers sing? I can't hear a fuckin' thing. Woah, woah, woah!"
If we all hadn't been so tired we deffo woulda strangled him!

CHAPTER TEN

SOCIAL REPORT MY ARSE!

We went out of the European Cup at the first hurdle for the second year running when we were absolutely trounced in Georgia 0-3. We were starting to lag behind in the League being in ninth place having won only two of our first seven matches. First Division newcomers Crystal Palace were unbeaten and topping the League on 12 points. Were they going to be another Forest and win the Championship in their first season back in the top flight? We really need a win in our next game at home to Bristol City to kick-start our season and get us challenging again. We got it emphatically with a 4-0 win. Johnno was again on the mark and goals followed from Kenny, Razor and Terry Mac. Inconsistency again plagued us when we were lucky to get a draw at Bolton with a goal from Kenny ten minutes from time. At least the weather was better than it was there the previous season; no freak snowstorms to contend with but it still wasn't the warmest up on that old Railway Embankment open end.

As I couldn't afford to go to Ipswich to see our 2-1 win I made my long-awaited debut in the Ormskirk Saturday League refereeing a game in Aintree between Athol and Newburgh. The secretary of Athol, Jim Daley, instantly struck me as a gentleman of the game. Jim made many complimentary remarks to me about my refereeing even though his team went down 0-4. I had enjoyed my first real taste of refereeing Saturday football, apart that is from the odd schoolboys game, but there was no way I could do it full time as it was bad enough flappin' and trying to find out the score from Portman Road; I just wouldn't have contemplated missing a home game. I could tell though the slight step up in class from the Sunday League. Some of these players had performed at a good semi-pro level and it told. Still, if it was to hone my refereeing skills it would do me no harm.

The Anfield Derby was played in glorious sunshine; it really was like a summer day. It must have affected the eyesight of Mike Lyons though as after eight minutes he tried to lob the ball back to George Wood from fully 35 yards out. The ball soared over Wood's head and nestled nicely in the top corner of the net for one of the great Derby goals. Certainly it was the best Derby goal since Sandy's effort nearly ten years earlier. Well in Mike! Everton equalised through Brian Kidd, one of the more horrible, nasty Everton players in my opinion in history. Ray Kennedy restored our lead in the second-half and then proceeded to miss a sitter that would have wrapped the game up. Kenny and Terry Mac were similarly profligate. We were made to pay for these missed chances when Andy King pounced on a long punt from Wood to salvage a point for Everton and score in three successive Derbies. Two minutes later came something unprecedented in the previous 85 year Merseyside Derby history. Jimmy Case and Everton's Gary Stanley were involved in a scramble for the ball that ended with Jimmy on the floor and Stanley standing over him. Terry Mac steamed into Stanley and a mass melee involving nearly every player on the pitch ensued. Stanley maintained his innocence and a case of mistaken identity. It must have been hard though for the referee to spot just exactly who were the perpetrators of that incident but it's now consigned to the history books that Gary Stanley and Terry McDermott were the first players ever to be sent off in a Merseyside Derby. There have been plenty of others since though!

"Dad, the letters 'ave come."

We used to call our Ste Hudson as, like the dutiful butler in "Upstairs Downstairs", he would announce the arrival of the mail and newspapers.

"Okay son, bring them up."

I opened the letter that brought me the dreaded news I knew had to come but was hoping would be delayed as long as possible.

"Shit!"

"What's the matter Peter?"

"It's the date for the Crown Court. November the fifth at Manchester Crown Court."

That was great wasn't it? A fortnight to prepare myself for possible incarceration.

"They've gorra do these Social Enquiry reports too so they're sayin' the Probation Office will be in touch. Fuckin' great, that's all I need!"

The Probation Office was indeed in touch and very quickly. I'm sure the Probation Office and the people employed by them by do, in the main, a very good, difficult job under trying circumstances. I'm sure also that they are a well-meaning body of people but the prick who came out to interview me was a right stuck up toffee nosed, "I'll look down my nose at you because I'm better than you" twat!

"Now then Peter, I wish to interview you to ascertain whether you are a good citizen and that if you are found guilty of the charges you are in Crown Court for that you will definitely not re-offend. I'll interview you and your wife together and then separately if I may."

Fuck off gobshite! Who the fuck're you? Fuckin' arse'ole comin' in my 'ouse that I pay rent for (sometimes) and lookin' down your toffee fuckin' nose at me. Go 'ead, fuck before I butt yer and kick yer outta the fuckin' door!

"Yes Sir, I understand."

"Are you involved in the local community at all?"

I fuckin' live in it don' I? Isn't that enough? Right in the middle of fuckin' Dog Shit City I am. What the fuck d'yer want me to do? Like, brush the fuckin' white dog shit up or somethin'? Where do you live? Up on fuckin' Knob 'Ill somewhere in yer fuckin' big posh 'ouse with yer big posh missus and yer big posh car. Get to fuck! I do what I can. I'm too busy goin' to work an' bringin' 'ome the dosh to look after me wife an' kids to be runnin' round doin' meals on fuckin' wheels or somethin'.

"Err…I don't really do anythin' I suppose. I don't know. What d'yer mean?"

"Do you do any voluntary work for instance or do anything for local charities."

Are you 'avin' a fuckin' laugh? Do shit I'm not paid for? You're on another fuckin' planet you mate!

"Err…I referee football matches. I get four quid a game but if I ref schoolboys matches I don't take any money, not even me bus fare. I don't know. Is that good enough?"

"It's a start I suppose."

Oh well whoopy fuckin do!

"What are your social habits Peter?"

I pick me nose, bite me nails, scratch me arse, piss in the bath, fart in the bath, fart in bed and then stick Ev's 'ead under the blankets, yeah smart that! That enough?

"Not sure what yer mean."
"For example, do you drink a lot? Do you gamble?"
Yeah, twenty-four pints on a Satdee night an' twelve for Sundee dinner! Take it easy through the week, just ten a night. Bet all me fuckin' wages away too I do. Prick!
"Nah, a few maybe at the weekend an' I never bet."
"Yeah, yer do. Yer 'ave a bet sometimes and yer always out at the match an' that."
Fuck off will yer Ev! Yer tryin' to get me sent to jail?
"Yeah, we go out an' that don't we Ev an' I go the match like but I'm not like always on the ale."
"Well we don' go out much. You do!"
AARRRRGGGGHHHHHHHHHHHHH!
"I'd like to interview you alone now Peter. Would you mind going in the other room please Evelyn?"
Never mind the other room! Just fuck off somewhere will yer an' don' fuckin' come back! It's pointless yer goin' in the other room anyway; yer'll only be usin' the cup to the ear and wall trick.
Once Timmy Twatface had got me on my own he really went for it!
"Peter, you do realise that these are very serious charges you face and that you could go to prison if found guilty?"
No! I thought like the judge was gonna give me a few bob or somethin' and say well done. Of fuckin' course I do yer prick. I've 'ad this fuckin' thing 'angin' over me for more than a year now. I'm fuckin' shittin' meself. Why fuckin' ask?
"Yeah, I know they're serious charges an' that I could get nick but I'm doin' me best to cooperate 'ere and you seem aggressive towards me."
I was gettin' exasperated by this time you see and I'd had nearly enough of his inane waffling. Then the fuckin' twat came out with the coup de grace:
"Do you want to go to prison?"
Well I suppose I'd get a decent scran for a change an' maybe get me shirts ironed. I won't get as much grief from the screws as I do from Big Ev so yeah, sounds okay. Might 'ave to watch me arse in the shower like but other than that, okay. Go 'ead I'll go for that. OF COURSE I DON' WANNA GO TO JAIL YER STUPID FUCKIN' TWAT!
"Of course I don't!"

"Well you see, this report is supposed to show you in a good light with a view to that if you are found guilty then a prison sentence might be commuted to maybe a suspended sentence and a fine. At the moment Peter I'm struggling."

You're *strugglin'?* ***You're*** *fuckin' strugglin'? Try supportin' a wife and a couple of kids by workin' every fuckin' hour God sends down to yer in a shitty fuckin' dirty stinkin' roastin' red 'ot factory an' then try comin' 'ome from work an' 'avin' a nark with yer bird cos yer fucked an' the 'ouse is a tip an' she's got a cob on with yer cos she's on the monthlies an' blames you an' doesn't fuckin' speak to yer for weeks. Try all that gobshite! Then fuckin' tell me yer strugglin'!*

"I am tryin' honestly. Yer know, I'm nothin' special. I go to work. I do me bit. I like a bevy now and again an' I go the match. I'm not the best person in the world but I'm not a bad man."

"Okay, send Evelyn back in. Will you stay in the other room please?"

Yeah I fuckin' will an' I don' give a fuck what yer've got to say abarr me. I might just fuck off to the Derby Arms anyway 'cos I've 'ad just abarr enough o'yer! Oh that's right, I can't go the Derby or any other fuckin' ale'ouse for that matter 'cos I've got no fuckin' dosh. Used it all so me kids could be fed this week yer see. Arse'ole!

"Okay, I'll tell 'er."

Ev was doing the cup to the wall and ear trick.

"Ee arr, Timmy wants yer in there."

"Is that 'is name – Timmy?"

Fuck off.

"Yeah, call 'im Timmy."

Ten minutes later I was ushered back to the inner sanctum.

"I'll be making my report to the court. Good Luck Peter."

Yeah, I think I might need it with you arsewipe!

"Okay, thanks a lot. Bye now."

Twat!

"What did yer tell 'im Ev?"

Of course I know anyway. I know we 'ave our narks an' that but yer'll've told 'im what a good 'usband and father I am an' 'ow I'm good to people an' 'elp old ladies across the road an' that. Yer'll've told 'im 'ow 'appy we are together an' 'ow we 'ardly ever nark. Yeah, because above all else yer love me an' yer wouldn't wanna see me go to nick. I mean, who'd pay for yer ciggies if I was in clink?

"I told 'im yer weren't a family man an' that yer more for yer mates than yer are for me an' the kids. Like yer never take our Ste fishin' or anythin'. I said you were more the outdoor type an' that yer like sports an' that yer go out a lot."

YOU FUCKIN' WHAT!

"Fuckin' 'ell Ev, why d'yer say all that?"

"'Cos it's the truth."

"It's not the fuckin' truth an' even if it was yer supposed to be tellin' 'im what a good man I am."

"It is the truth. Yer never take our Ste fishin'."

"'As our Ste ever fuckin' *asked* to go fishin'?"

"No, but 'e might want to an' yer could take 'im."

"Well 'e might wanna go to the fuckin' moon too but 'til 'e asks me I don't fuckin' know that. Besides, I'm as likely to take 'im to the fuckin' moon as take 'im fishin'. What fuckin' money 'ave I got to be buyin' fuckin' fishin' equipment? Anyway, the nearest I've ever come to a fuckin' fish is when it's been with a gang o' chips on me plate an' the nearest our Ste's been is the fish fuckin' fingers 'e 'as in school. I've never 'ad any interest in fishin' an' neither 'as our Ste."

"Well yer not a family man."

"What the fuck d'yer mean I'm not a family man? I go to fuckin' work don' I to support you an' the kids. Doesn't that make me a family man?"

"Well we don' go out anywhere as a family."

"Oh yer mean like they fuckin' do on the soap powder adverts an' in Corry an that? Oh yeah, all fuckin' 'appy smiley faces an' let's be all fuckin' nice to each other 'cos we're the Persil soap powder family an' we've got loadsa fuckin' money to do whatever we fuckin' want. It just doesn't fuckin' work like that in real life Ev!"

"Well yer more for yer mates than yer are for me an' the kids!"

"What the fuck's that supposed to mean? So I go to work an' when I get me wages I give them all to me mates do I?"

"No but yer'd rather go out with yer mates than stay in with us."

"Well I'm with yer on that fuckin' one an' can yer fuckin' blame me? A choice between 'avin' a laugh with me mates or stayin' to listen to all this shite? What the fuck d'yer think I'd choose?"

"Yer are the outdoor type though aren't yer?"

"Again Ev, I don' know what the fuck yer goin' on abarr! I go the

match an' I referee, yeah, that's outdoor. Fuckin' sorry, what d'yer want me to do, tell Liverpool and all the footy teams I ref to play all their matches indoors? That's abarr the only outdoors I get!"
"Yer know what I mean!"
"No, I don' what yer fuckin' mean. I'd love yer to tell me an' me to be able to know. Anyway, fuck all that, yer were supposed to be tellin' 'im what a great guy, good father an' good 'usband I am to keep me outta nick. D'yer know, if it wasn't for the fact that there'd be nobody to pay for yer ciggies I'd say I'm sure you want me to go to jail."
"Fuck off! An' 'is name wasn't Timmy!"
"You fuck off! An' if I wanna call 'im Timmy 'is name's fuckin' Timmy!"
Now don't please let me give you the impression that I had the last word here or that I won this argument because I never did have the last word nor win an argument with Big Ev in my life. She always had the ultimate weapon.

CHAPTER ELEVEN

COURT IN THE ACT

It was the Lesmobile to Maine Road. Christ, Les couldn't 'alf make that Ford Granada shift. I think we made it there in half-an-hour and that included a piss stop. We actually didn't go very close to the ground initially, instead stopping a couple of miles out and having a bevy in a very picturesque pub. Like, right off a jigsaw puzzle box it was. Made a change I suppose from the usual dens of iniquity we frequented when visiting Maine Road but it was also nice not to be worrying about getting your head kicked in. It wasn't quite the buzz of The Robin Hood though. Maybe it's a fact that the older the people are you go aways with the less chance you have of getting agro. Certainly worked out that way for us as I didn't get anything like the ag I normally got at Maine Road. The game was won by half-time with goals from Johnno and Kenny. Kenny added his second after 67 minutes before Razor finished the biz four minutes from time.

Whilst not exactly playing the toughest opposition in the world our League Cup run was going nicely. Exeter did well and brought a load of support but went down to two Davy Fairclough goals. I was gonna have to make sure I enjoyed the game against Wolves as it might have been my last for a while and enjoy it I did as Kenny netted twice and Razor once in the 3-0 home win.

"Dad, where'r'yer goin' all dressed up?"
Eight years old and bright as a button; my little Ste knew something was wrong.
"Oh, I'm just goin' for an interview for a job son."
"Yer've gorra job Dad where they make the elephants."
"The elements son, the elements. Yeah, I know I've gorra job but this'll be a better job."
"What time will yer be 'ome?"
Fuck me, yer beginnin' to sound like yer Ma!
"Err, I'm not sure Ste."
"Well, will yer be 'ome in time for the bommy and to set the fireworks off with me an' our Ev?"

"Yeah, I 'ope so Ste. I think so. If I get the job though I might not be able to come 'ome for a long time."
"Well if yer don' get the job Dad will yer set the fireworks off with us?"
"Yeah, I will son, promise."
"Will yer take me the bommy Dad?"
Little Ev. Bundle of blonde-haired fun. How could I not come home and take her the bommy? Shit, what if I got locked up? The thought, even though I was thinking it, didn't bear thinking about if you see what I mean. Maybe Big Ev and the kids would learn to live without me for a while but there was no way I was gonna be able to cope without them. If I didn't get shagged to death by some hairy arsed learies then I'd probably just commit sewer pipes anyway. Think I'd just do the sewer pipes to be on the safe side. At least I'd die with me arse intact!
"Yeah, of course I will love."
"I love you Dad."
"Yeah, I love you too Ste."
"Do yer love me too Dad?"
"Yeah, of course I love you Ev."
"I love yer too yer know."
"Yeah, I know yer do Big and I love you."
"Good Luck."
"Yeah, ta. I think I'm gonna need it."

"Ste's been in Risley yer know."
"'As 'e? I thought 'e was in Jersey."
"'E was but the bizzies nabbed 'im at the airport when 'e got back."
"Wasn't fuckin' there long then was 'e?"
"Nah, an' 'e's been locked up since."
"'Ow d'yer know anyway? We woulda 'eard wouldn't we?"
"'Is bird told my bird in the Conny last week."
"Why the fuck didn't 'e let us know?"
"Fuck knows."
We were in the hallowed portals of Manchester Crown Court waiting for the call to go into court and the certain black cap the judge would be wearing. It was no fun. Stu, Molly and Wooly seemed to be breezing through it but I was a bag of fuckin' nerves. Okay we'd

done wrong and deserved to be punished but my stomach didn't deserve what was going on inside it. Ev had finally deigned to speak to me and had bade me a tearful farewell, just in case, but not before we'd said our goodbyes in the appropriate and time-honoured fashion. What the fuck was I gonna do without her? I know we were always battlin' but I loved that woman so much I couldn't contemplate one day without her never mind six or more months. We were led into the dock and as we looked down we could see a screw escorting Charles Manson from a cell. It surely was Charles Manson wasn't it with that long, straggly black hair and full, scruffy beard?

"Yer fuckin' shower of fuckin' bastards! Why didn't yer fuckin' come an' see me?"

Why was Charles Manson shoutin' at us? We didn't know him nor done any harm to him.

"Who the fuck's that?"

"Shit! I think it's Ste!"

"Fuckin' 'ell it is too!"

"Fuckin' state of 'im!"

"Scruffy bastard!"

"See yer up there. Ack, ack, ack, ack, ack, ack, ack!"

FUCKIN' LOONBALL!

We were all pleading not guilty to all charges laid before us of course. Equally of course, we were all as guilty as sin. Some were more guilty than others but certainly we were all guilty to at least some degree. We'd had all our gear back from forensics only just a few weeks earlier. Fuck knows what they were doing with it all. Maybe somebody at the forensics lab in Chorley was wearing my kecks and shoes to go dancing in. I could have lent him those two-tone flares and pumps Ev had got me from the Oxfam shop if he'd wanted. Or maybe not. I got lost amidst all the jargon of depositions, submissions, exhibits etc. Did they really need to bring the beer barrel into court? The female prosecution barrister and our male defence barrister were locked in a head to head conflab for at least five minutes. Maybe they were neckin' and sortin' out where they were goin' for their after court shag. Judge Dread then got in on the act. Maybe they were gonna have a threesome! Ooh, can I watch?

Digression for old joke:

Lad comes into school with boss watch on. His mate says to him, "Where d'yer get that watch?"

Lad says, "I walked into me Ma's bedroom while me Da was at work an' me Uncle Tommy was on top of 'er in the bed. Me Ma said to me, 'Don't tell your Dad an' I'll buy yer anythin yer want.' So I said to 'er, 'I wanna watch. That one yer said yer couldn't afford to get me last Christmas.' Me Ma said, 'Okay, just get out and I'll buy yer it tomorrow but don't tell yer owld fella abarr 'is brother.' So, I've got a nice brand new watch 'aven' I?"

Lad's mate says, "Eh, my Uncle comes round to our 'ouse when my Da's at work too. I think I'll try that. Yeah, 'e normally comes round when me Da's on nights an' 'e's on nights tonight! Yeah, I'll get a watch off me Ma too."

Couple of days later the lad and his mate meet up again in the school playground. Lad's mate doesn't have a watch on. Lad says, "What 'appened? Where's yer watch?"

Lad's mate says, "Well I waited 'til me owld fella went to work. Then me Uncle Billy came round. I could hear me Ma an' me Uncle Billy in the bedroom. I wen' into the bedroom an' sure enough me Uncle Billy was on top o' me Ma. Me Uncle Billy said, 'What do you want you little twat? Get out!' I said, 'I wanna watch!' Me Uncle Billy said, 'Well come in an' close the door yer little fucker, me arse is fuckin' freezin' ere!"

Shit but it makes me laugh.

Meanwhile back at the court Judge Dread spoke, "Court will be adjourned for fifteen minutes."

Fifteen minutes? Was that long enough for them all to get it on together. I'm sure Judge Dread batted for England and bowled for Australia so he'd be having a go at everything. Surely fifteen minutes wasn't long enough for all that? The four miscreants in the dock were sent out to the corridor whilst Charles Manson was led back to his cell.

"What the fuck's goin' on Stu?"

"Not sure Wooly. They might be doin' a deal. What do you think Molly?"

"Same as you Stu. What abarr you Evo?"

"I think they've all gone to shag each other an' when they come back Judge Dread is gonna give us twelve months!"

"Oh you're a cheerful twat aren't yer?"

No I fuckin' wasn't! I just couldn't help thinking the worst. Our

barrister came along and talked a load of jargon blah blah to us. He was definitely fluent in Jargonese. Basically, what it all boiled down to was that the prosecution didn't consider they had enough evidence to secure a prosecution on me, Stu and Molly on either the smashed window or the break-in at the shop. They did however feel confident that they had enough forensic evidence to secure a conviction on Wooly for the smashed window as the glass in Wooly's shoes matched that from the window. Now that was very strange seeing as Wooly was nowhere near the window and it had been Stu who lashed the barrel. Maybe they'd mixed up Stu's and Wooly's shoes. Or maybe Danny Dancer from the forensic lab had borrowed Wooly's shoes, gone to Wigan for a night out, had a fight, smashed a window and got glass in the shoes. All very strange. Less strange was the fact that the prosecution felt they had enough forensic evidence to secure a conviction on Ste for the shop break-in. That was fair enough as you couldn't argue with blood, glass, fibres and fingerprints. How easy it would have all been if forensics had the DNA technology that exists today. Anyway, the upshot was that jiggery pokery had been done between prosecution and defence barristers. The conclusion of said jiggery pokery was that prosecution would drop all charges against me, Stu and Wooly in return for Wooly and Ste changing their pleas to guilty and accepting convictions. Wooly would be given a six months prison sentence suspended for two years. Ste would be given a six months prison sentence but as he had already served what would have been, with time off for good behaviour, the equivalent of that sentence in Risley he would not have to serve it. We had to go back into court obviously to complete the formalities but it all meant that we walked out of court free men. Maybe justice in some cases wasn't done but we weren't complaining.
"Right, let's get on the ale!"
"Too fuckin' right Evo, let's go!"
So on the ale we jolly well went!
"Why didn't you twats come to see me in Risley?"
"'Cos we knew fuck all abarr it. We only found out this mornin'."
"Me tart said she'd seen your tart an' told 'er."
"Yeah but she only fuckin' told me this mornin'!"
"Anyway, yer scruffy bastard, didn't yer get fuckin' razors in Risley?"

"Yeah, but I was on shavin' strike!"
"Shavin' strike? What the fuck's that and why?"
"I refused to get a shave 'cos I was locked up and you twats were on the out."
"Yeah but Ste, yer weren't locked up for this. Yer were on unconditional bail. Yer were locked up cos yer fucked off without payin' yer fines!"
"Doesn't fuckin' marrer, I was still locked up!"
It was useless trying to reason with Ste; he just wasn't having it. The drunker he got the more he went on about it and he did get very drunk as did we all!
"Right, how'd you fuckin' lot get 'ere anyway?"
"We got the bus from Skem an' the train from Wigan Ste."
"Fuck that fuckin' around with all that bus and train bollocks."
Oh no, please no! Don't even think abarr it! Please no, no, no!
Ten minutes later we were on our way back to Skem in some battered owld Tranny.
"I don' fuckin' believe this! We've just got outta jail, fuckin' literally in your case Ste an' 'ere we are fuckin' askin' to go back in!"
"Stop fuckin' moanin' Evo. If yer don' fuckin' like it fuck off out an' fuckin' walk!"
Molly did have a point I suppose – I could barely stand up let alone walk.
"Ee arr…let's stop an' 'ave a bevy 'ere."
We were outside an isolated pub somewhere out in the wet windy wilds. Must have been called THE SLAUGHTERED LAMB! The pub doors were open but there was not a sign of life – not even a barman.
"Shop! Anybody servin'?"
"Fuckin' shurrup will yer Evo."
"Why?" I whispered
I soon discovered why as ciggies, spirits and cigars were scooped in armfuls from behind the bar.
"Oh no! Oh fuckin' no!"
"Come on, let's fuck off."
"Yes, can I help you?"
I seemed to recognise the rather camp voice that came from behind the bar as we were on our way out of the door and into the Tranny.

"No ta mate. We've just helped ourselves. Ack, ack, ack, ack, ack, ack, ack!"
We were bound to get caught and when we did the key would be thrown away.
"This is fuckin' mad!"
"Shut the fuck up Evo an' get 'old of these."
"Ooh cigars, nice one. They'll do for me owld fella's Christmas box!"
Well one should not look a gift horse in the mouth. Or rather, one should not look a gift tin of King Eddies in King Eddie's kite!

"Where've *you* been?"
Why was that always Big Ev's favourite question?
"Been to court. Been on the ale. Been celebratin' with me mates. That okay?"
"No it fuckin' isn't! Yer shoulda been 'ome 'ere! Yer were supposed to be 'ome and at the bommy letting the fireworks off with the kids!"
Shoulda threw you on top of the fuckin' bommy!
Why was everythin' so fuckin' much hard work now? Why was everythin' an argument?
"Fuckin' 'ell Ev. I 'ad a bevy with me mates. So fuckin' what! I've 'ad this fuckin' thing 'angin' over me for more than a year, shittin' meself I'd go to jail. What's the fuckin' 'arm in celebratin' not getting locked up with a few ales with me mates?"
"Well I don' know 'ow yers got away with it cos yers done it!"
*We **did** it Ev. We **did** it. Not **done. Done** is the present tense or at least the very recent past, not fuckin' over a year ago. **Did** is the past tense. This was in the past so we **did** it not **done** it. Okay?*
"Yeah, well fuckin' Hitler killed thousands didn't 'e? 'E did it didn't 'e? 'E DIDN'T GET LOCKED UP THOUGH DID 'E? Yeah, of course we fuckin' did it but we got away with it didn't we? It 'appens! It also 'appens that people get locked up for things they didn't fuckin' do! That 'appens too! D'yer know what, I'm fuckin' sure you wanted me to go to jail!"
"I didn't. I just wanted yer to come 'ome an' let the fireworks off with the kids. They'd been lookin' forward to it. Yer didn't let me down yer let them down. See, I said yer weren't a family man."
"Fuck off!"

"You fuck off!"

Last word again eh Ev.

I suppose she did have a point though. I had promised the kids I'd be back to let the fireworks off. I shouldn't have promised them that anyway with the very real threat that having left home that morning I wouldn't actually be coming home until probably well after next Bommy Night but promise them I did. I had, indeed, let them down. It wasn't the first time I'd let them down and it wouldn't be the last.

"Cam on you fackin 'orrible little man!"

"What? What yer say? Whassamarra?"

"Cam on you fackin' twat! Get outta your fackin' bed!"

"What?"

"Get out your fackin' bed before I fackin boot you out of it you cant!"

Who the fuck was this Cockney twat callin' me a cant? What's a cant anyway?

"Cam on, go and get your fackin' shower before your fackin' breakfast!"

Shower? Shower? The only time I get a shower is after reffin' sometimes and only then if there's nobody else in there to laugh at me little dick. Like the sound of this brecky though! What're we 'avin', full English? Oh, right, okay, I'll get ourra me nice fuckin' warm bed and go gerra shower like yer fuckin' tellin' me to. I wanna big fuck off brekky though. It'd better be good and there'd better be plenty of it; enough to fill me belly twice over!

Eh, it's not bad in this shower. Nobody in here to giggle at me little will woll like the lads in school used to. I fuckin' 'ated those lads in school sometimes. Skittin' twats they were. Fuck them anyway! Yeah, it's quite nice in this shower. The owld donga's goin' quite 'ard too with all this nice, warm, soapy water cascadin' down on it. Hmm...yeah, I think I'll give it a little tug. Be nice that before brekky an' set up me up for the day. Whose is that 'and on me donga? It's not mine! Shit, whose is it?

"Come on big boy, let's do it!"

"Do what? Who the fuckin' 'ell are you?"

"You know what. Come on, you know you want it!"

Shit! It's that camp geezer from the bar where we robbed the ciggies and ale yesterday. Oh fuckin' no! Warra am I gonna do? Even worse

shit, I'm beginnin' to fuckin' like it! Todger 'asn't been this 'ard for ages! Bell end's about to spurt forth tadpole projectiles.
"Peter, come on, d'yer wan' it or what?"
"No, I fuckin' don't! Leave me alone yer fuckin' big jessy!"
"What'd'yer mean callin' me a jessy? Come on, let's 'ave a quick frolic before yer go to work."
There's only one person who describes rumblin' and tumblin' as a frolic! What a relief (well it will be in a minute) to realise it wasn't Lenny the Leary Lecher from Walton E Wing fondling my bits but none other than my darling wife.
"I can't luv. Look at the time. I'm gonna be late again!"
"Yeah yer can. Come on, just a quickie. Take the day off."
"Nah, I've gorra make an excuse up for yesterday. Got no chance if I stay off again today."
'Ang on though. It'd look dead sus me and Stu being off together yesterday anyway. Might look better if one of us (and why not me?) stayed off today as well. If I stayed off again today though I might as well take the rest of the week off. Yeah, that sounded good – a week off work. Probably wouldn't get ourra bed for a week! Yeah, deffo, 'appy days, 'ave the week off! Shit, who was Shift Manager this week though? If it was Eddie I'd 'ave no fuckin' chance; 'e'd probably be lookin' to sack me for bein' off yesterday anyway. If it was Ted I'd get away with it as long as Big Ev made up a fuckin' good excuse. Think, think, think! Yes! It's deffo Ted. Nice one! Week off work!
"Please Peter."
"Oh okay. Will yer ring in work though an' tell them I'll be off all week?"
"Yeah, yeah, just 'urry up."
"That was a great sleep. 'Ad this fuckin' mad dream though!"
"What dream?"
"Yer don' wanna know. Believe me, yer don' wanna know!"
"Yeah, yer right I don't. Come on, 'urry up!"
"Okay, but yer'll ring in work for me as soon as we've finished?"
"Yeah, yeah. For fuck sake, come on!"
She rang in work at four o'clock.

I couldn't have gone to Brighton even if I'd wanted to due to lack of finances but after a week of dingery dongery doos in the big binky bonky bed I was in no fit state anyway. Instead I was sent to an outpost of Lydiate called Lambshear Lane to referee Lambshear v Newburgh. Funny name that isn't it – Lambshear? Conjures up visions of little lambs running around the pitch shittin' them little selves before being sheared and probably shagged by twenty-two hairy-arsed footballers. Well it conjured that up in my mind anyway. You have to have those thoughts as a referee before a game though to replace the reality that very soon twenty-two players are gonna give you shit for ninety minutes. Time enough for all that during the game. For now, before the game and on the two buses journey to Lydiate, let's think about little lambs getting shagged. Might make those footballers seem a little less intimidating when they're shouting at me if I can think of them with a little lamb's back legs in their wellies.

My old mate, drinking partner and defender of my face Joey Laycock was playing for Newburgh.
"Alright Joey. 'Ow come yer playin' for these?"
"'Elpin out Peter. Good set o' lads. Normally play for the first team but the rezzies are short so I'm givin' them the benefit o' my experience.
Fuckin' 'ell those Lambshaggers, I mean Lambshear, won't know what's 'it them!
"Ah well Joe, yer know the score mate, no favours. Play fair and I'll play fair with you."
"I always do Peter. Yer know that."
My fuckin' arse!
"Yeah, no prob Joe."
Sure enough, two minutes into the game, Joey hit one of the Lambshaggers with one of his "special" tackles.
"Name?"
"Fuckin' 'ell Peter not again!"
"Yeah, sure is Joe. Bad tackle."
"Only two fuckin' minutes gone Peter. It's me first fuckin' tackle!"
"An' it'll be yer last if yer carry on talkin' to me like that. Name?"
I know it's mad asking somebody their name when you clearly know it quite well but even though I was becoming a lot less formal in the

procedure for issuing official cautions I still had to follow part of the drill.

"Joey fuckin' Laycock yer pancake!"

Now I know I should have been sending players off for using the terrible "f" word but Joey used to make me laugh when he called me a pancake, so much so that I'd come to regard it as a term of endearment rather than an insult, and I just couldn't bring myself to do it.

"Okay Joe, official caution. Do it again and yer off."

"Mumble, mumble, fuckin', fuckin', fuckin', shit ref. Mumble, mumble, pancake."

It was always the same with Joey. I think most refs were scared of him and so wouldn't have put him in the book if he'd fuckin' machine-gunned somebody but really he held no fears for me. In fact it was often said by opposing players that I was doing them no favours by booking Joey as he would then settle down to do what he did best – destroying them with pinpoint laser-like passes. So it proved in this match as Joey led Newburgh to an 8-2 victory, scoring, I think three, although I hope he forgives me if he actually scored more than that, along the way. One other booking in that game was for a right nasty fuckin' piece of work for Lambshear. This sly arse had deffo done something pretty nasty to a Newburgh player off the ball. I only caught the arse end of it so not enough to give him the early shower he probably deserved but enough to put him in the book for ungentlemanly conduct. Joey was over straight away.

"I know yer didn't see it properly Peter but that was fuckin' bang ourra order."

"I know Joe. Let me deal with it. Don't get involved. Yer've already been booked."

"Okay Peter but don't send 'im off."

I wondered why Joey one minute was screaming blue murder about sly arse and the next pleading his case for him to stay on the pitch. I found out later. Time now to sort this other fella out.

"Name please?"

"Bob Carolgees."

I had a fair idea that he wasn't Bob Carolgees as there was no sign of Spit the Dog but if he wanted to be known as Bob Carolgees then Bob Carolgees he was and that would be the name going into the County

FA; let them sort it out. Of course the bogus Bob Carolgees would receive another fine for giving a false name in but that was his problem, not mine. It wasn't for me to go leggin' round the changies later looking for the team card to verify that there was no Spit the Dog molester on the team card.

Fuck off yer fuckin lambshagger!

"Mr. Carolgees, I am issuing you with an official caution for ungentlemanly conduct."

"I'm not arsed. If 'e takes the piss again, I'll do 'im again."

Hmmm.....I somehow don't think yer will Bob.

"Well if I see you I'm afraid I'll have to dismiss you from the field of play for persisting in misconduct after having received a caution."

Me being formal again that.

I probably would have sent him off too as he deffo would have got up to something later on but he err…sort of…err…got carried off. All I knew at the time was that Joey's name was in the frame for laying him out while I was watching for a corner coming into the penalty area. Serves him right? Rough justice? Poetic justice? Whatever it was, sly gobshites usually get sorted out. I don't mind players clattering each other and having a go face to face. Most referees and indeed most players don't mind that but to do something sly off the ball is cowardly and usually results in said sly arse minus a tooth or two.

I got changed quick and was away to get the first of my buses home after the match. A car pulled up at the bus stop. Joey was in the back.

"Peter, come on. Come for a bevy. We'll give yer a lift back to Newburgh."

I thought about it for a minute or so but decided if I was gonna go on the ale with Joey and his mates I probably wouldn't get home til nearly midnight. Big Ev had been speaking to me for five consecutive days, which was, I think, a record at the time. I half expected Roy Castle and Norris McWhirter to turn up on my doorstep one morning.

"Hello Peter! You're a RECORD BREAKER!"

"Fuck off will yer Roy. I'm 'alfway through a shagfest 'ere!"

I didn't wanna spoil my good run so the little bit of common sense angel I had on my right shoulder took over from the gaggin' for a bevy devil on my left.

"Nah, yer okay Joe. Me missus is speakin' to me this week so don't wanna fuck it up."
"That makes a fuckin' change. Well, come on, we'll just give yer a lift to Skem."
"Nah, yer okay Joe. If yer give me a lift I'll only end up on the ale with youse and I'll be in the bastard dog'ouse again."
"Okay Peter, fair enough."
"What 'appened with the bloke who got carried off anyway? You do 'im?"
"Yeah, fuckin' right I did. Fuckin' twat volleyed one of our players off the ball when you weren't lookin'. Wasn't fuckin' 'avin' that Peter so I gave 'im a dig when yer back was turned."
Fair enough I suppose. I was though gonna have to keep a sharp eye (you know, that spare one refs have in the back of their heads) on Joey in the future. Couldn't have him thinking that he could get away with just anything.

Happy Days! Radio City was blasting out the news when I got home of our 4-1 win at Brighton. I was missing going to some of the away games but I wasn't half enjoying reffing on a Saturday too. Bit different to a Sunday. Moving around different grounds and seeing slightly better quality players than normally played on a Sunday. One of the great places to referee at in The Ormskirk Saturday League was Park Lane Hospital. Park Lane was a top security hospital and was the forerunner of what is now Ashworth Hospital. Park Lane had boss facilities, a football pitch Alex Higgins could have played snooker on, the refs always got well looked after and you could get a good bevy in the staff club afterwards. Their team was made up of mostly staff but the occasional patient would get a game and some of them were pretty good. Park Lane started the match against Westhead with only ten men 'til a bald as a coot guy turned up ten minutes into the game escorted by a member of staff who was absolutely pissin' himself laughing. As soon as the other Park Lane players saw Kojak they joined in with the merriment.
"What's the joke?" I asked one of the Park Lane players.
"We've been tryin' to get 'im to get a 'aircut for two years and 'e just wouldn't 'ave it. Then he told us before we were comin' out 'e 'ad somethin' to do. We didn't know he was gonna shave 'is 'ead!"

Maybe all that laughter contributed to Park Lane's 2-10 defeat. A Park Lane player who took my eye was a big Scottish guy who seemed to have taken a real liking to me – in a very manly kind of way I hasten to add. He was talking to me through the game telling me what a good ref I was and how he always enjoyed me reffin' there. I knew him to be a patient and was wondering how such a nice guy could end up in Park Lane, especially after him telling me he was only in there cos he robbed a bike. I decided to ask a staff member who was playing.

"It's a shame that big Jock's in 'ere isn't it? 'E's a crackin' player an' a really sound bloke. 'E said 'e's only in 'ere cos 'e robbed a bike."

"Yeah, and strangled 'is mother and father with the inner tube."

Errr…..shit!

Mind you, I would rather have dealt with Big Bobby the Bike Robber than the game I had the following day between Caledonia Reserves and Delta. That was fuckin' mad! You get one of these games at least once a season when all fuckin' hell breaks loose and you have twenty-two players scrapping on the pitch at the same time. Even Cally's Big Jim Mac the mild-mannered bespectacled Jock got involved. I eventually managed to restore order with one of my rousing Churchillian speeches.

"Right, it's up to you fuckin' lot. That was a fuckin' disgrace! I'm not 'ere to ref that shit; I'm 'ere to ref a football match. If that 'appens again I'm fuckin' off 'ome for me dinner and leavin' youse to it and shove me fee up yer fuckin' arse. I don't wan' it."

"Okay ref."

That was it. Simple as that. Not a bit bother after that. The stats before that didn't make pleasant reading though with six bookings and three sendings-off. Normally to get sent off by me you had to slit somebody's throat but that was a mad match.

Christmas came and everything was hunky bloody dory. The Reds were on another of our mad runs having not lost in the League since Forest back in September. Terry Mac was in particularly sparkling form scoring in nearly every match. The League stats from the defeat at Forest up to the second game of the Christmas period, a 2-0 win at West Brom, were very impressive – won 12 drew 3 scored 39 conceded 8. Even Jocky was getting the hang of this goal-scoring

lark netting in wins against Middlesbrough and brilliantly at Villa. Even better still, good old Roger Davies, the lanky bastard from Derby County who had been our pariah on more than one ocassion, chipped in, giving us a hand with an exquisite own goal (and how we laughed) in our 3-1 win at the Baseball Ground just before Christmas; wasn't in the Sandy/Mike Lyons league but it was a good 'un anyway. Fuckin' brilliant we were, it's gotta be said! Man U were our closest rivals being two points behind us and having played a game more. Just behind us in terms of points but there was no contest in class as our 2-0 win at Anfield on Boxing Day when we just wiped them away, swotting them like a particularly annoying little fly, proved.
THERE'S ONLY ONE UNITED – AND THAT'S A CHOCOLATE BISCUIT!
I was as happy as that dead happy fella called Larry everybody's always goin' on about; bird was speaking to me, kids were fine, had a boss Christmas, footy team was doing well, reffing was great and I was getting a good bevy in every now and then. Doesn't take much to make me happy does it?

CHAPTER TWELVE

FISH, FOREST AND FALSE NAMES

Seven thousand or so Mariners trawled themselves up from Grimsby to Anfield for the FA Cup third round tie. Fuckin' stunk of fish it did that day! Maybe they thought they were gonna have a jolly day out at the home of football, while watching their team get walloped but they really weren't gonna care too much about that as they were only in the Third Division anyway so weren't expected to do anything. They got their expected walloping to the tune of 5-0 with Davy Johnno getting a hat-trick but some of them most certainly didn't get their lovely day out. It all started peacefully enough with us in cruise control and two goals to the good well before half-time. The Kop were having fishy fun with songs like, "You only sing when yer fishin'."

Our players were getting the smelly fish treatment in turn too:
"Stingray Clemence."
"Phil Eel."
"There's only one Fillet Thompson."
"Stingray, Stingray Kennedy."
"Kenny Dogfish, Kenny Dogfish, hello, hello."
"Jimmy Plaice."
"Terry McDermcod."
"Souness is a walrus."

The Road End were having their own special kind of fun; wasn't often they had that many away fans to deal with. From our vantage point we could see that they were keeping Blackbeard, Flatnose and the rest of the best of those fine CONTstables very busy indeed. I often used to wonder did the likes of Blackbeard and Flatnose do any other type of police work outside of match days as they were absolute experts at what they did in the Anny and probably in the Park End at Goodison too. Anyway, it was all going very nicely, having a good laugh and pissing the match 'til Grimsby, in one of their rare attacks, nearly scored. A roar went up from the corner of the Kop near the tea bar on the Kemlyn Road side. There was a solid knot of maybe a hundred or so Grimsby fans in there. They probably only came into the Kop because they were locked out of the chocker Road End and possibly meant no trouble. That didn't appease some very indignant Kopites though. We might have been "gobshites" to the Road End but let me assure you, at that time, there were some right fuckin' loons in the Kop. Over the years Man U had brought a few lads into the Kop before they were summarily and unmercifully booted out. Chelsea too tried it on once before they suffered the same fate as Man U. Never before though had a shitty owld Third Division team the effrontery to come into the Kop. The inhabitants of our famous terrace were not at all happy. The scene at the tea bar and the toilets at half-time was one of pure madness with Grimsby fans getting launched everywhere. A salt and battery was going on. The Mariners were in the wrong plaice at the wrong time. Mariners were getting filleted in all over the plaice. I'm not codding there were fishmen getting battered everywhere. Okay, I maybe shouldn't be taking the piss and making light of the very scary situation the Grimsby lads found themselves in but they really shouldn't have come in the Kop. You might say I'm being two-faced as I've said elsewhere in my books of us going into opposition ends at away grounds. Yeah, but we got booted out of some of them too rather than actually taking them, apart from one famous occasion in the late 60's/early 70's when a very well known Liverpool lad, completely on his own, scattered a load of Geordies in their Leazes End. The fact he was whirling an axe around might have had something to with the dispersal of black and white shirts though. So, back to the fishies – that just would not happen today. Today, in 2004, a hundred or so Grimsby fans in the Kop would be garlanded and escorted to their seats by jester-hatted, face-painted, pin-badged up to fuck, self-appointed ushers with accents not dissimilar to theirs. Not having a go lads, just saying it how it is, how it was and marking the difference between 1980 and 2004.

"Hey, Remus, leave the lads alone!"
I don't know why but Billy Mac had christened Grimwood Foreman Jack Huyton Uncle Remus. I wasn't even sure who Uncle Remus was. Was he the one in Brer Rabbit? For whatever reason Billy had given Jack this nickname and it stuck with the lads. The Number One record, being the last of the 70's and the first of the 80's was Pink Floyd's "Another Brick In The Wall". The line from that was, "Hey,

teacher, leave those kids alone." I suppose then it was an easy line for Billy to copy when Jack was giving us shit but I still don't why he called him Uncle Remus. It always used to make me grin though.

Our unbeaten run ended with a 0-1 defeat at Coventry on January 19th. As was becoming the norm now for aways, I wasn't there and instead had the onerous task of refereeing Holy Angels v Ormskirk Tower Hill. Doesn't sound too bad does it. Holy Angels? They must be like a very well behaved Cathlic boys team or something? Not on your fuckin' life! Holy Angels were the most inappropriately named team ever in the history of inappropriately named football teams. They were from Kirkby and had some right hard cases playing for them. Don't run away with the idea though that they were just hatchet men. They had some very good, skilful players, none more so than their centre-forward who I'm sure was called Eddie Lundon, although that sounds far too much like the lead singer of China Crisis who were to become very big a few years later. Maybe it was Eddie before he started to make a career out of singing. Anyway, this Eddie, or whatever his name, was absolutely shit hot. He scored an amazing amount of goals that season – something like 70 odd I do believe. He scored all seven goals in this match. Maybe it was a fact that the hard cases would soften up the opposition for Eddie to do his stuff but whatever, he was a fine player and an even better goalscorer. To be fair to the (un)Holy Angels though they never really gave me a hard time. Maybe they knew of my reputation but certainly I had no cause to have any names in my book that day.

Forest away in the League Cup semi-final first leg on Wednesday night. Deffo going to that one. Nobody else I knew from Skem really fancied the trip though so I did it on Kenilworths's coaches from Litherland. Bad, terrible atmosphere when we arrived near the ground to park up. Forest loons were out in force and were well up for battle. They were surrounding our coaches as they parked and with very little evidence of police presence there were kick-offs everywhere. One of our lads was pushed against a shop window, nearly going through it before being battered senseless. I saw another lad get a fearful crack as he turned a corner only to run into a load of Forest. We were hopelessly outnumbered and could only hope that

once the specials got in retribution would be swift. Best case scenario for me on my Jack though was to get into the comparative safety of the ground. The game was awful with us setting our stall out for the 0-0 draw good result to take back to Anfield.
"We only sing when we're borin'."
And boring we fuckin' well were but it was effective. Effective that is 'til Forest were awarded another of those dodgy penalties they always seemed to get, especially against us, a minute from the end. Of course Cissy Mulhall arse - John fatty Robertson - wasn't gonna miss this was he? It was probably our own fault for playing too defensively (I can hardly remember us going over the halfway line, never mind having a shot) but we didn't deserve that cruel fate. More bedlam ensued after the match and although our lads battled manfully Forest were top dogs that night. The FA Cup 4th round tie back at Forest four days later would be interesting as would the second leg of the semi at Anfield in three weeks time.

As I was reffing Rainford North End v Bickerstaffe I wouldn't be going to the FA Cup tie at Forest. I felt shitty about that after the off-pitch mauling we'd taken in the League Cup match. I got mad pangs of guilt and ran around like a madman trying to get a ticket the night before the match. All to no avail though; the lads would have to manage without me. Not hard I know but when you've seen at close hand lads on their own getting battered you get the feeling you'd like to help out. There shouldn't be much of a problem at this one though as we'd be taking twice the 3,000 or so that went to Forest for the midweek game. So it proved too as tales later told of Liverpool being mob-handed and tooled up to fuck. Forest got back what they'd given us a few days earlier. I, meanwhile, was more concerned with Nobby Stiles aka Peter Bulcock. Explanations later.

After a hard night of drinking and looking for a Forest ticket with me on the Friday Delvesy had stayed at mine and would be coming to watch me ref the match at Rainford. I felt a bit sorry for Delvesy as by this time he was well parted from Mary and seemed intent on drinking himself to oblivion, not that my good mate Alan needed an excuse. We very nearly never made it to Rainford in time for the kick-off. We'd been in the taxi for about fifteen minutes when normally the speed merchants could do it in ten. We were also going completely the wrong way.

"Ee arr soft shite, we're yer goin'?"

Delvesy never was big on diplomacy, especially where taxi drivers were concerned.

"Preston."

"Preston? What the fuck're yer goin' to Preston for?"

I also would never have got a job in the Diplomatic Corps or in the "Be Nice To Taxi Drivers" campaign.

"Because that's what yer fuckin' asked for soft arse. Preston North End Football Club."

"No we fuckin' didn't. RAINFORD North End Football Club yer daft twat."

"Oh, sorry, mis'eard yer. No need to be fuckin' stroppy!"

My refereeing skills were to be put to the test, only this time it would be boxing not footy I was likely to be reffing.

"Okay mate, yeah, yer just mis'eard us. Just get us to Rainford as quick as poss please mate. Come on Delvesy, get off 'is back an' let 'im get us there."

We got to Rainford just as the players were taking to the field and looking for a replacement ref for the fat, lazy twat who wasn't turning up. The driver only charged us for the trip to Rainford, which was quite nice of him as he had no fuckin' chance of getting a tip off us two tight bastards.

"Fuckin' 'ell Peter, where've yer been? We thought yer'd gone to Forest and fucked us off."

Kevin Sultan was the captain of Rainford and a fine player he was too. I knew Kevin from my brief flirtation with playing for Grimwoods before I sensibly decided to hang up my boots and take up the whistle.

A humdinger of a game saw Rainford run out eventual 5-3 winners. Their last two goals came in the last minute of the match and were fairly contentious affairs. The Bickerstaffe players were none too happy at the final whistle, none more so, nor more vociferous, than their centre-forward although how he could pass an opinion on goals that were scored about seventy yards from where he was standing I don't know.

"The last goal was fuckin' well offside an' the one before that was fuckin' 'andball."
As this six-foot tall guy was right in my face as he was saying this I thought it best not to answer him and head for the sanctuary of the dressing room.
"Can yer 'ear me yer fuckin' twat?"
Well, yeah, I can fuckin' 'ear yer soft arse but for your fuckin' sake I'm pretending not to. Now fuck off an' let me get changed so I can go get a fuckin' pint in the Club.
"Please, go away or I shall be forced to send you from the field of play."
"Yer can't fuckin' send me off! The match is fuckin' finished yer cunt!"
I'm fuckin' losin' patience with you yer lanky twat. Now fuck off before I set Delvesy on yer!
"I can and I will send you off if you carry on. I should have sent you off already. Now please, go away."
"No, I fuckin' won't go away. You're the worst fuckin' ref we've ever fuckin' ad!"
Hmmm....yer couldn't 'ave 'ad Dickie then.
To be honest the situation was getting out of hand. This bloke, I felt sure, was gonna lamp me any minute. Fuck! Where was Delvesy when I needed him?
"Look, please, just go and get changed and we'll discuss it over a drink in the Club."
"No, I fuckin' won't! Fuckin' discuss it 'ere yer fuckin' fat, cheatin' bastard. Yer fuckin' cheat!"
Right, that was it! I could take being called a twat, cunt, the worst fuckin' referee ever and a fat bastard (like I'd never been called that before, although I did think Big Ev had the copyright on that particular insult) but I wasn't gonna take being called a cheat. I really fuckin' hated that. I wasn't there to cheat anybody. I never cheated anybody in normal life (except maybe Big Ev when unbeknown to her I stayed out on the ale) so I wasn't gonna cheat anybody at football. I was there to see that fair play was maintained as best I could, not UNFAIR play.
"Can I have your full name please?"
"Nobby Stiles."

Oh no, not another fuckin one. I 'ad enough with Bob fuckin' Carlogees a few months ago. Another few bob for the County FA when they find out yer've given the wrong name to the referee to go on top of the big fine and long ban yer gonna get from the boys down at Old Swan. Yer as fuckin' ugly an' as gummy as our 1966 World Cup hero to be sure but I bet yer can't fuckin' dance like 'im!
"Mr. Stiles, I am dismissing you from the field of play for using foul AND abusive language."
I never quite saw why the FA insisted on terming it foul OR abusive language. I found it very difficult to fathom how a footballer could use foul language, whether it be at a ref, a player or anybody else without it also being abusive. I suppose you could use abusive language without it actually being foul but I really couldn't see it. Prick? Wanker? Nob'ead? Foul AND abusive or just abusive? I'll let you decide. Ah, I've got it! One that's not foul but was meant to be abusive, although it always cracked me up – PANCAKE! Crafty owld bastard that Joey Laycock isn't he?
"Fuck off yer fuckin' cheat."
"Mr. Stiles, I would ask you to refrain from verbally abusing me as I have noted down everything you said to me and will mention every word in my report to the County FA."
"Fuck off!"
Mercifully some of "Nobby's" team-mates came and dragged the gap-toothed wonder away before he could get himself, and possibly me because I was fuckin' fumin' at being called a cheat, into any more bother. I'd decided if he called me a cheat once more I was gonna either chin him myself and fuck the whistle or get Delvesy to do it for me. Where was the golden-haired, Greek god lookalike (or he thought he was) fucker anyway? In the fuckin' Club getting pissed that's where!

"Alright Pete. 'Ow the game go?"
"Never fuckin' mind that. I thought I was gonna get filled in. Still might do."
"Who by?"
"Well don't fuckin' look now but by that fella behind yer who's givin' me fuckin' daggers. I sent 'im off."
So Delvesy just swivelled right round and glared at him.

"Fuck me, 'e's big 'im 'isn't 'e? If 'e comes anywhere near yer though Pete I'll crack 'is fuckin' skull."

I'm sure Delvesy would have made a good attempt at crackin' said skull before him and me were turned to mincemeat but I was glad of his support, if a little late, anyway.

"Let's just get fuckin' bladdered and worry abarr 'im startin' if 'e starts."

So royally bladdered we did get fortified by the news that we'd won 2-0 at Forest. "Nobby" had got off after a couple – wasn't a hardened drinker like me and Adonis I suppose. We staggered out of Rainford North End Football Club at half-past-eight (to make sure we got home in time to watch the Reds marvellous victory on Match Of The Day) with not a pot to piss in between us. It was a long walk home but funny as fuck.

"Yer stayin' at ours tonight Adonis?"

"Yeah, might as well. Fuck all to go 'ome for."

"Yer dinner tomorrer?"

"Yeah, sound's a bell."

"Well, get in that farmer's field an' earn yer dinner. Gerrus some carrots."

Delvesy came back with enough carrots to feed the western world.

"Right, your turn."

The great cabbage snatch done we were well set up for Sunday dinner.

"Peter, look at this!"

I turned to see Delvesy with his considerably sized lash in between a carrot and a cabbage.

"Meat an' two veg! Ha ha ha ha ha"

We arrived at the Derby Arms with about an hour to spare before MOTD started.

"Come on, let's ave a bevy"

"We've got no fuckin' dosh soft arse."

"Ee ah, we'll sell all this fuckin' veg. Some soft twat's bound to buy it off us."

"Yeah, okay an' I'll bum us a couple of pints, especially if me Ma and Da an' our Billy are in 'ere."

Delvesy was the world's best pint bummer, in a very nice way of course. His family were indeed in the Derby and some soft twat (can't remember who) did buy what should have been tomorrow's veg off us so we were well lubed up by the time we got home. Best part of watching the Reds win on MOTD was when Souness had weedy little John fuckin' McGovern by the throat, about to cack his nappy, in a strikingly similar pose to the famous picture of Billy Bremner pooing his pants when Dave Mackay had him in the same stance. Phoenix From The Flames? Souness had thought of it years before Baddiel and Skinner!

Delvesy did indeed stay the night, for his Sunday dinner and for about a week after that too! Great lad Delvesy but once you had him you couldn't fuckin' get rid of him! He turned up at our house one night, well, about two-o-clock in the morning actually to ask me the name of Norwich's ground and didn't leave for a fortnight! Great storyteller though but that's another story.

The postscript to the "Nobby" story is this, well, not quite a postscript as it's a bit long and postscripts are supposed to be short and snappy as in, "Ma said hello" or "Get us a pint of milk" or whatever but you know what I mean:

"Nobby" had requested a personal hearing before the Disciplinary Committee of the Liverpool County FA. Poor fella didn't know what he was letting himself in for! Chairing the Committee was a great old gentleman, sadly no longer with us, of the LCFA, Arthur Derbyshire. Now Arthur was a fair, firm man of the old school type and would give a player his say but would ALWAYS 100 per cent back the referee. If the referee said his report was truthful then that was the case – end of story. Arthur opened the meeting by reading, in full, as he always did, my three-page report on "Nobby's" tirade including every "f", "c" and "t" word contained therein.

"Now what have you got to say for yourself Mr. Bulcock, as we have now established from your Club Secretary that is your real name and not the one you gave to the referee?"

"Nobby" then fished his own three-page effort out of a bag. For the next five minutes or so "Nobby" read Hamlet's soliloquy; every last fuckin' Shakespearean word of it! Arthur looked at me. I looked at Arthur with equal puzzlement. What the fuck was goin' on 'ere! I seriously thought Sir "Nobby" Olivier had lost his marbles. Even the Bickerstaffe Club Secretary who was there to represent his player looked terminally embarrassed by it all. When Willy "Nobby" Shakey had finished his most marvellous recital he than said to Arthur, "I would like Mr. Etherington to repeat back to me every word I've just read."

YOU'RE FUCKIN' NUTS YOU!

"Repeat it? I didn't even understand it!"

"What was the point of that Mr. Bulcock?"

"The point is Mr. Derbyshire that if Mr. Etherington could not read that back to me then he could not possibly remember *everything* I said to him when he sent me off."

Yeah, fuckin' flipped – big style!

"Mr. Etherington, have you got anything to say or add to your report?"

"No Mr. Derbyshire. Everything I have to say is in my report."

Our training as referees, especially at Referee's Society meetings was to never add anything to our initial reports.

"Mr. Bulcock. Did you use foul and abusive language to Mr. Etherington?"

"Well, yes, I did swear at him but not all he says."

Shakey was sticking to his guns.

"Mr. Bulcock, you requested a personal hearing to this Disciplinary Committee to contest the referee's report of foul and abusive language. You have wasted a lot of your money and your club's. You have wasted a lot of your own time, the referee's time and the Disciplinary Committee's time. Mr. Etherington says in his report you used foul and abusive language. You admit you used foul and abusive language. We shouldn't even be sitting here. Could you please retire to the room next door while we consider our verdict. Mr. Etherington you may leave. Please collect your expenses on the way out."

Well that fuckin' told 'im didn't it!

I did actually feel a bit sorry for "Nobby". Arthur Derbyshire was a fearsome character to come up against. "Nobby" would probably be looking at something like an eight-week ban. I didn't want to stop anybody playing football but he had called me a cheat and I just couldn't take that. Worse was to come, or so I thought. I was to referee Bickerstaffe again on the Saturday after the hearing – a game that would probably be "Nobby's" last before his lengthy ban. He was bound to give me another volley. How wrong could I be?

I was huffing and puffing but just about managing, in my usual way, to keep up with play, when a delightful through ball found "Nobby" (when it was played that is; Law 15) just ahead of the last defender. "Nobby" rocketed the ball into the net. Sorry "Nobby" mate – offside. Right, I was bound to get a fearful earful now. Not a whisper! Shit, I wasn't prepared for this! Shortly after, "Nobby" went down under a fair challenge from a defender in the penalty-area. A great shout for a penalty went up from every Bickerstaffe player except one – "Nobby".
"Play on! Fair tackle!"
Not a word from "Nobby". Fair enough to the man, he didn't contest a single decision.
"Nobby" approached me after the game.
This is it. This is where I get the volley!
"Referee, you 'ad a great game there. Well done."
Eh?
"Oh, err, right, okay, thanks."
"I'm sorry for what I said to you the other week. You're not a cheat and I shouldn't have called you it. I'll serve my ban because I deserve it. You'll never get any more stick from me again."
Fair enough to Peter (I've give up calling him "Nobby" now) he was as true to his word as anybody possibly can be when caught up in the passion that a game of football, at any level, is. I refereed Peter many times after that and had absolutely no problems with him. I didn't like him calling me a cheat but it takes a big, brave man to admit he is wrong. "Nobby", I mean Peter – thanks. That Hamlet thing was fuckin' mad though!

CHAPTER THIRTEEN

BLACK PUDDINGS AND BROWN KECKS

Have I ever told you I've never been to Norwich? Probably, as I've told every other fucker. I hope to rectify that in the 2004-2005 season however as The Canaries have just won promo as I write. Hope Delvesy knows where they play now! Anyway, I didn't go this time, having to be content with watching it on MOTD. This game is celebrated as probably the best ever shown on the owld style MOTD; highlights only, before the mass showing of live games. We won the game 5-3 with a hat trick from Davy Fairclough; late goals from Kenny and Jimmy Case securing the victory. The match will be best remembered however for a truly stunning goal from Norwich's Justin Fashanu. Barney was marking Fashanu tightly but with his back to goal and about 20 yards out Fashanu flicked the ball up, let it drop, swivelled on the proverbial owld tanner and then hit a viciously swerving, dipping volley past the despairing dive of Clem. It had to be good to beat Clem from that distance and it certainly was a truly great goal. The goal was shown on the opening credits of MOTD for ages after that and probably got Fashanu his £1m move to Forest. Pity that Fashanu flopped at Forest. NICE BIT OF ALLITERATION THERE EVO! That might have had more to do with Brian Clough's managerial style than any shortcomings Fashanu had as a player because at Norwich he certainly looked every inch an England striker of the future. Poor lad's dead now. Shame he didn't have the glittering career he'd promised as a youngster; certainly would have been better than his "celebrity" (my arse) brother John.

Three days later we were out of the League Cup after once again being fucked by Forest; on the pitch that is but certainly not off it. We could hardly argue about Forest defending like fuck to get their 0-0 draw as that was exactly what we'd set out to do in the first leg but you just can't legislate for being Shiltoned out of a cup again. Shilton was a brilliant keeper no doubt but I'm sure he just used to pull that little bit extra out against us.

Thousands of Black Pudding Berthas from Bury invaded us for the

FA Cup 5th Round tie with their big hats, clogs and three foot long black puddings. They got the same treatment in the Road End as the fishies from Grimsby had but none of them came in the Kop. We had great fun singing Dvorak's New World Symphony at them. For those of you not too well up on classical music and TV adverts that was the tune used to advertise Hovis with the little woolyback lad cycling up and down Lancashire's cobbled streets to get his ma her Hovis. Soft cunt! Here's what the scenario should have been:
"Eeh ba gum yon lad. Willst tha go oop to baker's for thovis?"
"Nay but Ma I went t'other day. Why dust I 'ave ter go all time? Bloody legs are killin' me ridin oop and down yon 'ills. Can't thee send oor lass?"
"Nay, she went oop to baker's t'other day and as bike bumped on cobbles the saddle slipped oop 'er minge and broke 'er in. Or that's what she says. I've got me suspicions about Mr. Kiddy Fiddler the Baker me sen. Anyway, she's got 'er minge in a sling now so can't go."
"Well what abart fat lazy bastard in bed?"
"Nay lad, yon Father can't go. 'E says those cobbles play bloody 'avoc wi' 'is piles."
"Oh 'ere then. Gi' us fookin' money but I want new pair o' clogs for Christmas. There'll be yon Scouse cunts skittin' me for years o'er this!"

Nice little digression there! Alan Kennedy's bro Andy was playing for Bury so chant of:
"There's only two Barney Rubbles!"
Fuck that, we've got enough with one of the mad bastards never mind two! Davy Fairclough scored both goals in our 2-0 win. The 6th Round draw paired us away to Tottenham. Oh shit!

Forest came a visiting again in midweek but were royally fucked 2-0 with goals from Terry Mac and Razor. Wasn't much fun to be had off the pitch as the shitbags wouldn't venture to Anfield for a midweek League match. Give it a Cup game though and you'd have them all giving it the big one.

Upholland Working Men's Club were a funny team to referee. I

suppose it's only natural that a team will be okay with you when they were winning and not so when they were losing but UHWMC used to do it the opposite way round. Not sure if they were just trying to be different or what. Not that they were outright nasty either really...just sort of...well...funny. For a start their name was a bit of a misnomer as I don't think there were that many of them in the team who actually worked. They had a shit hot striker with an unpronouncable Polish sounding name. There were gangs of W's, X's and C's in there, that's all I know. I used to look at his name on the team sheet and think, "I 'ope I never have to book this fella."
Well, sure enough it happened one day didn't it? They were beating Kitt Green quite easily, something like 6-0 or something when I disallowed a goal by the latter day Gregorz Lato (leading scorer for Poland in the 1974 World Cup for those that don't know). If they'd been 6-0 down and I'd disallowed the goal I probably wouldn't have got as much grief but, as I say, they were a funny owd lot! Anyway, Mr. Pole took his protestations a little too far.
"Can I have your full name please?"
"Wryzickzyci."
At least I think that's what he said.
"Oh forget it. Just don't say anymore to me this match."
I'd had to have played half-an-hour extra time to get that fuckin' name in my book!

One of the great banes of my life, bus drivers, returned to haunt me making me nearly miss the match against Ipswich. The bus had got as far as the Pear Tree when the driver says, "Right, that's it, all off. We can't go past 'ere."
"What d'yer fuckin' mean yer can't go past 'ere?"
"Corpy bus drivers are on strike and this is the boundary so if we go past 'ere we'll be scabbin'."
"Fair enough mate, I understand that but 'ow the fuck am I gonna get to Anfield from 'ere?"
"I don't fuckin' know pal. That's your fuckin' problem."
"Well if yer knew yer were gonna fuck us off 'ere why did yer take full fuckin' fare to Anfield? If yer'd charged me 'alf bat as yer shoulda done I woulda 'ad enough to get a taxi. I'm fucked now."
No reply came the answer so there was no further point arguing the

fuckin' case. I had no more money to get a taxi or even a train. I didn't have the bus fare home even if I could have got a bus; I'd been planning on going to Ma's after the game and bumming it off her. Life hated me again. Thumb out! I walked for fuckin' ages before there was even a sniff of a lift. It was nearly quarter-to-three, I was only just out of Kirkby and no fuckin' chance at this rate of getting to Anfield in time for the second half never mind the kick-off. Fuckin' Ipswich again! I'd missed the match against them five years previously almost to the day as my Little Ev had been born. It had been Little Ev's birthday the day before and I'd spent all the money I had, apart from the bus fare to get to Anfield, on her birthday prezzy. It seemed I couldn't win. I'd let my kids down so often and felt so shitty about it that even when I did try to do the right thing life and God, if there is one, would just turn up and fuck me right up the arse.

"Come on mate, get in. D'yer wanna fuckin' lift or what. Yer goin' the match?"

In my feeling sorry for myself reverie I hadn't noticed a car pulling up.

"Fuckin' right. Ta mate."

Life loved me again. Never down for long, Evo. By the time we parked up it was well past three o'clock.

"I'm legging it up there mate if yer don't mind. Ta for the lift. See yer in there maybe."

I felt sorry for the poor owld fella but good enough as he'd been to give me a lift it was now every man for himself. Just as I'd got in through the turnstile, lucky that I had a season ticket, as all the pay gates were closed, even though it wasn't a full house, a fuckin' huge roar went up. Bastard, missed our goal! Fighting my way through the Kop to my favourite spec it became evident that Davy Fairclough had scored our goal at the Anny Road end. Made up we scored like but totally fuckin' pissed off at having missed it. Can't quite remember who equalised for Ipswich in a bad tempered, contentious game, Mariner maybe. We were awarded a penalty very near the end. Ipswich used all kinds of gamesmanship to delay the taking of the kick and also to put off Terry Mac, including Frans Thyssen throwing a lump of mud at the ball as Terry was about to take the kick. In those circumstances it was understandable that Terry missed the penalty, Ipswich 'keeper Paul Cooper denying us the win we deserved.

"Mam, lend's a squid for me bus fare 'ome."
I was forever doing this. Wouldn't have blamed her if she'd fucked me off.
"Okay but stay 'ere tonight an' go 'ome tomorrer. Come out with me and your Father for our Anniversary.
Fuckin shit, I'd forgotten it was their Anniversary! Hadn't bought them anything so I felt a right shitty twat.
"Sorry Mam, I didn't get yer anythin'. Forgot all abarr it."
"Don't worry, so did yer Dad 'til this mornin'. Come out with us. Yer Father'll pay fer yer ale."
"Nice one Ma."
Twenty-eight years they'd been married. I don't honestly know how she'd put up with 'im for that long, and vice-versa I suppose. It was like that in those days though – married couples stayed together. Not like now where a woman will fuckin' divorce a man if there's so much as a piss spot on the bathroom carpet!

A midweek 0-1 defeat at Wolves was followed by the Goodison Derby. I hadn't been able to get a ticket for the match but the Club Secretary of Bruges FC (Bruges from the Skem League that is – not our former European Cup Final opponents) who was also a commissionaire or something at Anfield, a lovely old fella called Fred, had very kindly offered me a letter of introduction (I know – I'd never heard of it either) which if handed in at the Everton ticket office would gain me admission. Fair enough! I had to pick the ticket up at Anfield an hour before the match. I also bought my ticket for the Cup match at Spurs. I did so with a certain amount of trepidation as there was bound to be unholy murder there. I didn't mind a bit of ag at matches, as I've said many times it was expected, you knew you were gonna get it, but this match had been talked up since the draw was made nearly a fortnight ago. There was a different feeling about what was likely to go on at Tottenham than there had been for any other match I'd ever known – even Man U matches. The spray-paint graffitists had been hard at work. All over the walls around Anfield were legends such as:
ALL ROAD END TO SPURS – NO RUNNERS!
8TH MARCH – KILL THE COCKNEYS.
Nice!

"Alright Fred. What 'appens with this letter of thingy?"
"Just give it in at the Ticket Office and they'll give you a ticket to get in."
"Sound. 'Ow much I owe yer mate."
"Nothin' Peter. You reffed our pre-season friendlies for nothin'. I haven't forgotten that so you take the ticket for nothin'."
Nice that people remember and appreciate favours you've done them. The letter of whatsit was exchanged for an envelope with my name on it. A ticket was a ticket and in's in I suppose but the best I could hope for was a Street End ticket. Fuckin' bingo! A Park End ticket! I LOVE YOU FRED! Davy Johnno did his old Everton chums in again and the game was virtually sealed before half time with a Phil Neal penalty. Of course it wasn't a penalty! Everton pulled one back with a goal from Peter Eastoe. Eastoe was on as a substitute for Geoff Nulty who had been very badly injured in a tackle with Jimmy Case. It was a bad tackle, no doubt, but Jimmy was never going to come out of that challenge second best. Jimmy would most certainly have been sent off for that tackle these days. Probably should even have been sent off then I suppose but all's fair and unfair in love and Merseyside Derbies. Anyway, 2-1 sent me and every other Red home happy. Now to look forward to the trip to Tottenham next week. Not!

The Derby Arms was full of Reds celebrating our Derby victory. Quite apt that isn't it? One of them was Gilly who was after a ticket for the Spurs match. Gilly was hard-core Road End and so, unlike me, wasn't pooing his pants at the prospect of taking on Tottenham and all they had to throw at us. In fact Gilly and the other Road End in the Derby that night were positively chomping at the bit to go. With all that in mind I sold my ticket to Gilly. Okay, I was a big scaredy cat shithouse but Gilly was happy, I was relieved, I got bladdered on the proceeds so everyone's a winner babe and that's the truth.

I knew in the end I'd do it. I had bad guilt pangs about having had a ticket for Tottenham and sold it on because I was too scared to go. I also didn't get to that many away games this season because of reffing so I should really have taken every opportunity I had to get to anywhere I could. For once I had a little bit of spare dosh so on the Friday night I went over to the Derby and bought a Tottenham ticket. Can't say who from as it was massively over the odds so wouldn't blow anybody up for touting. Neither Gilly nor any other of the local Road Enders were in there to make plans to meet up with so I decided it was off down to Ma's to spend the night to get the earliest possible special I could the following day.

Anything, and I mean anything, you ever hear about that mad day at Tottenham is the truth, I can assure you. You might think that over the years tales of that day have been over-exaggerated. Well I can tell you, if anything they were *under*-exaggerated! It was honestly fuckin' bedlam. We did quite well before the match, holding our own on the tubes and in the many battles on Seven Sisters Road and elsewhere around White Hart Lane. We'd been told there were Cockneys round the streets of White Hart Lane slamming early Scouse arrivals since six o'clock in the morning. Once the game was underway I was scanning the ground to assess the size of the Spurs mob and where the likely trouble spots would be. Of course there were plenty of loons in (or should that be on?) the shelf. There were also smaller crews dotted around other parts of the ground, especially in one corner of the Park Lane end that had been reserved for Spurs fans in what traditionally had been their end; I don't suppose they were too pleased at that. A few Spurs fans got on to the pitch in isolated incidents including one right scary looking fucker with a Mohican haircut who was making throat-slashing gestures at us before being pulled off by the bizzies. Those punk Red Indian look-alikes would do anything for a wank wouldn't they? I think there were about seven thousand Reds in the Park Lane end and most of them were up for the post-match battle we knew we were most certainly going to get. Plenty enough numbers I thought to deal with anything that came our way after the match. Those thoughts were well and truly scuppered though by the lovely lads from the Met Police. There were plenty of threats being made but not much actual fighting going on during the match. Terry Mac scored a wonder goal, even by his standards, to give us victory. Right, this is where the real "fun" starts.

The bizzies were holding us back for a bit inside the ground and the concourse at the back of the terraces. A good thing I thought at the time as we had a chance if we all went out together. We knew there was a massive mob of Spurs waiting for us outside.
"You'll never reach the station!"
Yeah, we'd heard it all before at many grounds and always held our own, well mostly anyway. We'd also sung it to away fans at Anfield; just all part of the match day ritual.
"Stick together! Don't run!"
Fuckin' right we were sticking together. I was gonna try stick to the biggest, fuckin' hardest Scouser I could find! The Met, and I'm sure they did it on purpose, fucked everything up by letting us out in groups of maybe fifty or a hundred at a time. The inevitable happened – we were leathered everywhere. I was probably in about the sixth or seventh group that was let out. I had never seen a mob that big, not even in Man U's heyday. It seemed all of London had turned out to get us. That could well have been true as most other London teams were either not playing that day because their teams had been knocked out of the Cup or were away so decided to go to WHL, join up with Tottenham and kill any Scouser they could find. We had the flimsiest of escorts so there was no stopping Spurs lads running into our lads and picking them off. Absolutely fuck all done by the Met but when we tried to have a go back the batons were out. We did have a go and one twat of a hot dog seller who was giving it large to us had his head shoved into his boiling fuckin' hot rancid onions and his stall turned over on to him. Spurs were weaponed up to fuck with knives, machetes and all kinds being flashed. There was even talk of a scalpel. Fuck me, even the medical profession were out to get us! The Spurs mob was growing by the minute as they were coming out of side streets and estates to join in the "fun". All of this was planned I'm absolutely sure and I'm almost as certain that the Met were in on it. Certainly they knew what was going to happen, didn't have enough men to deal with it and weren't interested in protecting us from getting a pasting. Our lads were getting forced by the Cockney hordes to be more and more tightly packed together on one side of Seven Sisters Road. Some of us were crushed against shop windows. Spurs were then running into us and pushing lads into shop windows. We were having a go back but were fighting against

impossible odds. One of our lads got into a broken hardware shop window and tried to start up a chainsaw. That scattered Spurs for a bit and fuckin' grateful we were for it too.

"WE ARE EVIL!"

Fuck me! I don't mind admitting it, I fuckin' shit meself when they sang that. There were thousands, and I do mean thousands *not* hundreds trying to do us in and yes, I fuckin' well believed they were *very* evil. Things brightened up for us slightly and we started gaining some retribution (the Cockney cunts weren't gonna have it all their own way) when the dispersed mobs of Scousers started to slowly join together having fucked off out of the escort. If that hadn't have happened I sincerely believe that some Scousers would have been killed; it really was that bad. That walk up Seven Sisters Road is bad enough as it is, probably half-hour or so in normal circs, but it felt like we'd been on that bastard road for about two hours when we eventually arrived at the station. It was going off all over the station and on the tubes but in a more confined space and with then somewhere nearer equal numbers at least we stood a bit of a chance. Mobs all over Euston too when we got there but again the numbers started equalling up as more and more Scousers were eventually reunited so we gave as good as we got. The specials were full of talk of the great Battle of Seven Sisters and, as I say, none of them were exaggerated. Seasoned, battle-hardened Road Enders and Kopites, never scared of a fight, were full of stories of how scary it all was. Thankfully though, apart from a few bust heads, eyes, noses, cuts, scrapes and bruises, everybody was more or less in one piece. The mental scars of that day would be far greater than the physical ones.

If you think I've just told you a big load of owld bollocks, maybe you aren't old enough to remember it or weren't there, then you ask anybody else who was there and they'll tell you, Spurs away in the Cup 1980 **WAS THE SCARIEST AWAY GAME EVER!**

CHAPTER FOURTEEN

SEMI-FINAL SAGA

By the time the League game at White Hart Lane came round we'd extended our consecutive League winning sequence to five with home wins against Manchester City, Leeds and Brighton and away at Bristol City. There was no fuckin' way I was going to put myself through that Seven Sisters mayhem again that season, if ever! I did hear though that quite a few lads had gone and given a good account of themselves. We lost the game 2-0 but got back on track with a 1-0 win against Stoke on April Fools Day. We went into the crucial match at Old Trafford on Easter Saturday six points ahead of United and looked likely to extend that margin when Kenny put us ahead with one of his specials in the first quarter-hour. Greenhoff J (how I hated him – and his brother. Sound familiar?) was our undoing again with the equaliser. Mickey Thomas (hated him too) added the winner. Still, we were four points ahead of them and it was going to take an awful lot for them to catch us with only six games left.

We tuned up nicely for the forthcoming FA Cup semi-final at Hillsborough against Arsenal with an easy midweek 2-0 win at home to Stoke.

I got one of the early specials to Sheffield so arrived in plenty of time for a bevy. I think it was the Waggon and Horses we congregated in and while it was mostly Liverpool in there the atmosphere was fine. That all changed when a crew of Arsenal meatheads came in and were obviously up and looking for a fight. They were soon going to get it. A load of Road End came in shortly after including Skem lads Gilly, Ronnie and Ashy. The atmosphere was getting more and more fraught and tense. It all kicked off when a big fuck off Cockney who looked more like a bulldog than a human being was showing off a swastika tattoo on his arm. Now one of Gilly's favourite sayings was, "It's mad that." That could have meant anything from "It's good" to "It's bad"; it wasn't meant to be an insult – just a saying. It was one just one of those mad sayings if you know what I mean. Anyway, Gunner Bulldog is showing off this shitty tattoo to anybody who cared to look and those who didn't.

Gilly: "That's fuckin' mad that!"
Bulldog took great exception to this and was making a move of murderous intent towards Gilly. Gilly always being one to get the first dig in and ask questions later threw a punch at the canine cunt. Unfortunately for Gilly he still had a glass in his hand when he threw the punch. I'm certain that there was no way Gilly was trying to glass Bulldog Hitler; it was just instinct at some meathead getting at him that made him instantly react. The punch, fortunately or unfortunately, whatever way you look at it missed.
"So that's the way you fackin' want it is it you fackin' Scarse cunt."
Fuckin' 'ell this was mad this! See, even I'm saying it now! It really was looking very ugly now. Somebody was gonna get seriously hurt soon. Gilly, having missed with his first punch, realised I think that he was no fuckin' match for this monster; especially if said monster was gonna glass him so slid off to retreat. The trouble spilled out on to the car park and the road outside the pub with several digs being exchanged on both sides but thankfully no glassing incidents and no real bloodshed. For my own part I decided it was time to get myself down to the ground. I wasn't being a shithouse but the Liverpool lads there were more than well up for a fight so felt easy leaving them to it. I just felt I could no longer get really seriously involved being as I had to think about the fact I was a married man with children. The whole thing just didn't sit right with me and felt I would be letting my wife and kids down even more than I already did should I get involved in stuff like that and come home with a mangled face or maybe worse.

The match itself was a big bag of shite. The nearest anybody came to scoring was when Talbot hit the bar for Arsenal. If penalty shoot-outs would have been in place then I'm sure both sets of fans would have been equally happy to get it over and done with there and then but, no, this was gonna go to a replay, or maybe more.

The replay at Villa Park wasn't much better, finishing 1-1 after extra time. Once again at Villa Park I had my fuckin' pocket dipped, this time in the Holte End. Freddie Fish had relieved me of a tenner, big money for me at the time. I'd only brought it out with me in case Big Ev went on the root while I was out and found where I'd stashed it.

The beautiful one knew by now most of my little hidey-holes but not all of them (he he). She should have been a bizzy my missus! She could always sense when I had a little stash going and invariably found it, but as I say, not always. There was one mad, fraught ocassion when I got three weeks of silent treatment after she found my well-hidden (or so I thought) collection of jack mags.
"Yer fuckin' perv!"
"I'm not a perv. They're only fuckin' magazines for fuck sake!"
"Yis yer fuckin' are! What d'yer wanna look at them for?"
"Ev, they're only fuckin' magazines. It's not like I've got a bird stashed in me wardrobe."
"Yeah, but why d'yer wanna look at them when yer've got me?"
"I don't fuckin' know! It's just what we do isn't it? All men read snatch mags."
"Yer are. Yer a fuckin' perv!"
"I'm not pervin' lookin at pictures of women. Now if I was lookin' at pictures of men…"
They just don't understand do they?
"Fuck off!"
Nah, she wasn't 'avin' it. No speaky for three weeks it was for me. I suppose I sort of deserved that one though. Did some fuckin' jackin' in those three weeks I can tell yer!

West Ham were patiently waiting for their Cup Final opponents after beating Everton in a replay in the other semi. They were gonna have to be mighty patient though as the third game in the Liverpool-Arsenal saga also finished level after extra time. Again Villa Park was the venue but I didn't get dipped this time. The game was an inestimably better affair than the first two games. Arsenal scored early on. We threw everything at them in what was looking like an increasingly vain bid for an equaliser to take the game into extra time. Kenny was once again our saviour scoring with virtually the last kick of normal time. The goal, as you would expect, was celebrated wildly in the Scouse half of the Holte End. I was with Baz who, in his wild celebrations, very nearly repeated his false teeth trick first perfected at West Brom the season before.

Sandwiched (somehow) in between the two Villa Park replays and in the space of just twelve days were League games against Arsenal (somewhat unsurprisingly finishing in a 1-1 draw), a 2-0 win at Stoke and a goalless draw at Crystal Palace. We could actually have won the League at Palace if we had won and United lost at Coventry. The Mancs though were on a fine run of their own; victory at Highfield Road being their sixth straight success. I'd thought it an unlikely scenario for us to win the League at Selhurst so didn't go, preferring instead to referee Ormskirk Saturday League champions-elect Argos' match at Bickerstaffe. Argos were a fine side and needed only a point to win the League but were beaten 4-2 by the less talented but very workmanlike Bickerstaffe side. Argos duly claimed their deserved League title though. They had some very good players in their team including the Baccino brothers (no, not Italian gangsters) Aldo and Paul. Paul was probably the better of the two players being a shit hot winger. Aldo was more of the man mountain type. He had a great, deft touch on the ball that belied his size – a size he used to good advantage on many occasions. Aldo took shit from nobody!

The highlight of my refereeing career so far was to take the whistle for the Skem Sunday League Founder Cup Final between Skelmersdale United "A" and Parkbrook. It really was a proud moment for me to ref my first Cup Final. The game was played at Skem United's ground, White Moss Park. I'd reffed at WMP before in friendlies and representative games but it was a good feeling to walk out to the middle of a "proper" ground and ref a Cup Final – the most important day of the players' season and the referees' too. I really felt as if I was somebody special - a thought I didn't have very often in those days. Skem "A" won the game quite easily being the far superior side but Parkbrook were a doughty little side having done well to get to the final. Parkbrook had a very young Gary Bennett in their side. Gary scored a sackful of goals that season. Even at the age of 17 and playing at Sunday League level Gary was showing that he was way too good for that standard. Gary's potential was of course realised when he went on to have a very good career in the Football League with Wigan, Chester, Wrexham, Southend and Tranmere. I had been invited pre-match (win, lose or draw) to the Parkbrook post-match piss up at The Roundabout in Skem. No, not on one of the many madly shaped roundabouts in Skem but at the hostelry of that

name. Although the game hadn't been contentious I thought I could expect a bit of stick when I walked in the boozer. Not a bit of it! After a bit of light-hearted booing I was cheered in and applauded to my seat. Parkbrook were a good club run by a real football man, Marty Garnett, brother of my fellow ref Paul. They made a big fuss of me, feeding and watering me. As you will well know by now, anybody who feeds me and buys me ale is a friend for life! I was pleased to be asked to present the Parkbrook annual awards. Not surprisingly Gary Bennett won the top goalscorer award. No surprise either at his other award – Crier of the Year. I presented Gary with the biggest dummy you've ever seen. Maybe it was a little harsh on Gary; yeah, he could moan with the best of them alright but mainly he got on with what he was best at, scoring goals, and didn't honestly give me too bad a time. Of the hundreds of trophies I've acquired over the years for reffing, linesmaning and quizzes the one for reffing my first Cup Final takes pride of place. It even managed to survive several of Big Ev's trophy-smashing frenzies when she had a cob on with me. Radios, baby-buggies and doors were my smashing specialities in a temper. Fuckin' mad I know but that's life eh! Anyway, back to the good stuff. Special day that. The day was rounded off by Big Ev deciding that this was the final day of my punishment for the great jack mag incident.
HAPPY DAYS!

Just three days after the second Villa Park replay we dragged our tired, weary, battered bodies and minds (players and supporters) to Highfield Road for the fourth game of the semi. The FA, in their wisdom, had very kindly informed everybody that should this game finish level then a fifth game would be played at Bramall Lane the following Monday (yeah, just four days later and with a League game at home to Villa, probably a Championship decider to fit in on the Saturday) and would then definitely be decided – penalty-kicks would be used to determine a winner if the game was level after extra time. I suppose, in a way, you couldn't really blame the FA as the Cup Final date was set in stone for May 10th, just five days after the proposed Bank Holiday Monday game at Sheffield United's ground so they had to get something sorted and quick. Maybe it was the thought of a fifth game weighing heavily on our players' minds but it

was a terribly lacklustre performance by us. Arsenal looked fitter and half a yard sharper. Perhaps they should have done, as they certainly hadn't had to fit in as many League games during this marathon as we had. Looking most tired of all our players (we were tragically to find out why years later but didn't know it at the time) was Ray Kennedy. It was Ray who was easily disposed on our own goal line, the ball being crossed for Brian Talbot to head in and finally bring the saga to an end. I remember Souness at the start of the second half urging us to give the team greater vocal support.
"Well you fuckin' give it to us and we'll fuckin' give it to you!"
I thought it was a bit shit of Souness to do that. I know the team were fucked and had given almost everything they had but so too had we. We were as fucked as them having travelled around to watch the games. The differences were that we were fucked and skint – they were fucked and loaded; they were travelling first class everywhere – we were bummin' lifts, getting our bones shattered on fuckin' crap owld rattlers and sitting on planks of wood disguised as seats on shitty thirty-year-old coaches. So fuck you Souness and yer extra fuckin' vocal support – yer got all of mine – and a bit fuckin' more yer didn't deserve! I felt even worse towards him when he fucked right off the pitch as soon as the final whistle ended. In fact I think he was actually shampooing his fuckin' perm in the shower even before the ref had finished the third blast on his whistle to signal the end of the game. He didn't even have the decency to put his sweaty fuckin' palms together a couple of times and thank us for following them around for those four matches. Fuck him!

The official crowd figure for that Highfield Road game was 35,335 but I'm sure the actual attendance must have been nearer 40,000 as there were so many forged tickets going around. The tickets printed by Coventry City Football Club were so bloody flimsy that a kid could have made good forgeries on his John Bull printing kit so they were no match for the master scammers we had in our ranks. I was pissed off that I had actually bough a ticket when I saw so many jarg tickets gaining entry including the two lads I went with, Eddie Physick (ta for the use of the couch Ed) and Dave Blanchard.

The final Saturday of the season saw us locked together with Man

United on 58 points. We had two games to play – that day's home game against Villa the following Tuesday at Middlesbrough. United were to finish their programme on that Saturday at Leeds. A win against Villa would definitely give us our 12th title no matter what United did as we had a vastly superior goal difference. Even a draw might suffice if United didn't win at Elland Road. We swept all doubts aside with a comprehensive victory. Johnno, sporting a huge black eye (a legacy of the bruising fourth battle against Arsenal I think but could have been a post-match row – it happened with us quite a lot back then) started the ball rolling as early as the third minute. Avi Cohen threw a bit of a spanner in the works with a peach of an own goal. Avi redeemed himself five minutes into the second half with an even better goal in the right end than his own goal. Johnno added a second and Noel Blake wrapped things up, returning Avi's kindness, with an oggy of his own. Man United had manfully tracked us all the way to try to keep in touch but they were never really as good as us that season. The icing on our cake was that the men from Old Trafford had lost 2-0 at Leeds so really the destiny of the Championship title that day was never seriously in doubt. Enjoying our title win in the post-match celebrations more than any other player, including other local lads, Thommo, Terry Mac, Jimmy Case and Davy Fairclough was little Sammy Lee. Sammy had been struggling to break into the side for a couple of years but this was one hell of a side to break into. Sammy had stuck to his task however and had been rewarded by replacing the injured Jimmy Case for the last half-dozen or so games. Sammy was loving every minute of the celebrations. There is a great picture of him standing on the fences of the Kop like a little monkey and screaming his head off. I'd forced my way near to the front and was celebrating with him. Celebrating with me and Sammy was the lad who had very kindly given me a lift that day and was to become a great mate of mine, Jimmy Brown. I'd known Jimmy for a couple of years through him playing for the Derby Arms in the Skem League. Fuckin' mad as a hatter Jimmy but we've now "enjoyed" a long, if somewhat chequered friendship, for 25 years. More, much more, about him later.

Boy, was I fuckin' glad we'd clinched the title against Villa! I just did not fancy at all another trip to the Mongworld that was

Middlesbrough. I mean, if we got all that ag from them last season when we'd already won the League what would it have been like if we'd actually clinched the title at their ground? Nah, best to stay away from that one methinks – so did a lot of others apparently! It was no surprise we lost the game 0-1.

It was an amazing feat for us to win the League that season given the way we had to finish it. Between April 1st and the last game at Ayresome Park on May 6th we played an amazing total of twelve League and Cup games. 36 days – 12 games! Now I know I've been on Countdown and it's easy for me but it doesn't take Carol Vorderman (phwoooarrr!) to work out that is one game every three days. No, it wouldn't happen now and it shouldn't have happened then but happen it did. We, in our own quiet little way, just gone it with though; didn't moan about it, didn't ask questions about it – just got on with it. That's the way it was then and the way it still should be – the Liverpool way. Great credit had to go to our players for that. Imagine asking some of the girls we've got playing for us today to do that? Fuck that, they'd be off crying to their tarts, the papers, their Ma, their agent or anybody else that would listen to their whinging.

Greatest credit of all however must go the man who had once again masterminded it all – BOB PAISLEY. What a man! What a manager! What a man manager! Bob hadn't changed players much during the season but had altered tactics now and again to suit certain games; it didn't always work but the proof was in what we had achieved. He'd also had the bravery to leave out his own big-money signing Frank McGarvey for the whole season, probably spotting early on that Frank was just not the Liverpool type player he thought he had been. Onwards and upwards Sir Bob! Let's go get that hat trick of League titles only twice previously accomplished in the dark mists of time by the men in baggy trousers (der, der, der) of Huddersfield and Arsenal. Oh, and getting our European Cup back would be nice!

CHAPTER FIFTEEN

ALL POMPEY TO ROAD END

"Ee Evo is tha gooin' Wembley for Charity Shield?"
Of course I'm fuckin' gooin', I mean goin', Lollipop.
"Do bears shit in the woods Lol?"
This reply sort of confused Lollipop who wasn't the most radiant element in Grimwoods.
"Yeah, I'm goin' Lol. Why yer wanna know?"
"Can Mam goo with thee?"
"Yer Ma's a Red?"
"Aye, 'as bin all 'er life."
"'Ow come yer Ma saw the righteous path when yer Da and the rest of yer are all Man U?"
"Granny must've dropped 'er art pram on yed when she were babby."
"Eh, now don't be fuckin' cheeky. That's my sayin'."
"Well she wants go but she's gettin nobody goo wi'."
"Yeah, no prob. She can come with me on the coach. Nice one."
It was a good job Mrs. Lollipop, otherwise known as Nell did go on the coach with me as I would have been right up the creek without a paddle otherwise. I would have had to walk to Ormskirk and back for the coach as I was absolutely Bernie Flint. Not a blind penny to my name. All I had was the coach ticket and match ticket. Lollipop's Dad Harold, sadly no longer with us, did the biz for us taking us to Ormskirk for the coach and picking us up when we got back. It was a boiling hot day and I really don't know how I would have survived without Nell buying me drinks and food all day. Nell obviously sussed that I was boracic so kept me fed and watered. Lollipop and his bros must have got their broad Skemese from their Pop as Nell had a lovely accent – sort of a cross between Scouse and wool but not all those thees and bloody thous her Lollipop was so fond of. I also liked her cos she called a lollyice a lollyice, not a lolly or an iced lolly. A lollyice is a lollyice and a lollipop is a lollipop – neither of them are lollies! Wools, take note! Then again they called mice moggies so there was no reasoning with them. Nell got off quite early outside the ground to take her place in the stand which was a good job too as there were mass battles going on all over the place.

We got off to another trophy-winning start, Terry Mac scoring the only goal. Things were once again looking good. Nell was the star of the day though. Thanks Nell – you're a good 'un!

Quiz question: What did Liverpool Football Club sell to Blackpool Football Club for £10,000 before the start of the 1980-81 season? Struggling? Well, think about it; I did say *what* not *who*. Still struggling? Okay, it was the set of fences that had been in front of the paddock since fences had been put up in front of all terraced areas at Anfield, in common with other grounds, two years earlier. The reason for taking down the fences and the consequent sale to Blackpool was that seats were now installed in the Paddock. This was the first stage in the tartifying Anfield process. I suppose it was inevitable really. More and more clubs were putting seats on to terraces to raise the level of seating accommodation as opposed to standing. Some clubs such as Coventry and Aberdeen had even gone so far as to put seats on all their terraces therefore making them all-seater stadiums. Richer, or supposedly richer, clubs such as Chelsea were actually knocking terraces down to make way for huge new stands. All this however was obviously decreasing the capacity of stadiums. Anfield would now hold less than 50,000 given that only about 1,500 seats could fit into the Paddock on a terrace that could hold 3,000 people standing. Therefore, the title-clinching game against Villa last season was the last time Anfield housed a crowd of 50,000. Now, in 2004, unless the plans for a new stadium are ditched, which doesn't look likely, and Anfield is rebuilt with a higher capacity, our famous old ground will never again see 50,000 people inside it. Quite sad really isn't it? Not as sad though as Liverpool Football Club *selling* a set of fences to a struggling club. Why didn't they just give the fences to Blackpool? Mingebags!

You know when I said earlier that I always get one match a season when there's a full on barney involving every player on the pitch? Well for the 1980-81 season I had two – in one day! Cricketers kicked it off against Little Digmoor in one of those classic Wools v Scousers battles. Funny, as whenever teams from outside Skem, say from Huyton or Kirkby, came to play in Liverpool County FA Cup games they would be calling the Skem teams wools, even though those teams were full of Scousers. Anyway, Cricks more than met their match as Little Digmoor had some right hard-cases in their team and they could also play a bit too. The battle ended with three bookings and two players sent off. In the usual way of these things both teams settled down to play football after I'd read them my very own, unique version of the Riot Act. Fuck all those words like sedition, I gave it to them straight: "Any fuckin' more o' that an' I'm fuckin' off 'ome to me missus!"

Maybe they took pity on me at the thought of me having to go home early to my missus but whatever they always seemed to sort themselves out after that. Little Digmoor won the fight and won the match 6-0.

It was a slightly different story in the afternoon game between UpHolland Labour and Delta. These teams just did not like each other at all, that is fair to say. Difference between the Cricks and Little Digmoor match though was that there were proper hard-cases on *both* sides in this match. That ended with four players booked and two players sent off. I always tried to stick to sending just two players off after these battles; if I got the original two scrapping miscreants that would appease everybody. I could actually have sent about four off from each side involved in these massive rumbles but to do so would have just ruined the game. As reports to the FA had to be in duplicate for bookings and triplicate for dismissals, as well as me keeping my own copy of every report, that was an awful lot of writing on a Sunday night. This was before these technologically advanced days of course so everything was handwritten (I couldn't even afford a typewriter) although quite how anybody down at LCFA understood my writing I'm not quite sure as it was once described by Grimwood foreman Jack Huyton as, "Like bloody fly's crawled o'er paper after it's bin in jar o' jam!"

Quite a good description I thought. Those reports would take hours to write and certainly scuppered any chance of my usual Sunday night Derby Arms bevy. Not that I was bevying much at all at that time as I was saving every last spare penny I could to get me to the European Cup Final I felt was our and my destiny this season. I'd decided that having missed the greatest night ever in the history of Liverpool Football Club in Rome 1977 that there was no way I was gonna miss the next European Final. Okay, I'd gone to Wembley when we the European Cup there the year after Rome but we played at Wembley that many times it was like going to a home game. Not that it wasn't special of course – it was – just I'd never been out of the country and I was desperate to go to a European match. I'd never really got started on the saving to go to the European Cup Finals of the two previous seasons due to our First Round exits each time but I was stashing dosh from an early date this time – just in case. I wouldn't be going to any of the games leading to the Final as I deffo wouldn't have afforded that and it would have ruled me out of the Final so I was just gonna have to save hard. I was jealous hearing tales of lads, a lot I knew, going all over Europe to follow the Reds. I was jealous hearing tales of the capers they'd get up to. I've gotta be honest I'd never even heard of Adidas Samba; they would have been well out of my price range. To hear tales of lads getting them for nothing and a lot of other "free" stuff that paid for their trips made me envious. I didn't begrudge them their good time of course, just that I wanted some of it. On the other hand most of the lads were a bit younger than me and didn't have a beautiful wife and two lovely children. I wouldn't have swapped what I had for what those Trans-Alpino boys would get up to but I would have liked just a smidgeon of it in addition. I think some of the lads would have swapped with me, well, at least the wife bit anyway, as many times I caught them casting envious, admiring, sometimes even lascivious glances at the beautiful one. And who the bloody hell could blame them? It was gonna be a tough task hiding my stash from her for the best part, hopefully, of nine months though. Operation Hideaway!

The first ten League games of the season had seen us make a decent enough start with six wins, three draws and only one defeat away at Leicester. The eleventh game pitted us at home against surprise League leaders, Ipswich. Ipswich had been a goodish side for a few years, winning the FA Cup in 1978, but under the astute management of Bobby Robson were now showing real Championship winning qualities. They left Anfield with a 1-1 draw, their unbeaten run intact and three points clear of us.

The twelfth game was at Goodison – my first away game of the season. It couldn't really be called an away game I know but Wembley, Goodison and hopefully the European Cup Final, which, it had been announced, would be staged at the Parc De Princes stadium in Paris, looked like they were the only "away" games I was gonna get this season. My enjoyment of reffing on Saturdays coupled with me saving like fuck for the European Cup Final meant my away trips would have to be strictly limited. Everton were two up in what seemed no time at all with a rare header from Asa Hartford (we were still singing that shit "There's a hole in your heart" song to him. It was shit when first sung eight years earlier and really just shittier now) and Joe McBride. Sammy Lee got us back into the game before half time. Kenny made sure the spoils were shared in the second half.

The first two rounds of the League Cup had given us no problems at all with both Bradford City and Swindon very easily dispatched. I wasn't always keen on the early rounds of the League Cup, still not, even in its present vogue, if the truth be told. I didn't begrudge the smaller clubs their big payday or their fans a big day out at the Mecca of footy. It was just that these clubs always brought about twice the number of fans that normally made up their average home attendance. Where did they all come from? Why did we have put up with their shenanigans of singing and dancing for 90 minutes? Sound if they wanted to sing decent songs but they were mainly shit. I think it was around this time that the oh so boring and oh so original "In your Liverpool slums" was first belted out by away fans, which was a bit rich coming from Bradford fans! Bradford isn't exactly the real estate capital of the UK now is it? And what did Swindon have to offer? Oh yeah, that's right, it's quite near a big pile of owld rocks where hippies and other assorted weirdoes congregate each summer. Well anyway I'm sure supporters of these clubs enjoyed their day/night out before going home with their tails firmly between their legs after being taught good manners and how to play football.

The Road End weren't involved in battle in the next round, certainly not *in* the ground anyway as they weren't in there. Our lovable (or not so lovable if you were an opposition fan) scalls had moved en bloc, lock, stock and darts to the Kop. The reason for this was that Portsmouth had about fifteen thousand fans inside Anfield; certainly the biggest away support I've seen at Anfield apart maybe from Celtic in testimonials. Portsmouth had been allocated the whole of the Anny and half of the Kremlin. A few fights went off in the Kop that night. I think maybe the rivalry between Road End and Kopites wasn't all good-natured. Most of it was I suppose and I'm not even gonna begin to venture to guess who got the better of the scraps. What I do know is that one Road Ender was up on a crush barrier giving it "Kopites are gobshites" for about 15 minutes non-stop 'til he was unceremoniously pulled off (ooh err missus – all he got in the Road End was a can of Fanta and a chewy off his mate) and cracked. That sparked a minor skirmish but nothing too bad; after all, we were all Liverpudlians (and I come from the Spion Kop). Pompey fans for their part were having a ball. There was nothing small-time or small town about these lads though. Pompey were doing well in the Third Division and were averaging gates of around 15,000 unlike, as I've said earlier, other clubs who would bring 7,000 fans and get 4,000 at their next home game. I never did quite understand what that was all about. One of the most amazing sites I've ever seen at any football ground, not just Anfield, was when DJ George played "Portsmouth" by Mike Oldfield before the match. Fifteen thousand Pompey fans stood as one dancing, jumping, and bouncing up and down for the full three minutes or so of the duration of the record. It was the usual dance (if you'll pardon the expression) on the field however. Portsmouth did give us a bit of a game for a while and were in fact only 2-1 down at half time but two late goals finished them off for a 4-1 scoreline.

We'd easily negotiated the first round of the European Cup with an 11-2 aggregate victory over the Finns of Oulu Palloseura. Souness and Terry Mac had both scored hat tricks in the 10-1 home win against them. We were up against a much tougher proposition in the second round, facing the Scottish Champions, who had broken the Old Firm domination, Aberdeen. A great early goal, one of his trademark chips, from Terry Mac, gave us victory at Pittodrie. We all expected a much harder game in the return at Anfield but easily overcame them 4-0, helped along the way with an own goal from Miller and Jocky chipping in with one of his rare goals. Aberdeen brought about five thousand fans with them. Not for the Jocks though the silly songs and dances of small-time English clubs. This lot were fuckin' solid! The Road End knew they'd been in a battle that night. So did Blackbeard and Flatnose!

Aston Villa's emergence as a major threat to our League title was even more surprising than that of Ipswich. Villa came to Anfield with 28 points, five ahead of us although we'd played 17 games, one less than Villa. Sandwiched in between Villa and us were Ipswich on 24 points from 16 games. Trying to spend as little dosh as possible to further my European Cup Final fund I'd cadged a lift off Eddie Physick. Sound lad Eddie but you couldn't get him to hurry up to do anything; more life in an urgent note and all that. Eddie insisted on going to the Saltbox in Litherland for our pre-match bevy rather than one of the favoured Anfield watering holes. Of course I liked it in the Saltbox as it was one of my old stamping grounds and I still enjoyed a bevy in there every now and again with Big Ev's bro John. It was too far from Anfield for a pre-match scoop for my liking though, especially as we didn't leave there in the Eddiemobile 'til about twenty-to-three. Our chances of getting in to see the kick-off were minimal to say the least. In a feat of driving worthy of a Formula One driver and parking like a big parker Eddie got us outside the Kop gates five minutes before kick-off. It was a good job we both had Season Tickets otherwise we would have both been stood outside, locked out with thousands of others. Villa, for once, I suppose reflecting their unusually elevated position, had brought a large following. Having battered away at the Villa defence Kenny finally made the breakthrough after 66 minutes. Villa were soon level though Allan Evans. Time was running out and we were desperate to cut Villa's lead at the top. Coming up was another of those wickedly curling deliciously beautiful efforts from Kenny. He was fuckin' great Kenny wasn't he. I could write a book just about Kenny's goals. The man was awesome. It's not exaggerating to say that at times during his career Kenny wasn't far off being the best player in the world. Scenes reminiscent of our last two home games against Villa when we clinched the League on each ocassion greeted the goal and the final whistle soon after. Only three points behind Villa now and a game in hand it was time to march on in our quest for a triple League Championship.

Err....maybe not. We were brought right back smack bang down to earth with a 1-4 defeat at Wolves. Guess who scored Wolves fourth? None other than our old favourite Emlyn Hughes. I don't know whether that was scripted or what but if it wasn't it should have been as shortly after scoring that goal and legging it round the ground in the grand manner of his celebration Emlyn ran straight into the arms of Eamon Andrews and his big red book: "Emlyn Hughes – THIS IS YOUR LIFE!" What a life it had been too! Certainly a great footballing career and I suppose nobody could begrudge Emlyn that glorious moment. I bet his Liverpool achievements topped all that though!

The yellow peril hoodoo of shit games in that shit kit was broken with a 4-2 win at Sunderland. Next up was Tottenham at home. A horrible, bloody, bruising encounter with Spurs playing the offside trap as if there lives depended on it was won by us 2-1. It was even more horrible, bruising and bloody off the pitch as the Road End sought, and got, sweet revenge for the mauling we'd taken at White Hart Lane in the Cup game nine months earlier. I was waiting at the Halfway House for the bus back to Skem when two Spurs supporters, cackin' themselves like two big cacky things, approached, pleading for me to help them get back to Lime Street. They had clearly already taken a severe beating. I have to say that it did occur to me to throw them back into the many packs of avenging lions roaming up and down County Road and Everton Valley in search of prey. I just couldn't bring myself to do it though. Okay, I'd suffered badly down that horrible Sisters Road last March and maybe these two twats had been part of all that but they would literally have been torn limb from limb had I alerted our lads to their presence.

"I'll flag a fast black down for yer. Ask the driver to let yer out right outside Lime Street station."

"We ain't got enough for a cab."

"Look, just gerrin the fuckin' cab. If yer 'aven't got enough just do a fuckin' runner when yer get there. If this lot get 'old o' yer they'll fuckin' kill yer."

"Thanks pal."

"I'm not yer fuckin' pal. Ee arr, 'ere's yer cab now fuck off yer

Cockney cunts and don't come back."
Whether they arrived safely back at Lime Street I obviously don't know but at least I'd done my bit. I'd done the same for a couple of Man U supporters stranded in the Boys Pen many years previously. I just hoped that I would be treated as benevolently should I be in a similar position in the future but I somehow doubted it.

We'd taken over from Ipswich at the top of the League when we visited Portman Road. Ipswich were still looking good however as they had played three games less than us and were only three points behind. Have a guess which player wore the number 7 shirt for us that day. No, not Kenny – he was injured. Give up? Okay, it was Ian Rush. Yes, the man who was to become one of the greatest strikers the world of football has ever known started his Liverpool career as a raw-boned, gangly, nervous youngster at Portman Road in the famous number 7 shirt worn with such great panache for years by Keegan and Dalglish. When Rushie's co-striker Johnno had to go off injured very early in that game, being replaced by Jimmy Case, little Sammy Lee was pushed up front to partner him to make a real long and the tall partnership. You would have thought that pairing would have no chance against two big hairy-arsed England international centre-halves in Osman and Butcher. On the contrary they did quite well although it was Jimmy Case, in his very own version of Supersub, that netted the equaliser in our 1-1 draw. Villa replaced us at the top by virtue of their 3-0 win against Birmingham.

One lesson I learnt very early in my refereeing career was to never underestimate the scale or importance of a match. That fact was brought starkly home to me in a Skem Sunday League First Division clash between top club Leigh Youth and Green Dragon floundering like a big slain thing at the bottom. Leigh Youth were supposed to win it in a doddle, just brushing aside their much inferior opponents with a scoreline of something like 8-0 and therefore no probs for me. Didn't turn out like that! Green Dragon went ahead very early on and threw up a veritable green wall in front of goal, breathing fire to keep the marauding hordes of Leigh Youth at bay. Leigh Youth didn't like this and became increasingly frustrated at their inability to break down the Dragon defence. As is usually the case Leigh Youth players and management team looked for somebody to blame. Guess who! Not the players who were missing chances galore; certainly not the Manager for maybe picking the wrong team or getting the tactics wrong. No, the man they blamed was good old, always wrong Mr. Referee! Okay, some marginal decisions went against them – shit happens – get over it! There was no need though for the torrent of abuse I was getting. My patience was getting sorely tried as the bookings count rose. The black book came out three times to administer the "official cautions". It could have come out many more times and red cards been flashed but I was bending over backwards to keep people on the pitch. That all changed when Green Dragon, in a rare attack, broke away to score a second goal. I was immediately surrounded by screaming Leigh players claiming for offside. Yeah, it might well have been offside but all I could say was that I certainly didn't think it was offside. See, thing is, a lot of Sunday League, parks players etc are under this misguided illusion that referees, even more unfit than themselves, can run 100 yards in about 3 seconds; that is, the time it takes for a ball booted out of one penalty area to land in the other. Impossible isn't it? I know that, you know that but try telling het up players who probably couldn't run 100 yards in 30 seconds that!

"Keep up with play yer fat bastard!"

"I would if I 'ad me fuckin' moped with me!"

The top came off the boiling volcano:

"Yer fuckin' cheatin' bastard!"

OFF!

"Why 'ave yer sent 'im off ref?"

"Cos 'e called me a cheatin' bastard. I think that's fair enough."

"'E's right, yer are a cheatin' bastard!"

OFF!

"You go off too."

The Leigh manager made sure I would get my dinner early:

"Right, come on lads. Get off the pitch. We're not stayin' on 'ere. Ref, that's it. We're not playin' any more."

Oh well I'll take me fuckin' ball 'ome shall I?

"Okay, fine, that's your decision. I must tell you though that by doing so you are causing the match to be abandoned. The matter will be reported and I think you will be in big trouble with the County FA. I

would therefore ask you to complete the match"
"I'm not bothered ref. I'm bringin' them off."
They'll be made up then won't they? All they get off the manager of their Saturday teams is an orange at 'alf time.
I know I've used that joke before but I do like it.
It was a long walk back from the pitch on Liverpool Road to the changing rooms at Blaguegate. To be fair to the Leigh Youth players they had wanted to finish the game and largely me left me alone on the long walk to sanctuary. Not so their Manager! Tommy Rogers had got wind of what had happened and was waiting for us when we arrived at Blaguegate. This was in the days before mobile phones remember so how the fuck he got to know about it I don't know! I think maybe he had radar in his ears. Wasn't much got past Tommy!
"Alright Peter, what's 'appened 'ere son? All the other games are still playin'."
Before I got a chance to answer, the Leigh manager chipped in, "'E abandoned the match."
"Er excuse me, I did *not* abandon the match. You took your players off the field causing the match to be abandoned. In effect *you* abandoned the match, *not* me."
"Yeah, but yer give us nothin' an' yer sent two of our players off."
Oh right, yeah, my fault. Give yer nothin'? It should be gave anyway. I'm not 'ere to 'and fuckin' presents out! Who the fuck d'yer think I am – Father fuckin' Christmas?
"I am not, nor am I takin' bein' called a cheatin' bastard!"
I was angry now you see and had given up talking in my posh (ish) official reffing voice.
"I didn't call yer a cheat."
"No, but two of yer players did. Yer know, those two I sent off."
"Tommy, we're not payin' 'im. 'E doesn't deserve 'is fee."
I lost it then.
"Shove it up yer fuckin' arse! I don' wan' it and I don' fuckin' need it."
That wasn't true by the way. I most definitely *did* both *want* and *need* it! My European Cup Final fund could do with the cash.
"Tommy, Tommy, you 'eard that! 'E swore at me!"
"I'm not fuckin' arsed! Report me to the FA. I couldn't give a fuck anymore. I'm sick to fuckin' death of being called a cheat!"

"Come on, come on, pack it in now, pack it in now, both of yers! Peter, go an' get changed. Ronnie, get round there with yer players!" Sound Tommy, I think he might just have saved me from losing my refereeing badge that day. I haven't named the Leigh Youth manager in this incident. It wouldn't be fair to as I think he went on to have some good jobs with clubs at a higher level. As so often happened in cases like this I was appointed to referee the offending team again the following week. Guess what – good as gold, no problems, I got an apology for the previous week from the manager and two fees, one for this game and from the one he hadn't paid me the week before. Double bubble – happy days! Half in the ECF fund and half in the Derby Arms later! Laughin'! Isn't Sunday League mad eh?

CHAPTER SIXTEEN

PASSING IT DOWN

Christmas was very good in the Evo household. Not so the footy. The three Christmas games yielded us one goal and four points; a 1-0 home win against Wolves a draw at Old Trafford and another at home to Leeds. Although we were just about edging out Villa at the top on goal difference, both on 34 points Ipswich still had those three games in hand and were only one point below. We were drawing too many games and really needed to string a good winning run together to keep up the dream of the treble title.

We spent a brilliant New Year's Eve night in the Saltbox with Big Ev's family. I knew some people thought I wasn't good enough for her and maybe at times they were right. I was nothing to look at while Ev was gorgeous. The Big one reassured me though: "I love you Peter. I'll never leave you an' we'll never get divorced; we love each other too much."
As the divorce rate seemed to be about 99% of all married couples that was good to hear. Amongst many tearful hugs and kisses we agreed to stop all the fighting and arguing, especially in front of the kids. Ah well, it was good while it lasted – 'til January 2nd.

The bizzies were still allowing Liverpool and Everton to play at home on the same day if FA Cup draws came out like that. I never did understand that. Non-League Altrincham were to visit us while Arsenal travelled to Goodison. Altrincham, led by their player-manager Johnny King brought the usual small town following of some 5,000 or so. It was surprising that Johnny King could even walk never mind take his place in the team for this match. In the second round replay a fortnight or so earlier he had been standing in front of Scunthorpe goalkeeper Joe Neenan to prevent Joe from booting the ball upfield. Whatever King said to Neenan I've no idea but Neenan took great exception to it and moved Johnny out of his way via the expeditious means of kneeing him violently in the bollocks. Now any man to have had that done to them (I'm sure most of us have) will know the excruciating agony it brings and also the fact you don't walk again properly for about three weeks. It still brings a tear to my eye thinking of when I was about fourteen (and a right little twat I was too) having had a barney with my sister Pauline when her mate intervened. I felt the full force of a meaty right knee full in the ball sac! I was carrying my bollocks round in a wheelbarrow for a month after that. Still am as it happens but that's now due to my enforced celibacy rather than any of our Po's mates travelling to Skem to wreak painful vengeance on me for smacking their mate around 40 years ago.

Altrincham, near Manchester? Yeah, they're Mancs – or so the Road End decided. So we had two lots of Scousers, Mancs and Cockneys all in Liverpool on the same day. Not good! We won our match 4-1 and Everton won theirs 2-0. That wasn't going to appease the Scouse hordes though, not while there were Mancs and Cockneys to have battle with. I'm sure there must have been about 10,000 lads that day battling in and around Stanley Park. Both sets of Scousers would be in Liverpool for the next round too. Just Scousers though, nobody else – the 4th Round draw came out Everton v Liverpool. Guess who was appointed to referee the match. None other than our fave Taffy – Clive Thomas. Happy days!

The ECF fund had taken a bit of a battering around Christmas (had to keep my darling sweet while she was in a good mood) so it wasn't a good idea to get into it to go to the top of the table clash at Villa. I was, as usual, scraping the bones of my arse on the deck otherwise. The Saturday League game I was due to ref had been postponed due to the bad weather so I plumped for, what seemed to be a good idea at the time, going to the Everton v Arsenal match where vouchers would be given out for the sale of tickets for the Cup game. I wasn't at all happy at having to put some of my hard-earned into the Goodison coffers but I had to make sure I got a Cup ticket (they would be like gold dust) and Everton were skint so I supposed it would be like helping a hard up neighbour. I'm a good lad aren't I?

Getting down to Goodison was not the best idea I've ever had. I went with Stu and his bro Michael, now sadly now longer with us, passing away at a tragically early age. I'd often been to Goodison as a kid when we were away. I used to go with my schoolmate John Shaw who promised me that he would go to Anfield with me the following week. He never did though, being very good at sliding his way out of it. Being in Goodison now though just didn't sit right with me. What made it worse was that I was in the Gwladys Street. I just felt like an alien invader. Things got worse when news of our match came through. A massive cheer went up when it was announced we were a goal down.

Bluenose bastards!

I was a guest though after all so just had to grin and bear it. It was almost too much when the news came through that Villa were two goals up and had therefore knocked us off the top of the League. Evertonians were celebrating like they'd won the League.

Fuckin' bluenose twats! I fuckin' 'ate yers!

It really was the epitome of suffering in silence. It was all I could do to contain myself when after having had to listen to all this shite going on Everton lost to two late goals from Stapleton and Vaessen after being a goal up through what was admittedly a great strike by O'Keefe.

Shove that up yer fuckin' arse yer blue shitbags! Fuckin' get in! Go 'ead Arsenal! Fuckin' great Gunners! Oh, Arsenal we love you!

I was almost singing with the 200 or so celebrating Gooners. All the angst had been worth it I felt as I was surely guaranteed one of 53,000 Cup tickets with a voucher from a match at which less than 30,000 people had attended. I was right too! Job done! Mission Accomplished! Not fuckin' goin' through that again though!

The daunting midweek trip to Maine Road for the League Cup semi-final first leg was made in some fuckin' clapped out owld Tranny that belonged, I think to George, who ran one of the Sunday League teams. It was okay really I suppose if you could put up with having a pickaxe or a shovel up your arse for an hour or so. George was a builder you see. The most comfortable seat I could find was on a bag of cement. Wilko was on board as were a load of other nutters; John Riley, his bro Jim – known to everybody in the world, even his Ma, as Bim and a right fuckin' 'eadcase whose name I honestly can't remember but will tell you more of later. We got there quite late so didn't have to put up with all the usual pre-match shite in the Kippax. It was a different story once we were inside as the usual Moss Side mixture of cans, bottles, steel bars, lumps of wood and coins came at us over the barrier. We'd only just got in as all this was going on with the match barely a minute old. Kevin Reeves scored a cracker of a goal at the far end from us. I think I was one of very few people who realised immediately that the goal had been disallowed as I was now in the habit of checking for a signal from the referee and linesman that the goal was valid. The referee was signalling for a free-kick to us. No problem – no goal. Clem had his head screwed on, taking the free-kick while half the City players were protesting and the other half (can you get half of eleven?) were still celebrating. City fans were still celebrating as if they had scored but clearly, to me anyway, the goal had been disallowed. No kick from the centre-mark to restart the game (OOH, YOU BIG OFFICIAL REFEREE YOU EVO – REF ON YER BIG REF!) so no goal. Easy to understand that isn't it? Not so it proved for some. We won the game with a goal from Razor that was celebrated wildly in our section of the Kippax. It was gonna be scary time outside though so I was sticking like shit to a blanket to Wilko. Too often I'd got lost at away grounds, especially Maine Road, and suffered pooy pants as a consequence. As it seemed we'd parked somewhere in the deepest South of Manchester, deffo somewhere I'd never seen before on my many trips to Moss Side, there was no way I was gonna find the Tranny without the aid of Radar Wilko. I was glad I was with him too as there were some horrible, moochy cunts around as we neared our parking spec.

"Let's wait 'ere for the others. Get ready to twat these if the cunts start."

I was ready but it was looking very dodgy with said cunts ready to start 'til the full Tranny complement turned up. The Moss Side Moochies fucked off once the numbers weren't right for them and we were on our way without further incident.

"Go 'ead! Fuckin' great win that wasn't it lads?"

"Yeah, sound. That should be enough to get us through."

"Yeah, we'll fuck them at Anfield."

Here comes the man with no name.

"Wha' d'yer mean a great win? It was a draw!"

"Was it fuck yer soft twat we won 1-0!"

"It was 1-1. They scored straight from the kick-off and we equalised near the end."

"Their goal was disallowed soft fuckin' arse! We won 1-0."

Funny as fuck to see the man with no name goin' absolutely fuckin' ballistic, jumping up and down on a bag of cement, in the back of the

Tranny celebrating a win he didn't know we'd got.
"Eh soft lad, get off that fuckin' cement. That's my seat!"
Soft lad wasn't the only one who thought the City goal had been allowed however. John Motson thought so too! Old Motty had commentated for the BBC throughout the first half as if City were a goal ahead. He only realised at half-time that the goal had been disallowed and so had to hurriedly dub a completely new commentary over the first-half action to be shown later on the televised highlights. If Motty got it wrong what chance did soft lad have?

Everton Football Club exchanged my Gwladys Street voucher for a ticket in the Goodison Road Enclosure for the FA Cup game. Don't quite know how that worked but I was glad of it anyway as I hadn't fancied going in the Street end. Clive Thomas was booed every inch of the way from the tunnel to the centre circle by the Evertonians. You could hardly blame them I suppose after his Maine Road shenanigans of 1977. We were winding the Blues up by cheering him but in truth apart from one monumental gift he'd given us that day four years earlier he'd never been one of our favourites. Clive had done us down on more than one ocassion and maybe, ever so slightly, went out of his way to make good his Maine Road mistake. That's not to take anything away from Everton that day though. Journeyman players like O'Keefe and Varadi were like men possessed and played as if their lives depended on beating us. Avi Cohen, showing lessons well learned in the Sandy Brown Academy of Own Goals, gave Everton the lead. Imre Varadi put Everton two up in the second half. The Evertonians were going mental. I felt so sick I felt like yacking everywhere. This was fuckin' bad news. There were probably about 15,000 Reds inside Goodison that day in a crowd of 53,000 (where were all those diehard Blues in the last home game against Arsenal a fortnight earlier? I was there!) but it felt like the ground was totally Blue and twice as many too. Jimmy Case pulled a goal back 15 minutes from time. We then threw everything at them in search of an equaliser but I don't think there was anything that could stop a Blue victory that day. Never has the phrase, "They wanted it more" been more apt. Mick Lyons was cavorting round the pitch like a latter day Nobby Stiles at the end along with the other Everton players and several thousand Evertonians. The shitty part of the Park End underneath the stand had now been blocked off (should have been years earlier – it was a shithole) and so wasn't housing nearly as many Reds as previous Derby games. Reds were spread out into the Goodison Road Enclosure and also in the Paddock. Evertonians moved on to the pitch mainly from the Street End and made a bit of a show of coming down to the other end to taunt us. There was a bit of bother as Reds at the front of the terraces bore the brunt of a few Evertonian boots. Some Reds got on to the pitch to have a go back but it was all over in a matter of seconds really. The torture continued outside as dancing Blues surrounded any Red they could find: "We're the pride of Merseyside!" Well they had to win the odd one didn't they? It was a long walk back to Stu's car. The three Blues in the car with me gave it as large as they could to me interspersed with talk of who they wanted in the next round. I had to suffer in silence as I needed the lift home. A black day indeed. It got worse the following week.

I'd decided it was high time I started passing the Red dynasty down. Of course both my kids were Reds, no question, but Stevo was chomping at his young leash to start going the match. Big Ev had been pestering me for ages to take him the match but how can you explain to a woman that you don't take a young kid, moreover your own child, into the cauldron of the Kop?
"He can sit down."
"No, 'e can't sit down."
"Your Price sat down when yer took 'im."
"Only on a crush barrier. Our Price was older. Our Ste's too young yet."
"Well I see loads sittin' when it's on the telly."
"They're in the stands."
"No they're not. They're in the seats."
"Yeah, that's the stands."
"If it's the stands, why are there seats?"
"They just call it the stands for fuck sake! I don' know fuckin' why but they do!"
"Well, take 'im in there then, in the seats."
"I can't."
"Why?"
"Cos my season ticket is for the Kop. Yer stand up in the Kop."

"Yeah, I've seen that when they all push to the front. Can't yer just take 'im in the stands or the seats whatever it's called for one match?"
"No I can't."
"Why?"
"Oh for fuck sake! I go in the Kop. I've always gone in the Kop an' always will. I'll take 'im in the Kop when 'e's old enough and the time's right."
Ste was now old enough and the time was indeed right. It was a nice, easy match I was taking him to. There would be no problem us winning, as Leicester were bottom of the First Division and we hadn't been beaten at home for 63 League games – 85 games in total in all competitions. The lad would love it and would be hooked. Once you go the match you never wanna stop. Ste knew all the songs as I was constantly singing them round the house. I would have to dip into the ECF fund for the extra quid or two to take him but it would be worth it. The lad was about to be christened in the Red faith.
"I'll take yer the match tomorrer son."
"Ah smart Dad."
Smart was Ste's favourite saying at the time. Anything remotely good was "smart". Bit like my "happy days" I suppose. It was smart though.
"Yeah, I'll take yer in the Kop but yer've gorra be good."
"I will be Dad, promise. Will yer get me sweets an' crisps an' pop?"
"Yeah but don't pester me."
"I won't. Smart!"

I did try to save the ECF fund a few bob by lifting the little fella over the turny but he actually wasn't that little so Tom The Turny man wasn't having it. We got in nice and early for prime position on a crush barrier.
"Ah, this is smart this isn't Dad?"
The little fella had only been inside Anfield five minutes and already he loved it. He was even more into it once the match got underway. I'm sure I heard a little "f" word slip out a couple of times. That shouldn't have been a surprise though listening to his Dad: "Yer stupid fuckin' bastard ref! Come on for fuck sake, get the ball up. Fuckin' mark up will yers. Fuck off Leicester yer shower o' twats!" Fair enough, you couldn't really blame an impressionable nine year old from copying what he'd just heard could you? There was no way

I was gonna check myself from swearing though. It was in me and had been in me since I first went the match when I was only slightly older than my son was now. I used to swear in the Boys Pen so why couldn't Ste in the Kop? Just hoped his Ma didn't find out that's all. Ste went as crackers as anybody else when we took the lead after 15 minutes. Okay, it was Leicester's Young who put through his own goal but it was cause for celebration anyway. Looking good and on course for another win. Leicester, having looked a poor side in the first half came out with a steely determination and a hitherto unseen footballing quality in the second half. They forced themselves back into the game with an equaliser from Byrne. A draw was looking on the cards, which wasn't good for us but would at least preserve our long unbeaten home record. Enter Jim Melrose to become a record-breaker. JIM WHO? Yeah, I know, I'd never heard of him before either. Fuckin' 'ell, this was bollocks. My son's first game and it looks like we're gonna get beat by bottom of the table Leicester. How bad is that? Plenty bad, I can tell you! We just couldn't break down the doughty Leicester defence again so that was it – we'd lost that proud record. There was only one person I blamed.

"'Ow come we lost Dad?"

Fuck off, yer fuckin' little jinx!

"These things just 'appen son. Can't win all the time."

"But I wanted us to win. It was my first match."

Yeah, an' it'll be yer last yer fuckin' Jonah!

"Never mind son. We'll win the next time I take yer."

"Can I go every match with yer now Dad?"

"Not every match son. I won't be able to afford it all the time."

"Okay, well some of the time?"

"Yeah, some of the time son. Some of the time."

It was a bit tight blaming Little Ste. If the fuckin' eleven galoots out on the pitch couldn't get it right how could a nine year old lad be expected to? Still, the lad had been blooded. The Evo Red dynasty would continue.

CHAPTER SEVENTEEN

ASSORTED LOONS AND RECORD BREAKERS

Terry's heart was pounding as all his pent up love, emotion and frustration was about to come cascading from him. Graeme was there for him, waiting, with open arms, for their previously unrequited love to be consummated. Terry landed in Graeme's arms and was whisked into the air, Graeme turning and spinning him round like a whirling dervish in one graceful movement. The two men's eyes met, faces fixed in manic grins. Terry thought the very life was about to be squeezed from him until Graeme's lips met his own. Terry's words of love were music to Graeme's ears; the words Graeme had waited, nay yearned, for his friend to say for so long:

"WHAT A FUCKIN' GOAL!"

Ah, 'ad yers fooled there lads didn't I? Thought old Evo had gone off his trolley and started writing for the gay section of one of those mad erotic literature websites didn't yer? Or maybe that Mills and Boon had signed me up to write their very first published gay novel. The reason for all this kissin', cuddlin' and tonsil hockey was that Kenny Dalglish's 30th birthday party was in full swing at Anfield inside the penalty area of Bulgaria's top football team CSKA Sofia. Graeme Souness had just scored his third goal of the night, every one of them a cracker, to clinch a 5-1 win for us. Terry Mac was swearing undying love, once he'd unwrapped his tongue from Souey's tonsils that is, for his midfield mate, even though they'd had a bet going since both got three goals in the 10-1 win against Oulu Palloseura as to who would score more goals in this season's European Cup competition. Souey's goal had just put them level on six each as Terry had also scored a whopper earlier in the match against the shell-shocked Bulgars. If ever the Kop's famous cry of, "GET INTO THEM!" had been heeded it was on this night. We never left CSKA alone from minute one. We well and truly got into them in a way that intimidated the Bulgarians into submission. Rolling back the years on the wing was Stevie Heighway. Steve was in the team only because of an injury to Johnno. Beep Beep was brilliant! CSKA just didn't know how to play him. While they were trying to take care of him it left loads of space for the others like the penalty area importuners, Graeme and Terry, to do their stuff. All that, allied to our best display of the season - passion, commitment, great football and stupendous goals – meant that we were all but through, barring a monumental collapse in Sofia, to the Semi Final of the European Cup.

Sunday League football throws up some great characters. Some of these characters also have a little bit of "scall" in them to give them that spark. Others though can be characters and yet still be true gentlemen, not only of football but of life. Mick Gray was one of those characters. I'd known Mick for a couple of years through bevying in the Derby Arms. Mick was a great mate of another Derby regular and fellow gent, John Farrimond, known to man and beast alike simply as Farrie. Farrie was manager of Dunlop Football Club in the Skem League. Many a battle I had with Farrie (or Omar as he was sometimes called due to him being the spitting image of Omar Sharif) during and after games and sometimes in toe-to-toe arguments later in the Derby. Those battles however would always end with a handshake, a bevy and these words from John, "You're a good ref Peter. You make mistakes and some bad decisions but you're never a cheat."

Fair comment Farrie lad. I could take that. I was never shy of a bit of criticism. It sometimes made me look at my own game and think of ways of improving myself as a referee. These blokes were all very experienced at running teams (far more experienced than I was at reffing matches) so I would listen to their comments if they were constructive. It was the people who would give me shit, screaming and shouting at me for no other reason than their team was losing that I had no time for. Mick had a great playing career with some good semi-pro teams and even now in his early forties was showing the way to much younger lads in the Derby Arms team. A man of many parts was Mick as he proved in one 3-3 draw against Ashfield when Derby goalkeeper Steve Rocke got injured during the game. Mick left his centre-forward position to go in goal and save two penalties. Not only that but when I also awarded Derby Arms two penalties (I did like those penalties) Mick ventured forward as he was normally penalty-taker anyway and slotted both. If you think that all sounds a bit Roy of the Rovers well maybe it was but that was Mick, great bloke and slightly larger than life. Mick came to me that night in the Derby for our usual post match Sunday night discussion where he would congratulate and chastise me in equal measure, backed up of course by Omar. Mick used to make me grin when he'd saunter over, thin moustache, cigar in mouth and blowing plumes of smoke like Skem's answer to Clint Eastwood.

"'Ow do I become a referee Peter?"

"You, a ref Mick?"

"Yeah, 'ad enough of playin' now Pete. Can't keep up with these young lads. I cracked two ribs there today in goal. It's not worth it anymore but I wanna stay involved so I'm thinkin' of takin' up the whistle."

"Okay Mick, I'll sort you a course with Tom Hughes."

Mick became a very good referee but sadly for only a couple of years or so. I'll tell you more about that in another chapter.

Another character was Steve Loren. Steve was a slippery eel of a winger for Busy Bee, Polaris and a few other teams during his playing days. If Steve got the ball on the wing and the centre-forward could head the ball a bit, as Eric Sealey could when they were playing in the same Polaris team together, then nine times out of ten it spelt goal. Steve should have gone into the Guinness Book of Records for one particular match. Let me set the scene:

"Ref, can I leave the pitch for a couple of minutes please?"

"Yeah, no problem Steve."

It was unusual for players to ask permission to leave the pitch for any reason, if they wanted to go off for anything they just got off, although technically by not doing so they should have had the old official caution. I thought maybe Steve needed to change his boots or something as he hared off the pitch (and boy was he quick) and legged it over to the changing rooms. He was back about five minutes later but still had the same boots on. Strange that. Maybe he'd wanted a pee but normally if a player needed to empty his bladder he would do it either at half-time or if absolutely desperate nip off the pitch for a minute, turn his back to any women or kids and water the grass right there. Ten minutes later:

"Ref, can I go off again please?"

"Yeah, go on Ste."

Same dance, gone for a slightly shorter period this time. I thought maybe if Steve had some sort of problem that the Busy Bee manager should substitute him but they didn't for the very good reason that they had no substitutes! It was getting beyond a joke when for the third time Steve asked:
"Ref, can I go off again?"
"Bloody 'ell Steve. What's wrong with yer mate?"
"Can't stop, tell yer when I come back."
Two minutes later Steve was back.
"What's up Steve? Why d'yer keep goin' the changies?"
"Got the shits ref. Should be okay now."
So there you go: Steve Loren – the only man in the history of football to have three shits in one match. Get that Guinness Book of Records down here!

Eric Sealey was a character too. Now I've known Eric for many years, worked with him for a few too, so I don't think he'll mind me saying he was a nasty piece of work on the pitch sometimes. Eric will say that he was only looking after himself and there were times I'm sure when that was the case. Eric was also sometimes the subject of racial remarks but woe betide anybody he heard hearing making them. One such ocassion, and I'm sure Eric won't mind me recounting the story, was when Polaris were playing a team new to the League on the first day of a season and unaware of how mad Eric was. We were only ten minutes into the match and Eric had scored two headed goals, from crosses by Steve Loren as it happened. One member of the new team turned to another and said, "Fuckin' 'ell, 'e's good with 'is 'ead isn't 'e?"
The other player said, "Yeah, 'e fuckin' should be. 'E's 'eadin' fuckin' coconuts all day."
Bad mistake!
I said, "Eh mate, yer can't be sayin' things like that yer know."
"Why fuckin' not?"
"Well for a start I could send yer off for it but worse than that if 'e 'ears yer 'e'll fuckin' kill yer!"
"Fuck 'im."
"Fair enough but I tell yer, if 'e 'ears yer 'e *will* do yer in and when 'e does do yer in 'e'll make sure I don't see it."

"Fuck 'im an' fuck you!"
Fuck you too. ***I'll*** *make sure* ***I*** *don't see it too!*
"Okay, but yer 'ave been warned."
Eric came to me and had a little word in my ear: "I 'eard it ref."
"Make sure I don't see it."
Ricky the racist lasted another five minutes before being carted off. Guess what – I didn't see it!

Having safely, but only just, got through the League Cup Semi Final against City thanks to a 1-1 draw at home giving us the aggregate 2-1 victory we faced West Ham in the Final. Oh deep fuckin' joy! Most Reds had wanted West Ham's semi-final opponents Coventry in the Final. Playing West Ham would be bound to bring unholy murder. There'd been bad enough trouble at the Charity Shield game at the start of the season. The two teams playing each other in a Cup Final would be bound to bring out the worst in everybody – Liverpool and West Ham alike. That's all what I thought at the time anyway but to be honest I didn't see an awful lot of bother apart from ticketless West Ham fans trying to storm a gate at our end at half-time. Plenty of reports circulated that there had been major bother in and around London the night before and on the day of the game but I hadn't actually witnessed them. There did seem to be more West Ham fans inside Wembley than ours but I suppose any London neutrals with tickets had sided with the underdog Hammers. The game itself was fairly nondescript. Phil Thompson was missing for us through injury so the team was captained by Razor. Also injured was Johnno, his place again being taken by Steve Heighway, quickly coming towards the end of his Anfield playing days. Stevie was waiting to take up a position with Minnesota Kicks in America but was staying at Anfield for as long as we needed him. Stevie was also due a testimonial match to be played on April 1st. It was, in fact, to prove to be the last of Stevie's 465 first team games for us; a marvellous record indeed for a man who hadn't really wanted to take up football as a living anyway, academia being his first choice of profession. Credit then to Shanks, Uncle Bob and the rest of the LFC coaching staff for knocking a raw, gangly, somewhat awkward youngster into one of the finest wingers LFC have ever had. Oh, and while we're at it, a big cheer too for the club who first nurtured Stevie's talent and gave him the chance to step up from the amateur game to the heady heights of the First Division and beyond – Skelmersdale United! The game was fairly dour with defences always on top; chances were few and far between. Colin Irwin, Thommo's replacement, looked jittery but my Granny could have played alongside Alan Hansen and kept most attacks at bay. The game belatedly burst into life two minutes from the end of extra-time with another controversial decision by Clive Thomas going our way. A high ball was played into the West Ham penalty area and was partially cleared. Sammy Lee was lying injured about ten yards from goal. The partially cleared ball fell at the feet of Barney Rubble just outside the area. No danger there then! No, Barney fairly smote the ball into the net. Cue wild celebrations in our end. No goal signalled the linesman, quite rightly as Sammy was lying in an offside position. Our fave Welshman took a quick look at the signalling linesman, nodded and headed back for the centre-circle. Goal said Clive, definitely a goal, Lee not interfering with play or seeking to gain an advantage by being in an offside position. Go 'ead Clive, get back to the centre-circle before yer change yer fuckin' mind! Right, go fuckin' mad again lads. The West Ham fans were going mad too but in a different way. Now there was bother. West Ham fans in our end were wading into Reds but were getting waded back into, as they were heavily outnumbered, twice over. Those, including me, with eyes still for the game rather than the battles going on at the front of our end could see that West Ham had won a free kick. Stewart's kick must have nearly broken Clem's hand as our keeper pulled off an astonishing save. The corner would be West Ham's last desperate throw of he gambler's dice. Three years earlier at the 1978 World Cup Clive had denied Brazil a winner in their 1-1 against Sweden when he blew for full time as the ball was in the air from a corner. A split second later Brazil had the ball in the net but no goal ruled Clive – time was up when the ball was in the air. Come on Clive, do it again this time. Neighbour took the corner. The ball floated high into our penalty area. Come on Clive - blow the whistle now! Alvin Martin's meaty head met the ball full on. The ball was on its way to goal. Come on Clive, for fuck sake blow that bleedin' whistle! The ball beat Clem all ends up but we had Terry Mac standing on the line like a stand in goalkeeper. Head it over Terry! Shit, the soft twat's saved it with his hand! To be honest it was the only thing Terry could do. No whistle save the one to signal a penalty to West Ham. So, no saved by a Clive Brazilian type ending. Terry Mac got yellow-carded for an offence that today carries an automatic red. West Ham had a penalty with the last kick of the game. Bollocks! Clem had no chance of saving this. I don't think Clemence and Shilton in the same goal would have saved it. Ray Stewart had, I think, a 100% record from penalties. Stewart had no technique, finesse or strategy for taking penalties, he just used to twat the ball as hard as he could – about 100 miles an hour! I wouldn't have got in front of a Ray Stewart penalty if you had paid me. Clem was being paid and still got nowhere near it but Stewart had kidded him. Instead of his customary blast Stewart placed the ball oh so delicately and sweet as a nut to Clem's left. So, 1-1, a bit of argey and bargey going back to the coach, away from Wembley and off to Villa Park to do it all again on April Fool's Day – Beep Beep's testimonial would have to wait. More dips into the ECF fund. There's gonna be fuck all left of it at this rate.

The formality of reaching the European Cup Semi Final was accomplished when we won the return in Sofia 1-0. The draw paired us with Bayern Munich. That was a tough draw but if we performed anything like we had in the games against CSKA then we might well be okay.

A John Bailey own goal gave us victory in the Anfield Derby. It wasn't as good as some of the other four own goals Everton had gifted us in the past twelve years, certainly not as good as Sandy's or Mick Lyons'. Nevertheless a deft near-post header from Jimmy Case's corner left Seamus (bizarrely changed from Jim) McDonagh helpless. A Derby win is, was and always will be cause for great celebrations by me. It doesn't matter how shit the game is or whether it matters in terms of winning the league, and we'd certainly blown our chances of a treble title by this time, a win over Everton leaves me ecstatic. Liverpool could beat Brazil in a match to decide who was the greatest team ever on the planet and it wouldn't mean as much to me as a Derby win. Due to new ground restrictions and the Paddock now being seated the crowd of 49,743 was the first Anfield Derby crowd below 50,000 since 1950. Our attendances in general this season were down anyway, struggling to reach 30,00 for some games and in fact below that for a couple of League games. Everton's crowds were down too as they were mostly all over the country. Nowhere did the recession caused by Thatcher's policies hit harder than on Merseyside, which I think might well have been exactly what Thatcher and her cronies wanted. A biting recession and high unemployment meant that some Scousers could no longer afford to go to every game as they had been used to for years. I was working, had a Season Ticket and it was a terrible struggle for me sometimes so imagine how it was for young out-of-work lads or men with families to support on the pittance of dole money.

"Get on your bike and find work" was Thatcher's right hand man Norman Tebbitt's answer to unemployment on Merseyside. Well just in case you hadn't noticed Mr. fuckin' Tebbitt there's no bastard work *to* find! These Tories might as well have lived on another fuckin' planet as they had fuck all idea what was going on down on this one!

I went to Villa Park with Alan Southern and his fellow Road Ender Larry Trencher in Alan's car and mighty glad I went with them I was too. I wouldn't have liked to have done that game on my own. No problems before the game; the Liverpool fans packed themselves into several pubs on a main road. I forget the name of the one we were in but it was wall-to-wall Red anyway. A few West Ham fans came to try to storm the pub but were well and truly wellied out. Thommo was fit again, taking his place in the team and resuming the captaincy. Jimmy Neighbour, on West Ham's right-wing, was causing us all sorts of problems and set up Paul Goddard for the header that gave West Ham a shock early lead took. Pulling the strings for us, surprisingly, was Steve Heighway's replacement, young Ian Rush. Rushie, the Ipswich game being his only other experience of first team football, showed a maturity well beyond his tender years and experience. A great effort from him inside the penalty area hit the bar as we laid siege to the Hammers goal. He even had the temerity to bollock Kenny for a misplaced pass. Neighbour again set Goddard up for a chance that should have put the Hammers two goals up, which would have been totally against the run of play but could well have put the game beyond our reach. We capitalised on that big let off after 25 minutes when Terry Mac played a delightful chipped through ball for Kenny to delicately volley the equaliser. We went ahead three minutes later when a Jimmy Case corner found the head of Alan Hansen. I'm not all that sure Jocky's header had the strength to reach the net 'til it hit Billy Bonds thigh and crept over the line to give us what turned out to be the eventual winner. Thommo went up to collect the trophy so therefore became the first man to be presented with a League Cup winners *medal*. Before this year tankards had been presented. It was scary after the goal and near the end of match when West Ham fans were trying to pull down the mesh fencing separating us and them in the Holte End. Fuckin' mad that lot!

Police and ambulance sirens mixed as they screamed up and down the roads surrounding Villa Park after the match. There were lads staggering round with cut heads and mashed faces all over the place. I'm not even sure who was who – Cockneys and Scousers. I just know there were some serious injuries that night. Alan had the right idea in getting us safely back to his car (an orange one if I remember rightly Alan – not sure of the make, might have been a Capri but then again it could have been a fuckin' Jag for all I know about cars) waiting for all the shite to die down and then parking ourselves in a nice quiet boozer for an hour or so to celebrate winning this trophy for the first time before making our way home. I remember that pub as being the first one outside London at which I paid 50p for a pint. Robbin' twats!

We were back in action two nights after winning the League Cup. Stoke City were our opponents in a game played on Friday night due to the Grand National being run the following day. A young lad called Ronnie Whelan, signed from Irish club Home Farm for a bag of spuds or something made his debut replacing the injured Ray Kennedy. Young Ronnie slotted in so well it looked like he'd been playing with players of the calibre of Souness and Dalglish for years. Ronnie's debut goal it was that put us ahead, a sharply taken half-volley that I'm sure even Kenny would have been proud to call his own. Terry Mac wrapped the win up with two second half goals. Older players like Stevie and Johnno were being gradually phased out, being replaced by new, fresh, energetic youngsters like Ronnie, Rushie and Sammy. We weren't going to win the League this season being now well off the pace in sixth place but one trophy had already been secured. The future looked bright and there was still the prospect of another European Cup although it would be a monumental task. Even if we overcame Bayern to reach the Final, our opponents would be either Inter Milan or Real Madrid. Fuck it – we're Liverpool – bring it on!

It was Friday night, the Reds had won, we had one trophy already under the belt with the prospect of another, all was well with the Evo world so time for a bevy! The Knowl Brow wasn't normally my pub of choice. It was okay for the odd bevy, normally after working the late shift as you could get a late drink there if your face fitted and you put on an accent with loads of thees and thous. Peter Whitty was in there. Oh shit! Nice lad but he'd got me into trouble once before when he'd asked me to go for a bevy with him one Friday night. That was fairly unusual for Whitty but I went along nonetheless. It was only when I got to the Viking I realised that I'd been set up as the stooge in a foursome. Peter had wanted to get off with a bird he'd fancied for a while so had invited her out for a bevy with her mate. I was the unwitting, unwilling partner for his prospective bird's mate. Err....I don't think so Whitty. Just as well that the bird's mate didn't fancy me. As a matter of fact I didn't fuckin' fancy her either and told her so in words to the effect of I had something twenty times better than her at home. Thankfully Stu arrived to save my bacon. If Big Ev had found out about that she'd have killed me. Not that I'd done anything wrong at all but then I didn't ever really need to do anything wrong for my darling to threaten to kill me. Just being in the company of two birds with another bloke would have had Big thinking I was slipping one of them the sos. Anyway, back to the plot (if there ever is one with my stories) this Friday night:
"Alright Evo. Been the match?"
No Whitty, Liverpool were at home but I thought I'd go up to St. Richard's and say a few prayers before coming to the Brow for a bevy.
"Yeah Pete. Been the match."
Whitty was an occasional matchgoer, in fact I think he had a Season Ticket but didn't use it all the time. He obviously hadn't been tonight as he was dressed up and slightly the worse for drink.
"Warra yer doin' in 'ere?"

Whitty wasn't much of a Brow man either.
"I could ask you the same thing."
"Ah Evo, I'm fuckin' pissed off. Me tart's fucked off. I'm looking for 'er. Come on; let's go down the Derby. She might be in there."
"'Ang on then, I've only just got this bevy. Let's finish this then we'll flag a cab down."
I could tell this wasn't gonna be a night for a quiet bevy.
"Nah, I've got me car outside."
"Fuck off Whitty, yer never drivin' in that fuckin' state!"
"I am. I'm okay."
The Whittymobile was some boss sports car; might have been an MG, I'm not sure but it couldn't half move. Whitty was driving the car quite well considering the amount of alcohol he'd obviously consumed but too fuckin' fast for my liking.
"Fuckin' 'ell Whitty, who d'yer think yer are, Donald Campbell?"
"Who?"
"Oh never fuckin' mind. We're 'ere now. Let's get in before Brian calls lazzies." Whitty's beloved (whoever she was at the time) wasn't in the Derby.
"Come on Evo. She's not 'ere, let's get back the Brow. She might be in there now."
"Fuck me Pete, I've only just got this pint. We might not even get a bev now in the Brow unless Lollipop's in an' gets us on the staybee."
"Down in one then."
Down in one it was.
"Yer fuckin' fish Evo!"
"That's me!"
Half a minute later we were back in the Brow, in one piece – just!
"Nah then, what's thee pair o' tusses doin' in 'ere?"
"Alright Lol, soft arse 'ere is lookin' for 'is bird. I'm just tryin' to get a bevy. Any chance of us getting a drink now?"
"Aye, leave it me."
Lollipop then spoke Woolese to the manager for five minutes before returning with three beautiful pints of the amber stuff.
"Gi' us a pound Evo and we'll call it reet."
Like fuck we'll call it reet, I mean right, it's 'is fuckin' round.
"Ee arr Whit, it's your round mate."
Whitty had been behind me but I was now talking to space. Whitty

was involved in earnest conversation with a bird.
"Ah, see 'e's found yon lass then."
"Yeah Lol. Fuckin' nuisance isn't 'e?"
Whitty came sauntering back with the swagger we all know that says, "I've copped!"
"Sorted then Whitty? Back with 'er now?"
"Nah, that's not me bird."
"Who was that yer were talkin' to then?"
"Don't know. Never saw 'er before in me life. Some wool bird. Got 'er phone number an' that. Might take 'er out next week."
"You're fuckin' mad you!"
"Come on, drink up. I'll take yer up to the Balc. We'll get a late bevy there."
"What is this, a fuckin' magical mystery pub crawl of Skem?"
"D'yer wanna bevy or wha' yer moaning twat? If yer do, get in the fuckin' car an' shut up!"
"Nah Peter, come on, let's get a cab. Yer can't drive now. Leave yer car 'ere."
"Fuck that, the wools'll 'ave it off!"
Whitty's rocket was flying up the dual carriageway when the inevitable happened.
NER NER NER NER NER NER!
The Plodmobile was struggling to catch us but eventually got alongside.
"Pull over!"
Whitty was making gestures as if to suggest to nice Plod that he couldn't hear him.
"Fuck sake Peter, pull over, we're gonna get well nicked 'ere!"
"Fuck them, I'll burn them off the road!"
OH SHIT!
Burn them indeed he did. The two Plod in the car though either knew, or had kept pace enough to see, where we were headed. They arrived in the pub car park about ten seconds after us.
"What the fuck do you think you're doing?"
They do ask the most pertinent questions Plod don't they?
"Just comin' ere for a bevy like."
"We were tellin' yer to pull over. Why the fuck didn't yer stop?"
"Where officer? When? We didn't see yer. We didn't did we Pete?"

Fuck you! I'm not getting involved in this. I just wanna bevy and get 'ome. I've 'ad my fuckin' share of police cells ta very fuckin' much!
"Err..I'm not sure."
"D'yer know 'ow fast yer were fuckin' goin' there?"
"No officer. Me speedo's broke."
"Right, get in the back of the car. You're coming with me. My fellow officer will drive your car to the station."
I was half expecting to be carted away myself under some such charge as, "Travelling in a rocket machine knowing or believing it to be a car exceeding the speed limit on Her Majesty's highway."
My nerves were shot to bits when I walked in the Balc. Joe O'Keefe, another lad from Grimwoods, was at the bar.
"Alright Pete. Bloody 'ell, what was goin' on there? 'Ave the police arrested Peter Whitty? Saw 'is car come bombin' it in the car park."
"'E's fuckin' nuts 'im Joe!"
"D'yer wanna drink Pete?"
"Yeah, a large fuckin' brandy!"
"I didn't know yer drink brandy."
"I don't. I just fuckin' need one now!"
My nerves calmed, it was time to settle down with a nice pint of my good lady friend.
"D'yer always get a late bevy 'ere Joe?"
"Yeah, the coppers from Wigan come 'ere after work. They get a drink so everybody else does."
I knew, just knew, that Ploddy Small Hands who'd knocked fuck out of me (without causing me an ounce of pain cos he was a fuckin' big wimp and couldn't hit properly) nearly three years earlier would be in there. Sure enough, PSH was staring at me across the bar. He had a puzzled look on his face as if to say, "I know that twat's face. I must've beaten the cheeky little get up once but I can't fuckin place 'im."
I fuckin' placed him alright! I was fuckin' dyin' to go round the bar and butt the twat but I'd had enough of the police for one night.
"D'yer know 'im Peter? 'E keeps starin' at yer."
"Yeah, sort of Joe. 'E's not sure who I am though."
"'E's one of the Wigan coppers."
"I know Joe. That's 'ow I know 'im."
Joe must have guessed the association between me and the small

handed twat and thought it politic to say no more. It was getting on for two o'clock in the morning when I left the Balc and started the long walk home. As usual I'd spent the money I was keeping back for a taxi. Long walk that from the Balc to New Church Farm; a good two hours worth at least, especially when you're tired, cold, wet, hungry and pissed. I'd been walking for about twenty minutes when a car approached me from the opposite direction. Hmmm...that looks suspiciously like Whitty's super dooper rocket machine sports car. Fuck me; it is Whitty's super dooper rocket machine sports car!

"What the fuck are you doin' out? I thought they'd lock yer up fer the weekend at least! An' what the fuck're yer doin' drivin' yer car?"

"Nah, they let me go. They gave me the breath test an' I passed it."

"There is no fuckin' way on earth they gave you the bag an' you passed. No fuckin' way!"

"Well I did, so fer fuck sake, get in an' I'll give yer a lift 'ome."

I'm not sure how Peter got away with that but I think it might have been some jiggery-pokery about not taking the test for a couple of hours, so when he did there wasn't sufficient alcohol in his blood to take him over the bag limit - something like that. I do know that he was one jammy bastard to have got away with it. I don't think he ever did find his bird either. LUCKY GIRL!

CHAPTER EIGHTEEN

FINDING THE FUND

Bayern came to Anfield and in a repeat of their "performance" in the 1971-72 European Cup Winners Cup match defended as if their lives depended on it. Knowing the Germans it probably did. They got the 0-0 draw they came for and that would, in all likelihood, be the end of our quest for our third European Cup.

For one horrible Sunday afternoon it looked as if even if we got to that Final in Paris they would have to play it without my presence.

I'd reffed my two matches and was well in pocket with the two fivers I'd got. Big Ev was tidying the bedrooms when I got in – she did mad things like that sometimes. Luckily enough for me, or so I thought at the time, she was occupied in our Ste's bedroom. Nice one! Enough time and away from prying eyes to surreptitiously shove my booty of two flims into my hidey-hole to top up what had become a diminished ECF fund. Little Ev was playing happily in our bedroom. I gave her a little kiss and thought no more of it. My mistake was in forgetting to shut the wardrobe door properly.
"Peter, come up 'ere!"
Big Ev had given no inkling of the monumental shit I was about to get. In fact, her voice was that soft I thought maybe it was frolic time. Good disguise there Big – well done.
The bedroom carpet was a sight to behold with pound notes (remember them?), flims and cock and hens all over the place. Jesus! I hadn't really been counting the fund that often, just sort of shoving what I'd saved into the hidey-hole in my wardrobe. There must have been a hundred nicker lying on the floor. It was like Sale Of The Century or one of those other quiz shows where they win a load of money at the end, take it out of a case and throw it all over the place. Little Ev stood there all cute and angelic with a lovely little smile on her face. She'd been playing in the wardrobe, dragging clothes and stuff out. It was a good job I'd moved my mag collection from the wardrobe to make space for the ECF fund. As well as dragging the clothes out my little cutie had also dragged my cache of cash out. My

ECF fund had been well and truly rumbled. It wasn't her fault I suppose as she was only six years old so her Dad's big wardrobe must have looked a great place to have adventures in.
"Where'd'yer get all that money? What's it for?"
Big Ev never did give me a chance to answer one question at a time. It was pointless lying. I'd been sussed well and truly so anything I said she wouldn't believe anyway. She probably wasn't even gonna believe the truth so I was fucked all ends up. I wouldn't have been able to think of a good lie in time anyway. I'm a boss liar and a quick thinking one too but this had me fucked. I was shittin' meself. You'd think I'd committed a crime wouldn't you?
"In that order – I saved it and it's so I can go to Paris for the European Cup Final."
"Yer fuckin' liar!"
Told you!
"It is! Why the fuck don't you ever believe anything I ever tell yer?"
"Cos yer always tellin' fuckin' lies!"
"'Ow d'yer know what's a lie if yer never believe *anything?"*
"Well yer shouldn't 'ave all that fuckin' money. Yer should give it to me!"
Fuck off, yer've 'ad yours an' fuckin' more!
"For fuck sake Ev, it's my money. I've saved it from my reffin' money. I missed fuckin' Rome didn't I? I'm fuckin' not gonna miss Paris!"
"Never mind that, yer shoulda give it to me so I can buy things for me an' the kids!"
Ah fuck it. I was fucked anyway so I might as well be brave.
"Why the fuck should I? You've 'ad yours. This is mine that I've saved!"
This was all reminding me of a fearful hiding I'd had from my Mam and Dad when I was twelve cos I'd found two quid, spent it on myself and not given it to them. I half expected Big Ev to come at me any minute with her very own 1981 version of Lily elbow. She had no chance though of emulating Lily eyes. There was only one woman in the world that could give Lily eyes and that was Lily. Those eyes could cut you into a million pieces. Sure, Big Ev could give you a fuckin' evil look with Big Ev eyes but they were like Debbie Harry asking you to come to bed with her eyes (no, not just her eyes, you

know what I mean) compared to Lily eyes.
"'Ow d'yer know they're gonna get to Paris?"
"Cos we fuckin' will and when we do I'm fuckin' gonna be there. Fuckin' end of!"
Fuckin' bollocks to it! It was mine. I'd worked hard for it. I was gonna keep it! I was just gonna have to suffer interminable silence for a month as punishment for my heinous deed. Fuckin' hard work being married isn't it?

Rather than stay in and have my nerves shredded to bits by Radio City's commentary on the match in Munich I decided to try to avoid the score 'til the highlights were on later by reffing B.I.C.C. V Newburgh in a midweek match of the Ormskirk Saturday League. I was having a bevy in the Commies with my mate and fellow ref Paul Garnett after he'd given me a lift back to Skem and did very well to avoid hearing anything about the match while I was in there. Mind you, there was a snooker match on and the world stopped when a snooker match was on in the Commies. It was nearly as bad as bingo in there on a Saturday night. Men have died for less than talking during a snooker match or bingo in the Commies. I'd timed it just right and walked through my front door just as the highlights were starting on BBC. Nice one, let's settle down now. Nerves still shredded to fuck even though I didn't know the score but it was better this way than having to put up with Elton Welsby making me shit myself every time the ball went over our halfway line.
"Well, I see yer goin' to Paris then."
I'm sure she didn't do it maliciously but I could really have strangled my wife on the spot for that. Mind you, at least she was speaking to me again now after the great ECF fund unveiling so I supposed I'd better make the most of it.
"I didn't know the score but yeah we're through."
"Oh sorry, I didn't know yer didn't know."
Like fuck yer didn't know!
"It's okay, it doesn't matter. The main thing is we won."
"Yers didn't win. Yers drew one all but it said on the radio yer went through on that away goals thingy."
Fuck off!
"Eh, you're gettin' good aren't yer love?"

Our team talk was given by Paul Breitner. Breitner, the Bayern captain, had said that we played "stupidly" in the first leg and that we would be easy meat for Bayern in the return. Bob just pinned that newspaper article on the dressing room wall. Team talk done. Kenny was injured early on and was replaced by Howard Gayle getting his first taste of European action. Bayern had built their game plan around trying to stop Kenny and so were completely disarmed by Bob's change of tactics. Bob employed Howie as an out and out winger. Bayern just didn't know how to play him apart from booting him viciously whenever they got the chance. Howie was running them ragged. The effect of getting booted so much allied to the fact that Howie's temper was about to snap and he might well have got himself sent off for retaliation meant that Bob took the unusual step of substituting a substitute, sending Jimmy Case on in his place. Howie's job had been done though. Only two substitutes were allowed so when Johnno also succumbed to the relentless kicking he'd had and was merely a walking wounded being put out on the wing only as nuisance value we were virtually down to ten men. The Bayern defence were tiring. Even they could only kick out so much and they'd had a harrowing chasing from Howie. Seven minutes from time, Johnno, from his wing position made a supreme effort to get the ball across to Razor just outside the penalty area. Ray swivelled and hit the ball firmly past the Bayern keeper to virtually seal our place in gay Paree. Bayern now needed two goals to win and although they did equalise on the night with a very late goal they never looked likely to stop our march.

LOOK OUT PARIS – 'ERE I FUCKIN' COME!

You've all seen Puskas haven't you? Anybody who has ever had the slightest interest in football will have seen old footage of Puskas ripping England apart in a famous Hungary victory at Wembley in 1956 or causing mayhem to European club defences in Real Madrid's halcyon days of five successive European Cup victories. Even if you haven't seen any of that you will surely have seen photographs of the Galloping Major as he was affectionately known. He was like a little fat pot-bellied pig but he couldn't half play football – probably the greatest player in the world at his peak and one of the greatest of all time. Get the picture? Well we had our very own Puskas refereeing in the Ormskirk Saturday League. Neil Leatherbarrow was to become a legend in his own lunchtime around the playing fields of Ormskirk. Neil was every inch of his 48 waist the size of Puskas. He was though only a misplaced pass behind me in being the worst footballer in the world - hence the irony of his schoolmates dubbing him Puskas – a name that has stuck to this day. Now don't get me wrong, Neil is Mr. Football through and through. Apart from myself I don't know anybody who loves the game of football like Puskas but he didn't half put me in the shit refereeing the 1980-81 Ormskirk Saturday League Agricultural Cup Final. Argos, having already won the League badly wanted this Cup to go alongside the League Championship they had so deservedly won. The game was played at my favourite reffing venue, White Moss Park, on a hot, sticky May Tuesday evening. In spite of the conditions the game was played at a blistering pace with no quarter asked or given from two very good and hard as nails teams. There hadn't been an ounce of bother in the 90 minutes which ended 2-2. Tackles were flying in during the extra-time period as they had been during normal time but again, no problem, players just got on with it. Enter Puskas to cause unholy murder. With only a couple of minutes left and the game looking likely to go to penalties, Argos winger Paul Baccino got to the byeline and crossed the ball which was headed out as far as the edge of the penalty area. Paul's bro Aldo fired the ball back towards goal through a mass of bodies. The ball rattled the back of the net. Goal as far as I was concerned, no problem. Quick glance over at my linesman, Puskas. Yes, waddling back towards the centre-circle. Goal. The ball was about to be put on the centre-spot for the restart of the game. No sign at all of protest from the J.J.Smith players.

"Peter! Peter!"

I looked across at Puskas who was waving his flag so frantically that trains were stopping at Ormskirk.

"Yes Neil."

"No goal Peter."

"What?"

"No goal. There was an Argos player in an offside position."

By this time players from both sides were surrounding both me and the tubby one.

"What's the problem ref?"

"I don't know yet. Let me talk to my linesman."
Ref, come on mate, it's a goal, let's get on with it."
There still wasn't much sign of protest from the J.J.Smith players but they could see a possibility that the goal might be disallowed.
"It was offside ref wasn't it? Yeah it was offside."
"Look, please. All go away. Let me talk to my linesman. I'm not talking to him 'til everybody gets outta the way."
"Right, Neil, what's the problem?"
"Argos player was in an offside position in the penalty area."
"Which one?"
"Aldo."
"Wasn't Aldo Neil, 'e scored the goal."
"No, not Aldo, his brother, Paul."
"Paul crossed the ball Neil. Wasn't 'im."
"Oh 'ang on. There was definitely somebody in an offside position."
"Why didn't yer flag straight away?"
"I wanted to be certain."
"Neil, we very nearly fuckin' kicked off again! Yer were a bit late weren't yer?"
"No goal Peter."
"Look, Neil, this is the last minute of a Cup Final. This is either the winning goal or not. You'd better be certain of this."
"I am Peter, I am."
"Was he interfering with play or seeking to gain an advantage."
"Yes Peter, in my opinion he was."
"Neil, I didn't even see anybody in an offside position never mind if they were interfering with play or not."
"I did Peter."
"Neil, you'd better be one hundred percent certain cos if I disallow this goal there's gonna be fuckin' murder."
"No goal Peter."
What could I do? My pre-match instructions to my linesmen in this match as they had been any time I had the luxury of linesmen was that all offsides were theirs. If they said offside it was offside. The uninitiated in the finer points of refereeing might well think that I should have overruled Puskas and allowed the goal to stand but I really couldn't go against my linesman after giving him specific instructions to flag for every offside and that he would be the judge

of it. Nowadays there would be no question that the goal would have stood. These days a forward has to be practically bumming the goalkeeper to be given offside. Back then though offside was offside and was given 99% of the time.

"No goal. Indirect free-kick to J.J. Smith for offside."

I was immediately surrounded by angry Argos players and I have to say I couldn't blame them. What happened next? Yes, you've guessed it, ten seconds later the ball was in the net at the other end. Oh fuckin' no! I never got away with anything like this. You could have bet a million pounds on J.J. Smith scoring straight after that just because I was reffing. Any contentious decisions I made would invariably lead to goals and more stick. For instance if there was an argument over a decision as to whether it was a goal-kick or a corner-kick and I gave the latter then you could guarantee that a goal would be scored from it leading to unholy shit for me from the defending team. If I could have found a reason to disallow this goal I would have done as clearly an injustice had been done. I looked across to the linesman at that end, John Grant, to help me out. No chance! John was like shit off a shovel and had legged it back to his position on the halfway line before the ball had rebounded from the back of the net. The Argos players were shattered, having seen their Cup dragged away from them in the space of ten seconds. They virtually gave up for the remaining half minute or so and just to add further insult to the massive injury J.J. Smith scored again right on the final, the very final, whistle. Argos had just lost a Cup Final 2-4 when they had every right to claim they should have won it 3-2. Guess who copped for all the shit? Yeah, fuckin' me, not Puskas. We'd collected our medals and while I was watching the players collect theirs Neil was in the sanctuary of the dressing room probably filling his face with a pork pie, a Mars bar or a radish (I'll tell you the tale of the radish another time) or knowing him most probably all three – at once! I really couldn't blame the Argos players and officials giving me flak but it wasn't my fault. I wasn't gonna drop Puskas in the shit though so I just had to take it. I didn't blame them for feeling robbed – I felt they'd been robbed! Not cheated, and nobody called me that thankfully, but definitely robbed. I hadn't had to book a single person in the match but I was getting that much stick after the game I had to do at least one. I picked on the most vociferous person, the Manager,

Tommy Maher. I felt shitty about that afterwards but I really had to take some action. Sorry Tommy. I could barely bring myself to speak to Puskas after the match. Neil hadn't done anything underhand, or technically wrong even, but if only he'd flagged straight away to disallow the goal instead of waiting all the aggravation might have been saved. It certainly made me think very carefully about my pre-match instructions to linesmen in the future.

Waiting for me outside the ground were Big Ev and the kids who'd come to see me referee this big Cup Final. I suppose they felt quite proud of me refereeing a Cup Final on a "proper" ground. Certainly Big Ev was taking much more of an interest in my reffing than she had before and was instrumental in persuading me to keep records of the matches I reffed, the very records I am now drawing on for statistical information. Why, she was even beginning to wash my kit!
"You alright Peter? I thought they were gonna 'it yer there."
"Yeah I'm okay Big. Nah, they wouldn't do that. They were just upset."
"Dad yer shoulda 'eard what they were callin' yer!"
"Yeah, I know what they were callin' me Ste."
"Yeah Dad, the men were sayin' sh.."
"I don't need to know what the men were sayin' thanks very much Ev."
All credit to the Argos players; as they came out of the ground they could see I was with my wife and kids so left me alone. In fact a few of them came over and shook my hand, including Tommy Maher, in a "no hard feelings" gesture. That was good of them and big of them.

CHAPTER NINETEEN

FROGS LEGS – EVO'S FIRST EUROPEAN TRIP

Two new players arrived late in the season; Craig Johnston signed from Middlesbrough in March and Bruce Grobbelaar from Vancouver Whitecaps followed him shortly after. Both were signed after the transfer deadline and so could play no part this season; that is even if they had been selected. Both were stating their intent to hold down regular places in the first team for the following season. Johnston had a chance. "Skippy", as he was known because he'd lived for a long time in Australia after being born in South Africa, had taken the eye at Middlesborough with his brand of attacking midfield play and lightning speed. In fact, so determined was he to make it in English football, that he had paid his own fare to come over from Australia for a trial at Ayresome Park. Now that's what I call wanting to make it! I'd have to be paid to go to Boro never mind me pay them! Grobbelaar however had no chance. Very little was known of this man save that he was a very eccentric goalkeeper who had once scored a penalty for Crewe Alexandra, the team he was playing for in between two spells at Vancouver. It was also known that he had fought guerrillas in the Zimbabwean Army and had actually killed men in battle. Clearly not a man to be messed with but he had no chance of getting Clem's jersey. Clem was still at least the joint best goalkeeper in the country. Shilton was brilliant, no doubt, but as I've said before I wouldn't have swapped him for Clem. Clem had his testimonial match a year earlier and had now been a fixture in our goal for eleven years. The way Ray was playing he'd be there for another eleven years too so the brash ex-soldier from Zimbabwe was going to have to do something extra special to replace him

Beep Beep's testimonial was eventually played on May 11th. The game was played between Liverpool players past and present and Everton players past and present. Some of the players of the recent past such as Tommy Smith and Peter Cormack were afforded heroes welcomes. Our very own knight, Sir Roger, was cheered to the rafters. Of course mad arse, Joey Jones, was there and doing all manner of mad things. The biggest cheer of the night though, from

Liverpudlians and Evertonians alike, was reserved for a player, coming on as substitute, who played for both Liverpool and Everton and had retired before a lot of the crowd were even born. He has the remarkable distinction of playing in Billy Liddell's testimonial in 1960 and Steve's in 1981. In two spells at Goodison he played 243 games scoring 111 goals. For us he played 67 games and scored 38 goals. Even at the back end of his career with his last Football League club, Tranmere Rovers, (becoming one of only a handful of players to have played for all three Merseyside clubs) he scored 21 goals in 45 games. Stats like that now for a striker would make him worth about a gazillion pounds. My Dad had often told me about him when I was a young lad; of how he was fearless and had a vile temper that used to get him into a lot of trouble with referees. I suspected that he was one of my Dad's favourite players even though he had played more for the enemy than he had for us. I had the pleasure of meeting this man a few years later at an Ormskirk Cricket Club Quiz Final where he was presenting the prizes and I can tell you his on-field temper was not matched by his off-field charm and pleasantness. He was a true giant and gent of the game. His name? Dave Hickson. If you've never heard of him then do yourself a favour and read some literature on him. Dave "Stormy Petrel" Hickson's story is a fascinating tale.

Our League campaign spluttered and farted to a fifth place finish. Our bid for the treble title was over long before the end of the season eventually finishing on 51 points, nine behind Champions Aston Villa. European Cup Final places were up for grabs though. Kenny was battling to be fit having missed the last four League games although Bob might have left him out in a deliberate bid to keep the King ready to face Real Madrid. Howie Gayle had slotted in well for Kenny in the maestro's absence and had scored what turned out to be his only Liverpool goal in a 1-1 draw at Tottenham. Johnno who had missed a few games near the end of the season should be fit as he'd played in the last match of the season in a 1-0 home win against Manchester City but if he wasn't there was a more than capable replacement in the young Rushie. Rushie hadn't scored yet in his nine first team appearances but was showing every likelihood of doing so very soon.

I'd applied for promotion to Class One status as a referee. I hadn't really been reffing long enough to even apply for this exalted status never mind achieve it but older, respected referees such as Tom Hughes, Chris Abbott and Eric Garner, a former Football League Referee from Ormskirk, had encouraged me to apply saying I was good enough. Eric had also very kindly said that if I started reffing on Saturdays then I was certainly good enough to make Football League status in time. That though would be a hard road; maybe another ten years down the line after working my way through,Contributory Leagues, Feeder Leagues etch such as Lancashire Combination and Northern Premier. That was all very well but I wouldn't be reffing on a regular Saturday basis anyway. I still felt now, nearly five years into my refereeing career, the way I had when I started – watching Liverpool at home came before anything else football related. My Class One assessment would take place in the Cup Final I was refereeing, Bruge v Derby Arms. I felt this was slightly unfair as Cup Finals are normally fraught affairs anyway with everybody wound up so wasn't really a fair test of a referee's ability due to the enormous pressure he was under. It worked out much that way too as I didn't have the greatest of games. Bruge won the game quite easily but I had ocassion to yellow card six players. That might have led the assessor to think I was over-officious but really it was down to nerves and maybe trying to over impress a bit. Whatever, it wasn't brilliant and I felt I'd blown my chance of Class One and would have to re-apply. Tell you who didn't help though – Jimmy friggin' Brown. Jimmy was supposed to be my mate, no that's a bit unfair, of course he was my mate but once we stepped on to the pitch that friendship was forgotten. Jimmy got nothing about of me and I got nothing out of him except a load of abuse. It wasn't that Jimmy just picked on me; he was like that with all referees. The inevitable happened however and I had to yellow card him. In fact I bent over backwards to keep him on the pitch but still the torrent came. I just about got away with not sending Jimmy off but I felt I'd done myself no favours in the eyes of the assessor and that he would think I was far too lenient to become Class One. It wasn't the fault of Jimmy or any of the other players I'd booked though. I just wasn't up to it that game and if I didn't get Class One it would be my own fault. The letter from the LCFA informing me of the results of the assessment came a few weeks later. I opened it with dread (was able to open this one myself you see as I got there just before Big Ev).

"Dear Peter, I enclose your assessment form and the result of the assessment with reference to your application for Class One Referee. Please take heed of the assessor's notes and constructive comments. I am pleased to inform you that your application for Class One has been successful and will take effect as from the start of the 1981-82 season."

FUCKIN' GET IN!

I've never taken a driving test but I've seen the reaction of plenty of people who have passed their test first time. That was my reaction to getting my Class One. I did of course take heed of the assessor's notes and constructive comments. These included, as I thought they would, comments about being too lenient and also about my fitness levels. They were fair enough comments. The assessor's sheet was signed by Tom Hughes. Christ, he must have been watching me from the Knowl Brow cos I deffo didn't see him at Blaguegate that day. Maybe he did the old assessor's trick of hiding behind a tree – he was certainly thin enough! Only messin' Tom – nice one.

I got a nice little surprise a week or so before my first ever trip abroad – Evo Reds was to be increased by one. Yes, Big Ev was pregnant again. I'm not quite sure how that happened – well I am but you know what I mean. I thought we'd been ever so careful. Big was on the pill and I thought we'd been extra careful on the odd ocassion she forgot to take it. But no, it seemed that The Tadpole Express had once again crashed through Edge Hill like a big crashy thing, hurtled on to Lime Street, deposited it's cargo and one of the pesky little taddies had slipped away to cop off with one of those sexy little eggs hanging around just waiting to be fertilised. Names? Would I get away with Kenny Dalglish Evo if it was a boy? Nah! Or Debbie Harry Evo if it was a girl? Nah again! We decided it was Angela, shortened to Angie, for a girl. I loved the name Angie. "Angie" by the Rolling Stones was one of my favourite songs, as was "Angie baby" by Helen Reddy. "Angel of the morning" by PP Arnold was another of my faves (pop pickers). Okay, that's sorted – Angie it is. What about a boy? Little Peter. Ahhh, little peewack. Due date? December 12th. Quick scan of the calendar. Shit! Saturday. Have to wait 'til next season's fixtures come out in July to see whether we're home or away. Knowing my luck, bound to be home. What is it with our kids and Saturday? Ste was due on a Saturday but had the good grace to arrive six days late. Little Ev was due on a Saturday; came exactly a week late and made me miss the home match against Ipswich. Now Peewack or Angie baby was gonna cause me similar angst.

As I mentioned earlier I'd never been abroad before much less ever been up in one of those big aeroplanes. Never really fancied flying anyway but even with a healthy ECF fund a flight, hotels etcetera was way beyond my budget. I settled for doing the straight there and back thing of going on the train. I had plenty enough dosh for that much cheaper option and there would be some left over to at least go toward my Season Ticket. Anyway, I wouldn't know what to do in a hotel; I'd never stayed in one before.

The sight in and around Lime Street on the afternoon of our departure the day before the match was a sight to behold for my untrained European eyes. Everybody it seemed was on the ale before boarding the train. I was in the Crown and the place was bouncing! All the songs were getting aired. I particularly liked this one: "On the dole, on the ale Gay Paree!"
There were flags draped in every conceivable drapeable spot:
HUYTON BADDIES
BOOTLE BADDIES
KIRKBY FUSILIERS
LIVERPOOL SCORE DE GAULLES
There were hundreds of them of all shapes, sizes and loads with mad sayings on them. My own favourite was: **TEBBIT'S SHAGGING THATCHER**. Okay, nothing to do with football but funny as fuck. I heard later that flag was confiscated by the bizzies on the train to Dover. If this was what following LFC in Europe was all about then I wanted more of it – and I hadn't even left Liverpool!

Although there were loads of lads from Skem going to Paris I somehow managed once again to end up on my own. I knew for a fact that Les, Peter Whitty and Wilko were somewhere around but it didn't look as if they were on the same train as me. The banter between lads on the train however meant that nobody was truly on their own. Some of the lads reckoned that this was the same train they'd travelled to Rome on in '77. British Rail had indeed thrown us on to probably the shittiest heap of old metal they could possibly find. To call the train a cattle truck would have been an insult to cattle. I'm not sure what the other trains were like (probably old rust buckets too) but they couldn't have been any worse than this. If the train journey had been bad then the ferry from Dover to Calais was a nightmare – for me anyway. While every other Red on that ship seemed to be carrying as much ale and ciggies as they possibly could I was being very ill. A salty sea dog I most certainly was not! Yeah, my belly had been full of my beautiful golden lady friend but it was soon emptied out as the ferry rolled and lurched. My belly was aping the ship's actions and sleep came as a welcome release for Pepe Le Spew.

Back on to another train when we reached Calais. The French rail authority had decided we not only liked travelling in shit heaps but that we were also partial to a gallon or ninety of stale piss. That train really was the fuckin' pits – absolutely disgusting! No water and no food, save for whatever the lads had managed to sneak off from the ferry's kitchens, or wherever they'd got them for the long journey to Paris. Salvation was on the way though in the shape of trackside vendors at certain stations we stopped at. You've seen these Charlies in foreign countries haven't you? Will sell you anything and everything that they've probably already robbed themselves. Nobody was supposed to get off the trains at these stops but most did and took advantage of the vendors. It was a bit tight I suppose robbing food from people who were nothing more than peasants themselves really trying to make a few bob but, as I say, they'd probably only robbed it themselves so needs must.
"Got any grub lads? I'm fuckin' 'Ank Marvin 'ere."
"Yeah, ee arr mate, 'ave that. No fucker 'ere'll touch it."
Evo was hungry and when Evo's hungry he'll eat anything! It wasn't good though. It looked like one of King Kong's bollocks and when I bit into it tasted like that too. I waded on though through the shitty

bit and was rewarded halfway down by a deliciously sweet tasting sensation. Turned out it was a mango. Must make a mental note to get some of them when I get home. Not stale ones though that tasted like cinematic monster's balls.

We arrived at Gare Du Nord (like the Frogspeak eh?) barely a couple of hours before kick off so no time for testing the strength or otherwise of French lager. Coaches were waiting to pick us up and drive us to the Parc De Princes. I'd seen mad drivers in London but they were 85 year-old women Reliant Robin drivers out for a nice Sunday afternoon pootle compared to these maddies. Traffic lights were there only for ornamentation. After an hour of that madness we arrived near the stadium, or at least where the coaches were dropping us off, to catch the arse end of a pitched battle between Madrid and Liverpool with the bizzies, the CRS, in the middle. It seemed smoke bombs and tear gas had been let off. Madrid fans were legging it down a subway with a few hundred Reds in hot pursuit. I just caught a glimpse of the bizzies' machine guns so was quite content to stay exactly where I was. After passing through three different sets of barriers, showing my ticket every time and also being searched on each ocassion I was eventually inside the stadium. Time to sample French lager. I shouldn't have bothered. Overpriced gnat's piss! Talking of piss – how disgusting are French bogs? For a start birds and lads go in the same bog; that is just not fuckin' right! Birds do bird things in bogs and men do man things. And what about that standing up to have a shite lark? That's fuckin bollocks! You've got to have a super dooper aim just to get your plop in the hole. If it's a sloppy one you've got no chance. Mind you, at least French blokes can't get nagged at by their birds for pissin' on the bog seat and not putting it down. I was almost beginning to wish I'd stayed at home – 'til I actually stepped up in to the seated area! Wow! I'd never seen anything like or as big as this. Parc De Princes was a 55,000 all-seater stadium – still quite a rare thing anywhere in the world. It seemed twice as big as Wembley but was probably only just larger if not the same size – it was just the all-seated aspect that gave it the illusion it was so much bigger. As kick-off time approached it became clear that our fans were heavily outnumbering Madrid fans inside. Our end was chocker and plenty of Reds were on both sides

of the stadium too. The Madrid end was a sight to behold; apart from a solid knot in the upper tier of the Madrid end that was all Liverpool too. There is a marvellous picture in the official Liverpool FC 1982 annual of the lower tier of that end completely Red and bedecked with all manner of flags. This was the fuckin' biz! What did catch the eye was that most of the Madrid fans had white polystyrene bowler hats on. What the fuck was all that about? You can bet that's how the fight had started outside – Scousers nicking those hats from the Madrid fans:
"Ee arr Manuel, giz that fuckin' 'at. I'm not standin' up to 'ave a shit for anybody!"

A German did our team talk for the Final. Awfully nice people those Germans aren't they, doing our jobs for us? This time it was Uli Stielike. Uli the Fooly had played against us for BMG in the '77 Final. Apparently he'd said we were lucky in that game and his side had deserved to win? Uli lad, not bein' fuckin' funny 'ere mate but what fuckin' drugs were you on when you were playin' in that game? He'd also said that this was his moment for revenge. Newspaper cutting. Drawing pin. Team talk done. Sound!

The game, to be honest, was awful. Laurie Cunningham, the ex-West Brom winger, was expected to cause us major headaches but was never in the game. For our part, we were definitely showing the effects of a long season. Quite a few players did indeed look as if they were carrying the injuries that had made them doubtful for the Final in the first place. Souness got into Stielike very early on so the German posed little threat to us. Nice one Souey. Souey though had been carrying an injury into the match so probably hadn't done himself much good clattering Stielike but he had to show him you couldn't get to Liverpool with mere talk, you had to back it up on the pitch. Stielike got his own back – on Johnno. Shithouse! He was avoiding Souey like the plague now. Thommo appeared to be struggling too but after missing the glory that was Rome you would have had to cut our skipper's leg off to stop him playing in this one. No, make that two legs you would have had to cut off – he would have played with one! Kenny finally succumbed to his injury and made way for Jimmy Case to play in his third European Cup Final. A couple of half chances for Souey and Johnno came and went before it all exploded into magnificent, vibrant, colourful Red life nine minutes from time. Ray Kennedy took a throw in on our left. There seemed little danger to the Real defence when the ball landed at the feet of Barney. It looked like the best thing Barney could do was to cross the ball into the penalty area and hope for the best. What did Barney do? Kenny must have left his brain on the pitch when he went off and Barney picked it up to replace his own. Kennyesque, Barney spotted the gap at the near post and fairly rocketed the ball past Rodriguez.

GOOOOOAAAAAALLLLLLLLLL!!!!!!!!!!!!!!!!!!!!!!!!

Kenny's brain also took Barney to the same goal celebration the King had done at Wembley three years earlier. Barney was nearly in our end with us before being swamped by his teammates. The next ten minutes were just pure celebration as the all-seater stadium became nearly, apart from the Spanish who'd fucked off anyway, all standing as we danced, cavorted and very nearly had sex with each other on the seats.

WIN THE EUROPEAN CUP FOR ME!
GAY PAREE, GAY PAREE, GAY PAREE!
ON THE DOLE, IN THE STANDS, DRINKING SCOTCH!
WE'RE GONNA KEEP THE EUROPEAN CUP!
ONE BARNEY RUBBLE, THERE'S ONLY ONE BARNEY RUBBLE!
EE AYE ADDIO BARNEY WON THE CUP!

And keep it we did. The Final whistle signalled our third successive European Cup triumph so UEFA were indeed gonna give us that particular trophy and make a new one.

AND WE'LL KEEP THAT FUCKIN' ONE TOO!

The atmosphere outside the stadium was a lot better than I thought it would be. Most Madrid fans had got off as soon as Barney scored but the ones that were milling around were friendliness personified. Hats, scarves etc were swapped, which was nice as Scousers were giving back the white bowlers they robbed from the Madrid fans in the first place. Just hoped they hadn't shit in them! We boarded our coaches to take us back to Gare Du Nord with very little incident. There was even a couple of hours before we were to catch our train to get a bevy or four. Whatever the make of the gnat's piss they were serving inside the stadium it certainly wasn't what they were serving in the bars around the station. The ale there was absolutely gorgeous. I met up with Wilko once again and it was nice to have a bevy with him. At least I wouldn't be travelling home on my tod. A few Reds had a spot of fun with the Frog prossies until Mr. Pimp, a John Shaft lookalike, turned up. His hat didn't last long though; that was well had off! What is it with Scousers and hats?

The train bounced back to Calais. Sleep was impossible. Who the fuck wanted to sleep anyway? No sleep 'til Skem! I'd got my sea legs now so was okay on the ferry. It was only the putrid smell of Wilko's rancid arse that made me sick on the return leg. I honestly didn't deliberately lose him getting off the ferry and on to the train at Dover. Maybe I'd get some sleep on the train back to Limey. No chance! I happened upon Peter Whitty and Les.
"Ah, that was great that wasn't it Peter?"
Nah, I thought it was shit Les.
"Yeah, sound Les."
"See Barney's goal?"
No I missed that one Les. Did Barney score?
"Yeah, what a goal eh Les!"
"Yeah, it was just like one I scored in the Army once Peter. Did I ever tell yer abarr that?"
ZZZZZZZZZZZZZZZZZZZZZZZZZZZZZZZZZZZZZZZZZZZZ

We got home maybe just about in time to possibly catch the victory parade. Well gone were the days of St. George's Hall, The Town Hall or the Library. Nah, if you were lucky you might just catch a ten second glimpse of the players on the top open deck of the bus along a road somewhere so it wasn't really worth the effort. No, we rounded this trip off in the only possible way these trips *can* be rounded off – on the ale in town! The Crown was reconstructed to look like the Parc De Princes. I'm sure people who hadn't been to Paris must have brought more flags down to the Crown as there was one that unless the maker of it was Septic Peg's Ma couldn't possibly have predicted pre-match:
BARNEY WON THE CUP!
Said it all didn't it? In fact, it might just come in handy again. Now, let's go an' get our League back!

CHAPTER TWENTY

THE DEATH OF A LEGEND

I attended the Ormskirk League Annual Presentation at Moss Side Social Club with Big Ev expecting to pick up just a trophy for the reffing the "Puskas" final. I was very pleasantly surprised when Sammy Lee, presenting the trophies, read out: Referee Of the Year – Peter Etherington. I couldn't really believe it. I knew I'd had a good season but not that good. I'd beaten some good refs of the calibre of John Grant, Ted Grant, Paul Garnett, Kenny Payne and even Eric Garner himself to that award. I must have been doing something right. Whatever it was I was up to the stage and pumping Sammy's hand as hard as I could. Not often you get to shake the hand of a European Cup Winner. We were on a table with Paul Garnett and his wife Rose. I don't know who was more made up, them or me. Certainly Big Ev seemed immensely proud that her husband had won this award. I was building up a nice little collection of trophies now. Many more to come hopefully.

Britain, and particularly its youth, went mad in the summer of '81. Riots started in Brixton in April and spread to Southall. The worst incidents however were in Toxteth where police used CS gas for the first time ever on the British mainland. Troubles soon spread to Bristol and other cities. It wasn't just cities either that felt the backlash of suppressed frustrations. Small towns and even villages were the scenes of rioting. Some might say that these were just copycat riots following on from Brixton, Southall and Toxteth and the many battles residents of that community had with the police. Now I'm not pretending to be any political analyst here but it didn't take a brain surgeon to work out that these, mainly young, people fed up of Thatcherite policies aimed at keeping them out of work, downtrodden and in their place had decided they weren't having this anymore and were gonna rebel against it. So what did we have in the middle of all this unrest? A bloody royal wedding! Who was it paid for Charlie and Di to tie the knot? Yeah, you've guessed it, us the taxpayer. Mad isn't it? Young lads with no job, no prospects and no hope were having this wedding, costing millions of pounds don't forget, shoved down their throats seemingly morning, noon and night. What was Number One in the middle of all this unrest? "Ghost Town" by The Specials. Very appropriate I thought.

Two major shock departures during the summer had seen Ray Clemence and Jimmy Case leave Anfield. The rumourmongers had it that Clem and Jimmy had a major fall out and it was a case of both of them had to leave. I never like hearing rumours and try to avoid them or anything ever unpleasant said about Liverpool FC but maybe the signings of Grobbelaar and Johnston had been made with this in mind. Clem went to White Hart Lane to continue his career as one of the two best goalies in the country. Tottenham's gain was I felt at the time our loss. Jimmy went to Brighton but I didn't feel his loss to be as great as that of Clem. Travelling the other way in part ex and our record club fee of £900,000 was centre-half Mark Lawrenson. Lawrenson was a very good player who could also play full-back or midfield. Bob had once again spent money very wisely. The chant the Kop had for him though was piss poor:
"Mark, Mark, Mark, Mark Lawrenson."
Sounded like a dog with a hair lip but there were just too many vowels in the moustachioed one's name to give him a decent song. Another outgoing was Colin Irwin who never really looked like making it with us so was offloaded, with a nice few bob to us to fund other transfers, to join John Toshack's Welsh revolution at newly-promoted Swansea City.

The Football League had decided that three points would now be awarded for a win with still the one point for a draw. This was supposed to be an incentive for teams to go for a win rather than playing for a draw. Having drawn 17 of our games last season it might be just what we needed to go for more wins this season. Didn't work in the first two games – a 0-1 defeat at Wolves and a midweek 1-1 draw at home to Middlesbrough. We got our first win of the season against Arsenal at Anfield. We were leading through a Terry Mac goal just before half-time. Arsenal would have equalised were it not for a breathtaking save by Grobbelaar. The ball was all but in the net when Brucie somehow twisted his body in mid air to keep it out. The crowd and particularly the Kop were quickly taking this eccentric man to their hearts. Yeah, he'd already shown signs of his madness, never being afraid to leave his penalty-area in pursuit of ball or man but so far he'd been more than effective.

Some amateur football pitches are very good while others are, well, to be honest, shit. I'd never before though reffed on one that was actually practically made of shit. I'd been given directions by the Aughton Men's Club Secretary and Manager Pete Webber on how to get to their pitch for the match against Westhead College: Get to the Red Lion at Aughton, get changed in the pub (liked the sound of that) and cross the road to the field at the side of the church. Climb over the stone wall and you're there. I didn't need the directions in the end as, top lift bummer that I was, I phoned Pete and managed to cadge a lift off him to the Red Lion and also back - win, lose or draw. Most Club Secretaries are like that. They'll bend over backwards to help you. Most Secs now knew that I couldn't drive and were more than willing to get me lifts to some of the far-flung outposts of the Ormskirk League. I thought Pete picking me up at The Derby Arms at one o'clock for the 20 minutes or so drive to Aughton for a two-thirty kick off was a bit early but Pete explained to me:
"We have to get on the pitch early to clear the sheep shit off."
I thought he was only messing and that in fact the early arrival would be maybe so some of the lads could have a sly pre-match pint.
He wasn't messing! The pitch actually belonged to a farmer and was next to one of his fields. The farmer very kindly allowed AMC the use of this pitch. The sheep weren't to know that very other Saturday (on me 'alf day off) twenty-two hairy arsed lads would be wanting to play footy on there.
"Ee arr Dolly, fancy a shag over there in between those white lines?"
"Yeah okay Rammie but I need a shit first."
"'Ave one over there. Those lads'll come along in a day or two an' clear it all off."
"Okay then."
Everybody had to get stuck into the shit clearing operation to make the pitch fit for play, including me. I know some refs who would have taken one look at the pitch and fucked off never mind shovelled shit but I wasn't arsed and besides I was restarting the old ECF fund 'cos we were deffo gonna get there again. The Final would be played

in Rotterdam. That would be nice. I'd try to look up Keret, that nice Dutch chap, a friend of my childhood next-door neighbour Mrs. Reid. I'd taken him to a match against Man City in 1968. Read all about it in OBAHK if you haven't already bought it! Keret was quite old then and might not even be alive now but it was worth a shot.
The Captain's name was Lugger. 'E was a dirty bugger. 'E wasn't fit to shovel shit from one place to another.
Why did that just come into my mind?
I had to let my wind wander to stuff like this to take it off the nauseating smell and look of sheep doodas. The shit, apart from the stink, was fairly easy to remove compared to one fuckin' belligerent sheep. It flatly refused to move despite the cajolings of the aforementioned twenty-two hairy arses.
"We'll kick off. It'll soon fuck off when we start running around."
No it didn't!
Dolly had been stood there for fully five minutes as we played around her. It had been my idea to kick off with the wooly twat still on the pitch so it was up to me to move her. I grabbed it with both arms (mine yer daft twat) and hauled it off the pitch.
"Get some wellies on an' shag it ref!"
I've got to admit the thought had crossed my mind as I wasn't getting much off Big Ev lately in her highly advanced state of pregnancy. I soon dismissed that thought. I mean, she was fuckin' ugly (the sheep that is, not Big Ev)! I didn't like the way a particularly nasty looking ram was looking at me either. He wasn't that happy at me just embracing his beloved never mind slipping her a bit of man sos.

Animals and their excrement safely removed we got on with playing a boss game that ended in a 2-2 draw. Quick change in the pub and a sharp slurp later we were on our way as Pete wanted to get back pretty handy. The closing minutes of Radio City's commentary on our match at West Ham that was about to finish 1-1 was interrupted by a newsflash.
"As yet unconfirmed reports say that Mr. Bill Shankly, former Manager of Liverpool Football Club, has had a heart attack and is in the Intensive Care Unit at Broadgreen Hospital."
I couldn't believe it. Shanks was still fit as a fiddle and anyway was only 68 – too young for a fit man like him to be having a heart attack.

Then I thought back to my mate Keith Horrocks, tragically taken from us a couple of years earlier at the age of twenty-one, and realised it can happen to anybody, any age. I got out at the Derby Arms, thanked Peter for the lift and legged it home as fast as I could.
"Ev, 'ave yer 'eard anythin' on the news about Bill Shankly?"
"Yeah, 'e's 'ad a heart attack. It said there's gonna be more on Radio City news."
Radio City news still couldn't give concrete confirmation but it was looking ominous.
"I'm goin' for the Footy Echo love. Keep listening for the news."
"Okay, I will do."
Talk between the lads waiting at Kidger's High Street newsagents for the Footy Echo varied between Shanks had just been admitted for tests to, he'd had a mild heart attack to he'd had a massive heart attack. The Footy Echo had only unconfirmed reports in the Stop Press.
"Anythin' on the news Ev."
"Yeah, it's been confirmed. 'E's 'ad a heart attack an' is in Broadgreen."

Three days later came the news (and I'm crying now as I write this nearly 23 years later) that Bill Shankly had suffered another massive heart attack after the mild one he had been admitted for on the Saturday and had passed away in Broadgreen Hospital. I sat in a chair and cried.
"Why are you crying Dad?"
"Cos Bill Shankly's dead Ev."
"Who's Bill Shankly Dad?"
Big Ev and Ste looked at me sobbing in the chair. They knew.

I felt like my Dad had passed away. That's how Liverpudlians looked upon Shanks. Depending on your age he was either your Granddad, your Dad or your big brother. Whatever way, he felt like a family member – one who always looked after you and one you couldn't do without. I think possibly his death affected fans of my age, or five years either way, most. We'd grown up with him. We'd been Liverpudlians possibly because of seeing and hearing Shanks tell us how great Liverpool were. We believed Shanks about how great we were. How could you not believe him? It was like your Dad telling you and you're not gonna disbelieve your Dad are you? In truth of course we weren't always as great as Bill said we were but we believed him and that was the main thing. Bill it was I think who mostly shaped my Socialist beliefs. If Bill was a man of the people why shouldn't I be?

Those events 23 years ago have been brought home to me, and I've been affected as I write this on July 12 2004 (30 years to the day since Bill resigned as Manager. He said he'd retired from football – he hadn't retired from life), by the sad news I've had today that one of our ex players, one of my all time favourites, is gravely ill. He might, by the time you read this, be no longer with us. Let's hope that's not the case and he makes a full recovery. This man's passion for football and love of all things Liverpool FC is matched only by that of Shanks himself. I met this man's son not so long ago so mate, whatever way it pans for your Dad, please take these words as a tribute to your Dad, in my opinion one of the greatest players ever to wear the Liverbird so proudly upon his chest.

A long, long time ago I can still remember how Bill Shankly made me cry.
And I knew if I had my chance I would see the great man dance a jig on Anfield's hallowed turf.
Peter Thompson made me shiver with every cross that he delivered.
Roger Hunt in the middle, even better than Billy Liddell.
I can't remember if I cried when we won the Cup with the '65 side.
But something touched me deep inside the day Bill Shankly died.
So bye, bye, Billy Shankly bye, bye. You brought us from the Second Division to rise
to Champions and Cup winners too, singing Billy how we're gonna miss you, Billy how we're gonna miss you.

The Kop was a massive sea of Red when Keegan put the ball on Toshack's head; Billy Shankly told me so.
And did you see Ian St. John's goal? Did Shankly lift your very soul? And can you teach me how to play like Cally?

Well I know that I'm in love with Shanks, 'cos he said Tommy Lawrence is better than Banks.
We all went on the booze when we stuffed five up the blues.
I was a teenage Kopite, a bit of a buck, but I really didn't give a f--k.
But I knew I was outa luck the day Bill Shankly died.

We were singin': Bye, bye Billy Shankly bye bye. You brought us from the Second Division to rise
to Champions and Cup Winners too, singin' Billy how we're gonna miss you, Billy how we're gonna miss you.

With no apologies to Don Maclean.

Bill Shankly R.I.P.

We beat Oulu Palloseura 7-0 in the second leg of the first round European Cup tie the night after Shanks' died. You could have heard a pin drop during the minute's silence observed before the game by the players of both sides and nearly 21,000 supporters. Not so the following Saturday.

The Football League had decided that there should be a one minute silence at all grounds on the Saturday following Bill's death. It was perhaps fitting that our opponents at Anfield on this day should be managed by a man who achieved much success as a player under Bill's management at Liverpool. John Toshack had started his managerial career very successfully at Swansea City and had probably been taught all he knew on that score by Bill and co during his time at Anfield. Shanks had helped Tosh during his managerial career. In fact Shanks had been at Old Trafford watching Swansea just four days before his first heart attack. Tosh had also, at Nessie Shankly's request, been a pallbearer at Bill's funeral just the day before this game. The teams came out side by side before the game. Swansea had brought thousands of fans with them. They were noisy and belligerent. Fair enough, their team was on the up over the past few years. They'd had a meteoric rise from being in the Fourth Division in 1977-78 season and now sat proudly in third place in the

First Division, their first season in the top flight, behind Ipswich and another of their fellow promoted teams West Ham - a magnificent feat. As the teams lined up for the silence Tosh took off his black Swansea tracksuit top to reveal a Liverpool Number 10 shirt. We saw this as a mark of respect for Shanks. The Swansea fans didn't see it quite like that though. The silence was interrupted after about twenty seconds by a handful of Swansea fans shouting obscenities about both Toshack and Shankly. I'm quite sure the majority of Swansea fans totally abhorred the actions of the lunatic few. Shock in the Kop turned to anger as threats were shouted back down to the Swansea fans. It only takes a few knobheads to spoil occasions like these. Sometimes it can be caused by latecomers not realising the silence has started. This time though there did seem to be a deliberate attempt by no more than a handful of Swansea fans, angered by their Manager wearing a shirt of the club they were playing, to ruin what should have been a great memory of a great man. Sensibly the more angry members of the crowd were persuaded to again be silent to salvage some dignity and silence was largely resumed. There really was mass anger though and some ugly scenes in the Anny Road end when the referee's whistle signalled the end of the silence. An amazing thing occurred shortly after. With no prompting from anybody, no word spread or anything, the Kop fell into a deathly silence. It didn't happen in other parts of the ground, just the Kop. Everybody in there felt it. It was as if 20,000 people had telepathically communicated their thoughts to each other that we weren't gonna let a few tossers spoil our tribute to Shanks. The players were still warming up and I'm sure they felt it too. Of all the occasions that have been described as the Kop's finest moment this, for me, was up there with the best.

Tosh had assembled a very good squad at the Vetch Field. As well as Colin Irwin, whom Tosh had installed as Captain, he had another ex-Red in Max Thompson on the playing staff. Tommy Smith, Chris Lawler and Cally had also earlier played under Tosh for Swansea on their way up the League divisions. Completing the strong Liverpool element were Assistant Manager Phil Boersma and Coach Doug Livermore. There was also a strong ex-Everton contingent in Dai Davies, Neil Robinson and last but by every means least, Bob

Latchford. Big Bob had never scored against us in Derby games but the big galoot managed to do just that in the second half of this match to put the Swans 2-0 up. Their first goal had been scored by possibly (Tommy Smith would say definitely) the most horrible, snidey, sneaky, shitty, nasty piece of work ever to don a football shirt – Leighton James. Tommy Smith hated him! He once spat at Smith after a game, Tommy having to be restrained from ripping the little shit's head off and shoving it up his arse. James' goal in this game came from the penalty spot and how he loved celebrating in front of the Kop. The atmosphere was already bad following the breaking of the silence – this little twat was making it worse. Terry Mac got us back into the game with a penalty just on the hour mark. Five minutes later referee Arnold Challinor awarded us another penalty. LOVELY JUBBLY! He loved those penalties did Mr. Challinor! Terry sent Dai Davies the wrong way again and booted the ball back into the net in celebration after it had rebounded to him. Well "Loadsateeth" wasn't happy with that was he? The toothless wonder first of all tried to welly Terry and then gave him a sly dig to the ribs. Terry was lying in the net in agony. Souness came steaming in to sort it out but the gummy twat got out of the way sharpish. A draw was the right result in a great game of football played on a very emotional day. Pity it had been spoiled by a few idiots – and they weren't all on the terraces.

Tosh got quite a bit of stick over the shirt incident for a good while after that from Swansea fans. Even wearing a Swansea Number 10 shirt before their next home match against Arsenal didn't fully appease some of the fans. They had seen his wearing of a Liverpool shirt as an act of treachery and that he should have been more concerned about his present club than a former one. That was sad as I'm sure Tosh meant no harm by it and had only done so to commemorate a great friend and mentor.

CHAPTER TWENTY-ONE

RUSH 'N' RIOTS

Having scored his first Liverpool goal in the home win over Oulu Palloseura, Rushie followed it up with two in the 5-0 win at Exeter in the League Cup 2nd Round first leg match. Three days later he opened his League account with two goals in the 3-0 home win over Leeds. A much needed win that was too as it was only our third League victory of the season having drawn three and lost three of the other games. This three points for a win lark wasn't working brilliantly for us. The three points for a win did show though how a team could move a few places up the table with just one victory – more if you could string a good winning run together. The three points for this game moved us up from 13th to 8th. Happy days!

The Leeds match had been our fourth home game in 11 days and finances were terribly tight. It was getting really hard work to keep up with it all and I hadn't even started this season's ECF fund yet. I was gonna have to sort it soon or my Rotterdam trip would be in the balance.

Our European Cup tie against AZ '67 Alkmaar should really have been sown up in the first leg in Holland. We were two goals up and cruising – well cruising according to the Radio City commentary but you never knew with them. You'd be screaming for a goal when the ball was actually at the other end but you couldn't make that out from the commentary. Johnno's first half strike and Sammy's early second half effort were cancelled out by Kist and Tol. This was the second match in succession we'd thrown away a two-goal lead, having done so at Brighton, that match eventually ending 3-3. What Radio City did get right, describing it as "English boots meet Dutch boots on the terraces" was that there was some bother in the stadium at Alkmaar.

Rushie scored another two of our six goals in the return at Exeter so was now well in the groove.

We very nearly blew the Alkmaar tie completely at Anfield. All looked to be going well when Terry Mac put us ahead from the penalty spot three minutes before half-time after the Dutch goalkeeper Treytel had brought Kenny down who was about to score. Kist equalised for Alkmaar. Rushie put us back into the lead with twenty minutes left. Brucie however was having one of those nightmare games that were beginning to get just a little too prevalent with him now. A speculative effort from distance by Jonny Metgod (later to star for Forest) should have been easily saved but Bruce was way off his line. The ball sailed over Brucie's head, hit the bar and rebounded into the net off Phil Thompson, desperately trying to get back to salvage his goalkeeper's mistake. Another long distance Metgod shot hit the bar shortly afterwards and we looked in big trouble. It was left to Alan Hansen to save the day five minutes from time with a goal any forward would have been proud of. Alan went dribbling through the defence like a latter day Peter Thompson before slotting past Treytel. No, hang on, Thommo Mark 1 wouldn't have scored that, preferring instead, having beaten six defenders, to go back and beat them again! It was honestly though a brilliant goal from Alan that won us the tie and saved Brucie's bacon into the bargain.

Rushie's first Derby goal came in his debut match of that particular fixture, albeit a bit of a fluke as the ball rebounded from somewhere around his conk (and what a conk!) after a defender had tried to clear. Added to two earlier goals from Kenny it gave us a 3-1 victory. The number 9 shirt was now claimed as his own but Johnno was still knocking around as a more than capable deputy should the need arise. Eamonn O'Keefe was sent off in this game for a terrible tackle on Ronnie Whelan as blue frustration boiled over. The Derby win bumped us up to seventh place – the highest we'd been this season.

The quest to retain the Football League Cup continued with an easy 4-1 home win over Middlesbrough. Rushie was on the mark again as was Johnno with two goals after young Kevin Sheedy had opened the scoring. Sheedy looked a very good player with a peach of a left foot on him but Uncle Bob preferred Ronnie Whelan mostly in that position. Another young player was signed from Ayr United – Steve Nicol. Ronnie and Kevin could probably have got both their left feet into Steve's left boot. Steve took a huge size 14. The 19 year old came with a big reputation from the Honest Men (Ayr's nickname. Quiz on Evo you big quiz man!) with a reputation as big as his feet as a play anywhere man although his preferred position was full back. Well he was just gonna have to wait a while to get in the team wasn't he? Get in the rezzies young Steve and learn your trade!

The arrival of Nicol meant the end of the road as far as his Liverpool career was concerned for Avi Cohen. Avi, to be honest, hadn't quiet looked up to the job. He was particularly found wanting in the Cup defeat at Goodison last season. Being ripped apart by the likes of Eamonn O'Keefe and Imre Varadi hadn't done his long-term first team prospects much good at all. It was a pity really as he was solid enough in his own quiet sort of way but lacked maybe the pace to get him through several hard English seasons. Ah well, at least he could start going the synagogue again on a Saturday.

It was time to forgive young Evo for jinxing the result against Leicester last season and take him the match again. I wish I hadn't bothered! What was it with our Ste and teams that played in blue? Steve Moran's strike gave the Saints a 1-0 win. I deffo wasn't taking him again.

The West Sutton Labour Club V Tanhouse Tommy Rogers Cup tie in the Skelmersdale Sunday League played on 29th November 1981 is still talked about to this day. What a game it had been for one hundred and nineteen minutes! The score was locked on 3-3 after a pulsating game that ebbed and flowed, the lead changing hands several teams. The game was being played on a horse's field disguised as a footy pitch. Players were tired; tackles were being mistimed making them look more malicious than they were so leading inevitably to official cautions – five of them. Well that's giving the players the benefit of extreme doubt at least. These two teams didn't like each other. A full-blooded Cup tie was made even more frenetic by the usual slanging matches. The West Sutton players jibes of "Scouse cunts!" were returned with interest by Tanhouse's "Woolyback, sheepshaggin' bastards!" I would always turn a couple of deaf ears to this type of raggery unless it got too out

of control. By the way, official cautions did not carry with them yellow cards for a while. The previous January the FA had sent out one of it's strange edicts that yellow cards were no longer to be shown to players officially cautioned. The FA in their wisdom (not) decided it was seen as provocative by players for referees to be brandishing yellow and red cards at them and could inflame already volatile situations.
WHAT?
Anyway, it was a roughy-toughy old game with tackles flying in all over the place but generally I'd had the game well under control.

West Sutton won a corner in the last minute of a match that now looked destined to go to a replay. Tired bodies were hauled into the penalty area in either a last gasp effort to win the match or to save it to do it all again next week. The corner came over. Now if I had been a Clive type referee I would have blown the whistle there and then while the ball was in the air. That then would have prevented what was about to happen. I was as knackered as the players, soaking wet and muddied to fuck. I needed a rest before I went out to referee my afternoon game. I know – I'm mad. But no, I'm Mr. Fuckin' honest Pete aren't I? 90 minutes is 90, or, in this case, 120 minutes is 120 minutes, not 119 and let's all get in the changies for a warm. Those minutes include time added on for stoppages of course in that if there was a stoppage I thought warranted time adding on for I would stop my trusty stop watch. So the stop watch, once 90 or 120 minutes were up would say 90 or 120 minutes while my ordinary watch might say 93 or 123. Anyway, you get my drift. I actually think there was about 30 seconds left so that would have been enough time in normal circumstances if a goal was scored to get the ball to the centre, kick off again and give the team who had just conceded the goal maybe just about enough time to have one last go at equalising. A goal was scored. Alec Morris, the Tanhouse centre half, in a desperate attempt to either head the ball upfield or away from goal in any case succeeded only in allowing the ball to skewer wildly off his head and give the Tanhouse keeper no chance. The West Sutton players went mad! After a hard, gruelling game they were only seconds from going through to the next round. I honestly think their cavorting was in celebration only and not trying to wind up Tanhouse in general or

Alec in particular. Alec was NOT a man you wound up lightly! Alec didn't see it that way and saw it as his duty to himself and his teammates to flatten as many West Sutton players as he could. He did a good job on two of them before I could get over to him to tell him I was sending him off. Bang! I turned round just in time to see the Tanhouse keeper, Dave the Rave, performing a perfect Bruce Lee Kung Fu kick on his opposite number. Fuck! How did he get up this end that quick? Shit! Tanhouse striker Ian Davies was seemingly trying to drown one of his opponents in a big patch of mud. For fuck sake! Stinky, stop fuckin' 'ittin' that bloke with my linesman's flags; I've gotta fuckin' use them again next week! Jesus fuckin' Christ! It was going off everywhere now. Punches to the right of me, butts to the left, onwards into the valley of death rode the poor owld fuckin' referee. How the fuck am I gonna stop this? I stepped back. It was honestly like watching the most surreal martial arts/cowboy/Rocky film you've ever seen! It was fuckin' bedlam! John Wayne, Bruce Lee and Sly Stallone all in one film. Imagine how mad that is. Well this was fuckin' madder! Then, right in the middle of all this something dead funny happened. Tanhouse Club Secretary Tony McKenna had been subbed about twenty minutes from time, gone back to the changies, got showered and changed into his nice clean clothes. Macca was walking back to the pitch when he saw all the commotion. He was having that! He was gonna get stuck in and help his mates out. Macca ran onto the pitch to get stuck in and walked into a right hook that put him firmly on his arse in a sea of mud. After that comic interlude (well not that comical for Macca who had a busted nose and shitted up clothes) the mayhem continued unabated. There was no way this lot we're gonna stop until they just kicked, punched, butted and linesman's flagged themselves to the point of exhaustion. I picked up the ball.

"Match abandoned!"

"Where the fuck are yer goin' ref?"

I swear a Tanhouse player actually asked me that in between punching the fuckin' 'ead off a West Sutton player.

"I'm fuckin' off, that's where I'm goin'! That's fuckin' mad."

"Ref, ref, ref! Come back. Eee arr it's okay now."

"Fuck that!"

"'Ow long was left ref?"

"'Alf a minute."
"Yer can't abandon a game with only 'alf a minute left."
"I can and I 'ave!"
I looked behind and even more surreal than John Wayne and co was the fact that they had all now stopped fighting. Crazy! There was no way back for me now; I'd made my decision to abandon the match so I was sticking to it.
I bellowed across the pitch, "The match is abandoned due to serious misconduct!"
So they all started fighting again.
"Eh ref. That was your fault. You shoulda stopped that."
I think the spectator who said that to me was only messin' in a trying to wind me up sort of way, not really meaning it but just saying it for a laugh.
I wasn't for messin', windin' up or laughin'.
"Yeah, like you'da fuckin' stopped it! Yer fuckin' jokin' aren't yer? Giant Fuckin 'Aystacks wouldna stopped that – in a fuckin' tag team with Big fuckin' Daddy!"
I was annoyed you see.
I was refereeing my afternoon game on the same pitch. I think the fighting had just about stopped when I went out to ref Alexandra v Dunlop.

Tanhouse won the fight by the way but then you would expect them to with nicknames like "Gringo", "Jaffa", "Maggot", "Nipper", "Mowy", "Macca", "Dave the Rave" and last and definitely least "Stinky". I still see a lot of the Tanhouse players involved in that match when I'm out drinking and conversation ALWAYS gets round, even 23 years later, to the game. Of course I had to write the report up as I saw it and it was my opinion that Tanhouse were to blame. I had nothing against them at all and still remain firm friends with Tony McKenna (he of the mashed face and muddy kecks). I think they were fined about £50 and warned as to their future conduct. Tony took that at the FA Disciplinary hearing with good grace. It's funny to look back on but it honestly was fuckin' mad at the time. If you're ever in a boozer in Skem, especially Tanhouse way, ask anybody about that match. They'll tell you all about it. Oh by the way, while you're there, ask Stinky can I have my linesman's flag back.

Then it all happened again! Oh fuckin' no, please! Alexandra v Dunlop didn't go off as badly as West Sutton v Tanhouse but go off it did after about half an hour. It was a cup-tie in the same competition so once again full-blooded bodily contacts were being made. One bad tackle led to a punch (off) led to another punch (off) led to a shove, led to a push, four players involved now, led to a little scrap here, a scuffle there, fuckin' 'ell everybody involved now! It didn't ever reach the grand scale of the previous match but it was bad enough. After I'd done my usual in these circs of sending off the two instigators of the mass battle I called all the players to the centre of the pitch:
"Right, yer all know what went on 'ere this mornin'. I'm not fuckin' 'avin' two o' them in one day! Yer saw I abandoned that match; I'm not gonna be frightened to abandon this one too! So 'ere's the score – yer just gerron with it an' sort yerselves out. Any more of it an' I fuck off. Understood?"
I made that speech through chattering teeth. Whether my shivering fit was brought on by the pressure I was under, anger or just the fact that I was fuckin' freezin' cos I was absolutely soaked to the skin – it had actually started snowing now - I'm not sure but it was a truly great Evo effort to get all that out.
"Understood ref."
Sound as! No more problems. Dunlop won 4-0. Let's get home. Get warm. Write reports – oh those fuckin' reports! Get me dinner. Get a bath an' get out for a damn good bevy! I did all that except for the bevy bit. By the time I'd done everything else, and it must have taken three hours to write those reports in duplicate, triplicate and fuckin' quadruplicate for the various bodies they had to go to (no word processor for Evo in those dark days), I was too fucked, stiff and cramped up to even think about walking over to the Derby. Aitchoo! Headache – bang, bang! Shivering. Oh deep joy! On top of everything else I'm now gettin' the 'flu! Is this reffin' lark worth it for a flim a throw? Yeah, course it is! I'd do it for nothin'. I love it. Yeah, I am, I'm mad!

We had a great 2-0 win at Forest with goals from Lawro, who'd slotted into the side like he'd been at Anfield all his life, and Razor.

I, meanwhile, was dying of 'flu and reffing two games in one day - Salesian High School Under 19's v Deyes and Newburgh v Athol – in the snow! If a game could only just about be played on a just about playable pitch then I played it. The players didn't mind (they wanted their game), I didn't mind as I too, flued up or not, wanted my game. I also needed the dosh for the ECF fund which stood at that moment at precisely err….nil! I'd dipped into and then wiped out the fund to buy all the essentials you need to bring a new life into the world. Prams, cots, blankets, nappies, toys, rattles, sterilising units (what are they all about? Does anybody ever use them?) etc cost, and they're only for me! Only messin' – Little Evo 3 was gonna be sorted when he/she made the grand entrance. Sometimes priorities have to be got right. No good me having a load of dosh stashed away for a trip I might not even be making if it meant we were gonna struggle (struggle some more that is cos we were already struggling) for stuff for new babby. Peewack or Angie tucked away in his/her Mum's belly didn't know what the ECF was all about. He/she was due in a few days and was playin' footy like a good 'un in Mum's belly. If I were you kid I'd stay were you are for as long as poss in yer Mum's nice, warm belly. It's bloody freezin' out 'ere! Yeah, good idea, stay where yer are for an extra few days. It was a good job I'd enjoyed those two games at Salesian and Newburgh as that was the last amateur footy there was gonna be for six weeks. Britain was in the grip of a cold snap – the worst spell of weather since err….last year. Do I sound like a weatherman? Nah, Evo the weatherman – doesn't quite go does it?

December 8th 1981 – now that was a *proper* cold night. Yer wouldn't have sent a dog out in that! Why did people say that? Did people wait 'til it got dead cold and say, "Oh, I think I'll send my dog out. Go on Rover, away you go!", open the door to be hit by this mad blizzard, then say, "Oh no Rover, it's much too cold for you to go out in that. Come back in and lay at my feet near the crackling log fire while I sit, in my slippers, smoking my pipe, reading my favourite newspaper with Mozart on my stereo playing gently in the background and a foaming jug of my home-brewed real ale by my side." (Bloody 'ell, sounded good that didn't it? I want some of that!) I mean, the poor dog wouldn't know whether it was coming or

going would it? Nice and warm one minute, licking its bollocks (nice trick if you can do it – I've got a video like that) and picking its fleas off itself. The next minute freezing it's freshly licked bollocks off for a few mad seconds then being told it can go back, get warm again and resume its nether nuzzling. Mad isn't it?
"Look at that dog lickin' its bollocks. Wish I could do that!"
"Throw it a bone an' it might let yer."
Anyway, digression over, it was bloody freezin' but Arsenal were to be our visitors in the League Cup 4th Round replay. The first game at Highbury had finished goalless. Ninety minutes of the most appalling dross later and this game had the same scoreline. You can put up sometimes with shite games as long as your feet don't feel like they're in a fridge, your arms don't feel like your hands have been chopped off and your little willie doesn't look like a Walnut Whip when you go for a piss. It was honestly absolutely freezing. The game should not have been started on that frozen pitch never mind be allowed to carry on as the night grew colder. The only highlight of that depressing 90 minutes was seeing Souey getting stuck into Peter Nicholas. Nicholas was another nasty piece of work from the valleys (was he related to Leighton James?) and had snidely, off the ball, done Razor at Highbury. As soon as Souey saw his chance he took it, leaving Nicholas body-skidding along the pitch in a crumpled heap. Nicholas was carried off but might actually have been glad to get off and in the warmth of the shower to play with his Walnut Whip.
LOST THE WELSH VOTE THERE EVO!
Of the 21,000 brave, hardy souls that had turned up to watch this shite I reckon at least a quarter of that number got off without watching the extra time. Those that stayed were rewarded by us sparking to life and scoring three goals without reply.

Oh deepest of deep joys – as soon as we got out of the ground it started snowing – and I mean snowing properly – like a big blizzardy thing! Standing at the bus stop at the Halfway House waiting for a bus that should have arrived over an hour ago is no place to be even in good weather never mind when you're now up to your knees almost in snow. Good job I had a decent conversationalist with me. Terry O'Toole helped to run the Dunlop footy team with Farrie. Terry, as well as being a football man through and through, was a

Trades Union and political activist. I used to love listening to him talk. Skem at the time was a hotbed of political activists. Good that lads wouldn't just lie down and let Thatcher, Tebbitt, Whitelaw and the likes steamroller us. My mate Alan was in the same mould as Terry. The same applied to John Simmo who was, I think I'm right in saying this, the local representative of the Workers Revolutionary Party. I know that sounds a bit "Citizen Smith" but it was a bona fide political party. Vanessa Redgrave was something like Chairman or President of the party. I've gotta be honest and say a millionaire actress at the helm of an extreme left wing political party didn't sit right with me but she made all the right noises and seemed sincere about her Socialist beliefs. More joy for Terry, me and the other frozen souls on the bus was that the clapped out owld fuckin' heap of rusting shite that Ribble had sent out to get us broke down at the Old Roan. We waited an hour for a replacement bus to come out as we chatted, chattered and nearly froze the little Walnut Whips off ourselves. The driver of the replacement bus, when he eventually arrived, informed us that it would take at least another hour to get back to Skem as he wasn't gonna drive more than twenty miles an hour in this.

"Eh mate, can't yer go any faster? My missus is about to drop!"

"I'll drop you if yer don't shut the fuck up! I'm goin' as fast as I can."

That was fair enough I suppose. He was only doing his job. Besides, I was too cold to even argue with him, never mind fight, and he was a big fucker. The size of your prospective opponent should always be the main thing you look for when picking a fight with somebody. It doesn't *always* work, I've had some terrible hidings from blokes much smaller than me, but it is a good guideline. By the time we got home, at past one o' clock in the morning, me and Terry had shot Thatcher, Whitelaw and Tebbitt, threw the Queen in the Tower, sent Dukey Phil back to Greece and installed Simmo as Prime Minister. So it was all worth it in the end wasn't it? Course it was!

CHAPTER TWENTY-TWO

WHEN A CHILD IS BORN

Somebody at FIFA liked me. The thorny issue of my knotty problem (I'm sure that must be mixed metaphors or something) of Babby Evo 3 being due the same day as Liverpool were at home to Birmingham was solved by FIFA insisting that we play in the World Club Championship match against Brazilian side Flamengo in Tokyo on December 13th. Yeah, like that was gonna be worth playing wasn't it? We were gonna win that though weren't we? They had Zico, Nunes, Adillio, Junior, Andrade and every other boss Brazilian player of the time you could name. We had no chance. We had been forced by FIFA to take part although I don't think Peter Robinson's arm was that far up his back as the new fangled one-off game way of deciding the Championship in some footballing outpost with loads of dosh in the country's coffers carried huge sponsorship money. The World Club Championship used to be a really big thing in the sixties. Then it used to be played on a two-legged basis at the respective clubs' home stadiums. Any club winning it in the sixties really could claim to be footballing Champions of the World. Celtic came very close in 1967. They had won the home leg 1-0, then lost away to Racing Club Buenos Aires 1-2. Away goals didn't count double then so Celtic had to stay in Buenos Aires for a third match. They had been kicked to fuck in their own home leg so were treated far worse in Argentina. Racing Club supporters were not only attacking Celtic supporters but also Celtic players – while the game was in progress! Allegations about the match officials concerning bribery and corruption were rife. It was no surprise therefore that they lost the third game 0-1.

Man U had a go the following year but, in much the same circs as Celtic before them, lost 0-1 away and drew 1-1 at home to another Argentinian club, Estudiantes. Both Celtic and Man U deserved to be crowned Champions of the World at that time. They were certainly both good enough. Having seen the experiences of Celtic and United, European clubs saw it as not worth the hassle and in the seventies many European Cup winners refused to play in it. Sometimes the beaten European Cup finalists would take the place of the winners, as

BMG did in '77 and Malmo when Forest were European Champions two years later. Other times the games weren't even played at all as when we were European Champions in '78. Forest did take part after their second European Cup success when the "tournament" had been moved to Tokyo, losing 0-1 to Nacional of Uruguay. The whole farce was now no more than a glorified friendly – a sort of Charity Shield of the world but if it was gonna make sure I didn't miss a home match then I'd put up with it.

Flamengo, unsurprisingly, wiped the floor with us. Nunes scored two and Zico (their Zico that is, not ours) added one of his specials to complete a 3-0 rout. Had it all been worth it? Liverpool Football Club must have thought so with a few extra grand in Barclays for them.

I needn't have worried anyway; if FIFA hadn't intervened then the Divine would have done as most of the country's football was called off due to the terrible weather. Even I called my game off in the Ormskirk League. I'd decided to take the game only the night before as Little Peewack/Angie was showing no sign of leaving the warmth of his/her Mum. Can't say I blamed the little blighter. I was glad I'd stayed in my nice warm home – I just didn't fancy clearing sheep shite off Aughton's pitch in this weather.

The little fella/lass was four days overdue when we went to the ante-natal clinic. We were told what we expected to hear, "The time is nigh." Well not exactly nigh but certainly within a few hours. There was though enough time to go in the ambulance with Big, settle her in, get home to pick the kids up from school, feed them and sort somebody to look after them 'til they were ready to leave for their (non) starring roles in the Trinity School Nativity play. When I got back to the hospital after doing all that the birth of Little Evo Number 3 was indeed imminent. I hadn't been at the birth of our Ste, having to wait outside the delivery room, but had been present when Little Ev popped her gorgeous head into the world. That had been a fairly traumatic experience for Big Ev. This birth seemed to be going a lot better but that was easy for me to say – I wasn't the one huffing, puffing, panting and pushing. Maybe it's the way my mind chooses

to remember it but it did seem to be over a lot quicker and with far less mess than my Little Ev.
"Go on Ev, yer nearly there."
"I'm not 'avin' any more!"
"That's what yer said last time. Go on love, one more push."
"I 'ate you!"
"Yer said that too."
Aren't midwives brilliant? They must have seen this scenario a million times of the mother cursing the father; had to put up with all the screaming and hollering going on and yet they all seem to love their job and take the greatest of pleasure in delivering a new life into the world.
"There you go Evelyn. Here's your baby now. You've got a (cue drum roll – I'd rather have a chicken roll I'm starvin'. Midwife fed me when Little Ev was born. Where's she? I 'aven' 'ad any dinner. I want some!) little girl!
Thank Christ for that Evo. We thought you were never gonna tell us!
What a beautiful little girl she was too. Dark hair atop a lovely little face. Slightly chub of chop and with a lovely little button nose. She was an Evo alright. Little Angie Evo – welcome to the world. Yer gonna be a Red. Yer know that don't yer?

I was standing at the bus stop outside Ormskirk Hospital panicking about whether or not I'd get back in time to pick the kids up from the school play. What's more I didn't have any money for bus fare. I was just gonna have to hope that the driver would take pity on me in my hour of need. I certainly wasn't even gonna attempt to walk it. I'd never have got back in time for the kids and anyway it was blizzarding again. Really was shit weather for weeks at that time. Alan Southern driving past in his British Gas Board (I think) van spotted me shivering at the bus stop and kindly gave me a lift to the school. Good lad Alan. Abarr as good a footballer as Wilko but in the same mould of top ladness.

I arrived at Trinty School just in time to hear the choir and entire cast finish the show with the most spookily appropriate song there could have been for me right there and then.

"This comes to pass, when a child is born."
I just stood at the back of the hall in floods of tears. What a song that is! It still brings goose bumps to me and makes my scalp stand on end when I hear it even now. You only really hear it at Christmas as it is the definitive Christmas song. It was the Christmas Number One of 1976. If I had my way it would be Number One every Christmas. I still play it at times other than Christmas though, especially when I'm feeling a little down now and again. I'm never down for long anyway but hearing that song and thinking of my Little Angie's glowing cheeks – then and now, even now when she's all grown up, never fails to lift my spirits. Yeah I know I'm gettin' all sloppy and slushy and sentimental but that's big soft Evo for yer isn't it? I looked at my Steven and Evelyn singing there on the stage and felt so proud of them, of their Mum, of myself and of the fact that they had a little baby sister. The two kids spotted me standing at the back of the hall and waved. They obviously knew by now that they had a little bro or sis. I could see them bursting to get off stage as Mr. Bain, who has been Headmaster at Trinity since Adam and Eve went to school and is still there, gave his closing Christmas speech. Little Ev was first off the stage.
"Dad, Dad, 'ave I got a little brother or a little sister?"
"You've got a little sister Ev."
"Can I push 'er in 'er pram when she comes 'ome?"
"Yeah, you can love."
Steven was 10 now so he was all grown up about it and summed it up in his favourite word.
"Smart!"

Tears were in my eyes but great joy in my heart
The day my little Angie's life here on earth did start.
"Don't You Want Me" was number one on a cold December morn
But the song that most reminds me of Ange is "When A Child Is Born."

Aah, aah, aah, aah, aaah, aah, aah, aah.

Baby years, full of joy, in those big happy eyes
Twinkling, shining, full of life, never failing to surprise.

Unconditional love and blood is thicker than water
There's no love on earth like a man's love for his daughter.

Canaletto, Rembrandt and Van Gogh painted things of such great beauty
But they never painted anything as good my little Angie cutie.
My little Jelly Bean with your gorgeous face and laugh that's sounds so mad.
It makes me very proud for me to be your Dad.

Aah, aah, aah, aah, aah, aah, aah, aah, aah.

The lowest point so far of what had not been a brilliant season came on Boxing Day. We crashed, and I do mean crashed properly, 1-3 at home to Manchester City. We were giving stick to Asa Hartford, the ex Everton player and to Kevin Bond who was getting "Daddy's boy" taunts as his Dad, John, managed City. So obviously Hartford opened the scoring, right in front of the Kop. Bond got his revenge too from the penalty spot after a terrible error from Brucie. Thommo's attempted clearance that looped high into the air in the penalty-area should have been easy meat for Brucie but no, he flapped at it like a big flappy apprentice wallpaperer. The ball fell to City winger Kinsey who fairly hammered the ball for what seemed a certain goal. Thommo was back on the line by now but had to do what his goalkeeper had summarily failed to do. Perhaps Thommo and Brucie should have changed places before the start of the match. There were those who were saying Thommo was a better goalkeeper than Brucie anyway. Bond stepped up to slot the penalty with ease. Mind you, I reckon his owld fella could have come on and beaten Brucie from the spot the form our 'keeper was in! I think *my* owld fella would have had a chance of slotting past Brucie from twelve yards! Ronnie Whelan's 85th minute goal gave us some hope but City scored again in the last minute after another bad mistake by Brucie, letting what was no more than a hopeful near-post flick from Kevin Reeves to squirm under his body. Some of Brucie's eccentricities at times had to be seen to be believed. In fact he was getting more erratic than eccentric. To complete a fuckin' horrible shit of a day some fuckin' dead'ead threw a bottle from the Kop. I think the bottle hit City keeper Joe Corrigan somewhere around the shoulder. Great credit must go to Corrigan as rather than make a big fuss about it Joe just calmly picked up the bottle and placed it behind the goal. The incident had been well noted by the police and of course the club would get bounced by the FA because of it but the whole thing could have been made a lot worse had Joe reacted badly. Attempts were made by outraged Kopites to get the culprit out but I don't think that happened. Joe was applauded by the Kop for that. Joe in turn applauded the Kop at the end of the game; he knew it was only one idiot that had been gunning for him. We chanted Joe's name as he was leaving the pitch in respect of the man. The fuckin' mindless act of one cretin could have had dire consequences for the club and us fans. The ground could have been closed for a few games; certainly the Kop might well have been. The fact that neither of these things happened is, I'm sure, as a direct result of Joe not wanting a fuss made. Nice one Joe. I'll never forget you for that.

My culinary prowess (or lack of it) was to be put to the test by cooking the Christmas dinner – On December 27th! Big Ev was suffering terribly from post-natal depression. Not that I would have known post-natal depression at the time from the hole in my arse. I don't think I'd even heard of it then. Maybe I did realise what it was but didn't want to know; that might have been nearer the truth. I was about as much use to Ev at the time as an ashtray on a motorbike. Certainly I was brought to task when the midwife called one day, I think Christmas Eve, on a visit to see how mother and baby were doing. Ev was totally washed out and I was lying in bed like a big, fat, lazy pig. I heard middy asking Ev where I was. I also heard her voice raised in disgust telling Ev to get me out of bed after Ev had replied. I came downstairs to receive my deserved volley.

"What are you doing in bed?"

"I'm tired."

"*You're* tired? Your wife is the one that's tired. Look at her. She should be the one in bed, not you! You should be looking after her."

I couldn't argue with her for the very good reason that she was right. It didn't help though that Ev wasn't speaking to me. There was no way in her state that Ev was going to cook Christmas dinner. There was no way either that I was gonna attempt it. I was okay cooking a wagonload of chips and a couple of fried eggs but a monstrous turkey, an ovenful of roasties and a big gang of veg was beyond me.

I decided the day after Boxing Day that fuck it, I was gonna have a bash. The turkey had been in the fridge for a few days now and if not cooked soon would go off - even I knew that.
How long can you keep a turkey in a freezer?
I don't know, about six months I think. Why?
Oh right, I put one in last night and it was dead this morning.
BOLLOCKS TO THE JOKES GET ON WITH IT! THIS IS A SERIOUS STORY!
'Ow the fuck d'yer cook a turkey? Yeah, whack it in the oven, top shelf, at full tilt for a couple of hours. Roasties on the bottom shelf. Laughin'! Yeah, that should do it.
WRONG!
A couple of hours later we had roasties like Ghandi's bollocks and turkey although burnt on the outside was quite nice once you cut into it but was as raw as a good smacked arse further in. How the fuck we didn't all die of salmonella, food poisoning or botulism whatever I'll never know. What I do know is that this wasn't a happy time for me; my wife was ill, she wasn't speaking to me, our lovely little new baby girl, beautiful though she was, was making sure nobody got any sleep by demonstrating what a good pair of lungs she had, my footy team was shite and to top it all off like a great big toppy-offy thing I had the raging shits right through to New Year. Death by salmonella would have been a blessed release.

Bob was under pressure to replace Brucie. Bob was not one to bow to pressure and kept faith with his man. Bob would make changes when he was ready, in his time, at his own leisurely pace and when they were for the good of Liverpool Football Club. He was saying nothing just now but Bob had changes planned one of which was to have a dramatic effect on the club's fortunes.

Phil Thompson had been a proud and honourable Captain of Liverpool Football Club. He was a local lad with a fierce passion and determination to do well and win for the club. Thommo wore the Liverbird on his chest and his heart on his Liverpool sleeve. Bob took the captaincy from Phil and handed it to Graeme Souness. It was known at the time that Phil was none too happy at this to put it mildly. What did he do – go off and sulk? No, Thommo was made of sterner stuff than that and just got on with it, although I'm sure he was mightily upset. Phil was as Red as any Kopite and it must have hurt. It was however one of Bob's best ever managerial decisions. Who knows what actually went on behind the scenes and how the actual scenario of Bob telling Phil and Graeme that the captaincy would change hands was played out. Maybe Bob got them both together quietly in his office, or maybe the bootroom, and informed them of his decision. Perhaps he had the two men in his office separately and told them. There was talk later that Souness had been in to see Bob after the Man City debacle and had touted for the captaincy. Whether that was true or not only a handful of people will know. Even if it was true I'm sure Bob would have made his own mind up. Bob had spotted that Souness was a born leader of men and was destined to be Liverpool Football Club Captain one day anyway. Whatever way the deed was done though I'm sure it was in a dignified manner befitting of Bob and Liverpool Football Club. I could be one hundred per cent certain however that Bob didn't do it in the same way that Tommy Docherty once changed Manchester United captains. Willie Morgan was captain of Man U at the time and was waiting in the tunnel, holding the ball (come on, keep it clean) as captains do, at Old Trafford with his teammates behind him to lead the team out. Docherty snatched the ball from Morgan, thrust it into the arms of George Graham and said to Graham, "Get in front of him. You're Captain now."

No surprise then that United were relegated that season. Happy Days!

The effect of the change in captaincy was dramatic. Swansea were trounced at the Vetch Field in the FA Cup 3rd Round by four goals to nil. The League positions before the home game against West Ham saw us in twelfth place. The table was slightly misleading in that clubs had mostly played a vastly different number of games. We had 24 points from 17 games while the leaders, Man City, had 34 from 20. Not much difference you might think – win the three games in hand and, with the new three points for a win, we're only 1 point behind.

Only problem there was that we hadn't strung more than two League wins together all season and certainly didn't look like doing so now. The likely League Champions to me and many other people looked like Ipswich. They were in fifth place with 32 points from 16 games. So, if they won the game in hand they had on us it would put us 11 points behind them. No chance of catching that up is there? I mean, put it this way, we would have to win four consecutive games and Ipswich lose four on the bounce to overtake them. That wasn't going to happen was it? No, the stark truth was that we were nearer the relegation area than the top of the League. We were only 7 points ahead of Notts County who occupied the last relegation position in 20th spot. Wasn't looking good was it? Relegation wasn't really a possibility (not one that I or any other Red wanted to think of) but we had no chance of winning the League. So we'll just consolidate our position and settle for the obscurity, anonymity, whatever you want to call it of a respectable finishing position in mid-table shall we?
MY ARSE!

We embarked on a run of four consecutive League wins beating West Ham and Wolves at home and Notts County and Aston Villa away. Included in the 4-0 win at Meadow Lane was Rushie's first ever hat-trick for us. Things were most definitely on the up!
LIVERPOOL, LIVERPOOL, LIVERPOOL!

In between those games we'd had an easy FA Cup 4th Round win, 3-0, at Sunderland and a couple of bruising, hard fought encounters with Barnsley in Round 5 of The League Cup. The first game at Anfield ended goalless. Barnsley seemed to have brought every miner in Yorkshire with them. Certainly most supporters I saw had donkey jackets with NCB emblazoned on the back. I don't think the Road End boys would be robbing many of them. I think Wilko was after one like but Bally persuaded him it wouldn't be a good idea to be baaaaed at for the rest of the season. Anyway, all the Barnsley lads seemed to be about seven foot tall and as wide. Imagine the scenario of Wilko trying to have one of them off:
"Eh, yer fuckin' Yorkshire cunt, giz yer jacket."
"Why? Does want it for blanket? It'll never fit thee. Yon's only a weedy Scouse bastard."

"Just fuckin giz it yer twat before I knock yer out!"
"Now look son, yon jacket 'as bin signed by Arthur Scargill so it's goin' nowhere."
"Come on Gary. Let's fuck off before 'e shoves a sack o' coal up yer arse. Anyway, yer not a fuckin' wool. Yer'd only get shit in the Anny."
"Ah fuck it anyway. I only wanted it to swap for a 1970 Leeds scarf."

It looked as if we were going out of the League Cup in the replay at a fog-shrouded Oakwell when Barnsley took the lead. Souness equalised before half-time. Late goals from Johnno and Kenny put is through to the next round.

We had a brilliant 2-0 win at Ipswich in the first leg of the semi-final. Terry Mac gave us the lead two minutes after half-time. Rushie added the second two minutes later. A more daunting prospect though looked to be the League game at Anfield against the Portman Road side four days later.

By this time Ray Kennedy had left the club. Razor had joined up with Tosh at Swansea. Nobody worked harder to improve their game than Ray. Maybe Ray thought Bob was nuts when told that he would no longer be employed as a striker but as a left midfield player. Ray's transformation once he'd got used to that position was amazing. With 384 appearances and 72 goals Razor had been pivotal to our success. Never hogging the limelight Ray was largely unappreciated by the media. Not so by his fellow players or his fans. There was no better sight in football at one time than to see Razor dropping forty yards bombs into the penalty area for Terry Mac, Kenny or the fledgling Rushie to volley into the net. Ray had won four League Championship winners medals, three European Cup winners medals and one League Cup winners medal when he left the club. Ray's contribution to the success of Liverpool Football Club in his eight years at Anfield should never be understated.

Our four successive League wins had rocketed us up the table to fifth place having 36 points from 21 games. Surprise package Southampton now topped the table with 40 points from 22 games.

Ipswich were still very well placed in third spot with 38 points from 29 games. This game was crucial to our season. The four wins on the bounce had been great but we really couldn't afford anything else other than a win. Boy, did we get that win? We were absolutely brilliant! The game was won by half-time with goals from Terry Mac, Rushie and Kenny. Ronnie Whelan's second half goal just put the cap on an outstanding performance – our best of the season.

Ipswich were back at Anfield three days later for the second leg of the League Cup semi-final. Hardly worth them going home was it? They must have wished they had gone home and stayed there when they found themselves two goals down on the night and four overall early in the second half – Rushie and Kenny getting the goals. They did score two themselves later on to give them a respectable draw on the night but it was us who would face Tottenham in the Final at Wembley on March 13th. Funniest moment of that game against Ipswich was when John Wark took a full-blooded volley from Terry Mac (and how he could hit them) right in his nutsack. Poor Warky was down in a heap for ages. He deffo wasn't gonna shag his bird that night! The Kop struck up with an amazingly high-pitched "Johnny Wark, Johnny Wark, Johnny Wark." Great stuff – except for Warky that is!

Back down to earth we came and how! Dumped out of the FA Cup 0-2 at Chelsea. I didn't go to that game but tales of Chelsea fans being nuts in the ground and jumping into our end are legion. I've seen photos of that day and even they scare me! Lads who did go talk about it in almost the same terms as I and every other Red at Tottenham two years earlier talk about that. Scary shit!

We had good wins in the next two League games, 4-0 at home to Coventry and 2-0 at Leeds.

CSKA returned to Anfield for the European Cup 3rd Round first leg game. They looked altogether a better, fitter, much more organised side than they had a year earlier. Ronnie Whelan scored the goal that gave us a slender lead to take to Sofia but this was gonna be no easy tie.

The ECF fund was at the princely total of fuckin' zero! Just couldn't save anything when there was baby stuff needed. If we got to Rotterdam I'd have to borrow the dosh or do something drastic but there was no way I was gonna get there on my own ackers.
"Can I go the match with yer tomorrer Dad?"
No fuckin' chance! We've lost the two games yer've been to. What're yer tryin' to do – get us relegated?
"Yer can't son. I 'aven' got enough money."
"I've got me own money Dad. I've been savin' it an' doin' little jobs for people an' that."
Fuckin' good lad our Ste. Even at ten years of age he had the work ethic that had been instilled in me and handed down through generations of Evos. He was prepared to use his own dosh to go the match. Sound that. What a lad! What a Red!
"Ow much yer got son?"
"Abarr a fiver Dad."
A flim! Fuckin' 'ell, that's more than I've got an' I'm working every bastard hour God sends!
"Yer've got a fiver Ste? That's good isn't it?"
"Yeah Dad, I've got it in me little piggy bank."
He'd had that little plassy piggy bank since Kitty, Big Ev's Mum had bought it for him when he was about six months old. I think he's still got it! Hmm....wonder if I could get into it for my ECF fund. Nah, don't even think abarr that Peter. I used to feel bad enough when I was robbin' money outta me Ma's purse to go the match when I was a kid, never mind do that to my son.
"Okay son, yer can come"
"Smart! I 'ope we win this time."
"So do I or yer not goin again."
I was only jokin'. Or I thought I was. We wouldn't lose at home to Brighton. Would we?

Shit! We lost at home to Brighton. The memories I have of that game are a big, powerful striker running our defence ragged – a lad by the name of Michael Robinson, Jimmy Case, on his first return to Anfield, getting a great reception from the Kop and an Ian Rush shot sticking in the mud on the Kop goal-line as we tried to will the ball in. The Anfield pitch, which for years you could have ate your dinner off, was an absolute disgrace and had been nearly all season. Where in previous seasons it had been green and lush this time it was brown and sandy. Tons and tons of sand had been poured onto the pitch in an effort to get it something like right but it looked awful. In the end the groundsmen had actually dyed the sand green to disguise how bad the pitch really was. That didn't work – we all knew it was shit. Andy Ritchie, ex Man U to make it worse, scored the Brighton goal. Three games, three defeats and three times to teams playing in blue eh Ste? You're not a jinx though are yer? I didn't push him off the crush barrier at the end of the game! Honest! He fell off. Honest!

We recovered to wallop Stoke on their own midden the following week 5-1. The goals were scored by five different players - McDermott, Dalglish, Souness, Lee and Whelan. This was more like it! Let's get off now to Wembley to win the League Cup again, then on to Sofia, beat those pesky Bulgars and go on to retain our European Cup.

CHAPTER TWENTY-THREE

THE LAND OF MILK AND MONEY

We were very slight favourites to win the League Cup. Okay it was now called the Milk Cup and there was a new trophy for winning it. As well as the old three-handled League Cup, which was a strange looking trophy anyway, the winners would receive a smart looking new cup that looked not unlike a bottle of milk, a bottle of sterry milk but a bottle of milk nonetheless, if you looked at in a certain way. I don't know whether it was designed that way but that's how it looked to me. Yes, the great new God of football – sponsorship – had given us the bottle of milk cup. There was also a substantial amount of sponsorship money coming to the winner from the Milk Marketing Board. I KNOW!

Alan Southern called at mine the night before the game to discuss final travel plans etc for the next day.
"Eh Dad, it's been on Radio City all day yer know that yer'll 'ave ter leave early cos there's loads o' roadworks an' that on the motorways. It said yer should go on the M40 or something."
"Christ, 'e's clever isn't 'e? Yer don't get many lads 'is age know about stuff like that."
Alan's assertion was totally correct. Ste was the brightest ten-year-old I'd ever known, certainly miles ahead of me when I was his age. Ste was also the best maker of a cup of tea in the Evo household. Good lad, I'd take him to Wembley one day.

We did indeed leave early so arrived in good time. Memory might be playing tricks but I think Larry Trencher and maybe one other was with us. I was definitely very glad of the lift off Alan as I would have really struggled to come up with the dosh for a coach. We witnessed a few minor scuffles but nothing too bad in and around the car parks. There was a bit of a heave-ho in that sort of downhill bit outside our end of Wembley as a big cry of, "The Road End united will never be defeated!" went up. I think Larry was particularly keen to join in that one before the bizz bobs moved in and sorted it.

We were in the West Terrace at Wembley. It was considered to be the lucky end and as we were in that end for most of our Wembley visits I suppose it was just that. The FA choosing which end your fans are housed though doesn't win you cups. Teams have to do that for themselves. Superstition might help a little but it's down to the players on the park to perform. The fans of course can play their part and certainly we did that day.

We were a goal down after little more than ten minutes when Steve Archibald turned on the edge of the area, leaving Jocky for dead and scored a great goal. As was the case the year before there were plenty of Cockneys in our end and more than a few fights broke out at the bottom of the terrace. Sammy should have netted the equaliser but sent a weak header wide. Well, come on, you wouldn't expect heading to be Sammy's forte would you?

Ray Clemence got a stunning reception, one he seemed almost overwhelmed by, when he took up his position to defend his goal at our end for the start of the second half. Clem, for so many years our saviour, was threatening to be our heartbreaker this time. Stunning saves from Terry Mac and Kenny kept Spurs in the lead. We were the superior team in the second half and it looked only a mater of time before Spurs cracked. There was one almighty scare for us though when Archibald's shot looked destined to give Spurs a two-goal and probably winning lead until Souey, summoning up all his energy, got back on the line and managed to clear. What a player this man was! What a captain too. Coaxing and cajoling his players, Graeme led by example. This man was a winner!

Roared on by the most vociferous support I'd ever heard from us at Wembley we got our just rewards three minutes from time. Bob had sent on a pair of fresh legs and extra attacking options in Johnno to replace Terry Mac. Johnno's pass it was that found Ronnie Whelan who thumped the ball past Clemence. Our end went ballistic. Extra time was round the corner and we knew, just knew, we were gonna win it. The players knew it also.

THERE'S ONLY ONE RONNIE WHELAN! ONE RONNIE WHELAN, THERE'S ONLY ONE RONNIE WHELAN!

Try getting your tongue round that a few times! If you're not careful it comes out sounding like ONE WONNIE WHELAN!

It's hard work being a footy fan yer know!

Spurs players slumped to the ground during the break before extra time while their coaching and physio staff ran round frantically trying to massage life back into tired legs. Meanwhile Bob had ordered our players to stay on their feet. Indeed Souness and co looked fired up, ready to go and impatient to get at the bedraggled Spurs.

There were no goals in the first period of extra time. We were once again kicking towards our own fans in the second half. Believe me, that was a big advantage to us. The Spurs supporters sounded as tired as their players looked now and could barely raise a whimper as a great, surging wall of sound came from our end. Kenny got the ball in the Spurs penalty area. A lesser player, a lesser man would have opted to shoot. Kenny's superb footballing brain was in overdrive and instead of shooting bided his time for our players to come rushing in droves in support past the weary Spurs players. Kenny could then have picked out any one of three players but Ronnie was there first for a goal that shook the very foundations of Wembley as we joyously bounced up and down in celebration. That was it – we'd won! There were still nearly ten minutes left but Spurs didn't look to have the heart, never mind the energy to come back at us. Sammy played a superb, curling 40 yard ball with the outside of his foot to Rushie that if Glen(da) Hoddle had played it would have had the assembled media and telly pundits creaming their crackers with delight. Rushie took the ball on and passed to Johnno who looked certain to score. Johnno tried to round Clem but was foiled first time. Johnno got the run of the ball to collect the rebound and square the ball to Rushie. Rushie made no mistake as Clem fell crestfallen to the Wembley turf. What a performance that was!

With two trophies to collect Souey would have been well entitled to pick up the new one. Instead he climbed Wembley's 39 steps to the Royal box and lifted the three-handled League Cup. An ear-splitting roar from our fans was followed by an even louder one when Thommo raised the (sterry) Milk (bottle) Cup aloft.

A big bag of skill, passion and commitment had won us that final. Most of all though it had been won by sheer bloody hard work. There

was joy unbounded on the lap of honour. None more so than Brucie. This man was a nutter! Brucie had his medal in his mouth and walking on his hands round the side of the pitch in a display of post-match lunacy never been seen before at Wembley.
BRUCIE, BRUCIE GROBBELAAR, BRUCIE GROBBELAAR IN OUR GOAL!
BRUCIE, BRUCIE GROBBELAAR, BRUCIE GROBBELAAR IN OUR GOAL!
(SOMETIMES!)

I was glad I hadn't gone by coach when I saw the commotion going on down in the coach parks. It was difficult to see who was doing what to whom but there was definitely a mass battle. Talk later said that one Spurs fan had an axe. Not good! We had no trouble getting back to Alan's car. Those rip-off vendors were making a fortune.
"'Alf a quid for a can of Coke! I can get a pint o' Stella for that in Skem!"
They never take any notice of you though do they? Just pocket the money and call you a Scouse twat under their breath.

We were stuck in traffic near that massive NCP car park at Wembley. There was a van in front of us with probably about a dozen Reds in it. The van had been sussed by a few moochy Cockneys. The moochies waited 'til a few more of them arrived and then made threatening moves towards the van – a couple of bottles being thrown in the process too. The van emptied of lads tooled up to fuck. I'm sure one lad had a trowel. Needles to say (*needles* not a typo for *needless*, just something Albert Steptoe said once. You'd have to see it to be funny – visual humour you see) the mooch men beat a hasty retreat.

We ended up in the grip of the roadworks young Evo had warned us about and so had to divert through Northampton. Well that's a bonus isn't it? It seemed loads of other Reds had the same idea and Northampton town centre became Red for an hour or two. Most of us were in one boozer and enjoyed a good few bevvies before wending our weary way home. That really was a great day and a great Final. We'd triumphed against the odds and that made it sweeter.
WE LOVE YOU LIVERPOOL WE DO! OH, LIVERPOOL WE LOVE YOU!

I didn't have to worry any more about this season's ECF fund or how I was gonna get the money to go to Rotterdam. We were out! Well beaten in Sofia 2-0 and to compound our defeat Mark Lawrenson became the first Liverpool player to be sent off in European competition. Most of the blame was laid fairly and squarely on the shoulders of Brucie. Certainly he made at least one appalling error for one of the goals, maybe even two. He was getting a reputation as a clown. He was a very good goalkeeper, no doubt, but his eccentricities and erratic behaviour were costing us dear. It seemed at times that he couldn't catch a cold. More calls were made to get him out of the team. Bob again resisted.

After another Rushie goal had given us a home win over Sunderland we went to Goodison for the 126th Merseyside Derby. In a parody of the many times Gordon West was presented with a handbag prior to Anfield Derbies, Brucie was given a cardboard clown's face from a Gwladys Street Blue. Brucie took this in the spirit it was meant; the same way Westy had taken it for all those years. Brucie put the clown at the back of the goal. It certainly smiled on us that day and it was jubilant Reds who were laughing at the end. Ronnie opened the scoring when his cross was headed on to the bar by Craig Johnson. Ronnie seized on the rebound and smashed it home. Everton were level shortly after through Sharp. Souness restored our lead with an unstoppable shot after Kenny had done the spadework by holding off not one but two defenders with his arse – one with each cheek. What an arse that was! Skippy secured the result nine minutes from time when his mishit shot looped wildly over the stranded Southall. For the last couple of minutes, with the game safe, Brucie was twatting about around his area winding the Evertonians up for calling him a clown. Like Alan Waddle nine years earlier, Brucie rammed "clown" taunts down blue throats. Clowns always have the last laugh.

That win brought us level with the Blues on 44 League Derby wins each. We'd always been behind them in that particular race; in fact it was the first time we'd even been level. Would be good to get our noses in front of them next season.

The winning League streak was stretched to four with an impressive

3-1 midweek victory at home to Birmingham. We hit the top of the table for the first time this season with a 1-0 Bad Friday night (if you haven't read MYMK buy it now for explanation) victory over Notts County. Great stuff! From twelfth to first in 14 games. Not bad eh? So I went to the Derby Arms when I got back to Skem to celebrate us reaching the top? Not bloody likely! This was Bad Friday remember. Sunday hours. No bevy. Se ya later!

The Football League actually gave us five days rest (that was nice of them wasn't it?) before our visit to Old Trafford. That was a really boss victory. Skippy, now gradually pushing Terry Mac out of the side such were the level of his performances - they had to be good to displace Terry, scored the goal to give us a marvellous win. The much maligned Brucie played a major part saving a Frank Stapleton penalty. Good job Brucie had been reading the match programme before the game as he saw a photo of a Stapleton penalty in an earlier match and guessed that should he take one in this match Stapleton would put it to the same side. Brucie guessed right. See, he wasn't *that* mad!

Six on the trot and then we *really* kicked into gear! Manchester City must have hated our visits to Maine Road. Sammy started it off with a 30 yard free kick that wouldn't have stopped at Old Trafford if there hadn't been a net in the way. Phil Neal stepped up to take a 42nd minute penalty and shit high into the net. *Shit* isn't my typo – it was in the Manc version of our Footy Echo. It's the best typo of all time and I've still got the paper to prove it.
Quote verbatim: "Neal stepped up to take the penalty and shit high into the net."
Classic!
Skippy, Barnie and Rushie added to Phil's shit to give us another thumping victory at Maine Road. Barney's was a strange goal. His shot from an acute angle on the left floated in. It was probably a cross actually but you never knew with Barney's goals. He scored a good few goals like that so they couldn't have all been flukes.

Roll on yer big rollers! Another Barney "special" and Skippy's effort put paid to Stoke as did Kenny's goal against West Brom.

Victory at Southampton would equal our club record of ten successive League wins. Southampton nearly stopped that. The game stood at 2-2, Rushie and Ronnie scoring for us. Ronnie produced a winner, like a rabbit from a hat two minutes from time to maintain our run and equal the record.
The record-breaking win (send for Roy Castle!) came with Skippy's two goals against Forest at Anfield. Craig had really settled into the team very well now. His all action style and goalscoring prowess were establishing him as a real crowd favourite.

That was some feat under any circs – 11 wins on the bounce. There was still a lot of hard work to be done though to win the League. Our run in was daunting to say the least. We had five games left – three away on the trot against Spurs, Birmingham and Arsenal, then the home return against Spurs, finishing the season off, once again, at Middlesbrough. Oh shit! Why did we seemingly have to visit Boro last game of every season? It was never any fun to go to Boro (still isn't) but having to go there to win the League would ensure lots of cloth touching. Ipswich had caught up their games in hand and had in fact overtaken us in those terms. The Ipswich run in was two away against West Brom and Brighton followed by two home against Forest and Spurs. We had the advantage in points – 78 to their 74. Our miles better goal difference was also worth virtually a point should it come down to that to separate us.

At half time in North London it looked as if not only was our winning run coming to an end but that we were on our way to a defeat that could be disastrous for our League hopes. Spurs were 2-0 up through Perryman and Archibald and seemed to be on their way to avenging their League Cup Final mauling. Cometh the hour – cometh the man. But this wasn't a man. This was a God. This was Kenny! Millions of words have been written about Kenny and I could write a million more without ever doing him justice. He pulled this game round almost single-handedly with the two goals that gave us a deserved draw. Mind you he was helped by the fact that he had Souey, who had played in only part of one of the last eight games, alongside him after coming on as sub.
I'D WALK A MILLION MILES FOR ONE (OR TWO) OF YOUR GOALS OH KENNY!

I picked some mad away games to go to! Because of my burgeoning (I do like that word) refereeing career I'd only been to a handful of aways this season. The Ormskirk Saturday League season was over so I was now free to spend the best day of the week however I chose. I chose to spend it doing my best to get myself beaten up by going to Birmingham. I hadn't been to St. Andrews since the Tilton Army had tried to decapitate me and a few thousand other Scousers by throwing a knocked down housing estate at us nearly four years earlier. This time however it was a piece of piss. I really don't know what happened that day but I hardly saw a Brummie, apart from in the ground, let alone have a fight with one. The lads on the specials, of which I was one, were being bussed from New Street station to the coach park right outside the ground. Souey's magnificent crossfield ball that must have travelled sixty yards or so from the position he struck it right on the touchline was met with a thunderous volley from Rushie. Another great away win and no agro at all. Life was sweet.

We made up our game in hand on Ipswich with the match at Highbury. Rushie scored our goal in the 1-1 draw. Those three away games on the trot were vital to our season. We hadn't been found wanting; eight points from those three games was a fair return. With just the two games left for both ourselves and Ipswich the destiny of the Championship was in our hands.

The situation on the morning of the Spurs game was quite clear – a win would give us our 13th Football League Championship. We were on 83 points, Ipswich had 80, that goal difference was worth an extra point so a win would do, no matter what Ipswich did in their last two games.

Anfield was in League title winning mood. It was going to be no easy game against Spurs, we knew that from our two previous meetings this season, but optimism prevailed and it was carnival time in the Kop. We ran out to a deafening roar. A couple of lads got on the pitch towards Thommo. One of the lads was waving a flag and had this mad mask on. It was usual in these circs for a player to go nuts at the fans and tell them to get off the pitch, or words to that effect. Thommo though was a local lad, Red through and through and Kirkby to the core. Phil stood there pissin' himself laughing at the monster mask and shook hands with both of the lads. I'm not sure if the lads got lashed and didn't see the match but I bet they'll never forget the day Thommo had a laugh with them and shook their hands. Thommo was looking to make a little piece (well, quite a big piece actually) of history in this match. If we won the League this would be Thommo's sixth League Championship winners medal – a feat never before accomplished by a player with one club. Come on Thommo lad!

At half-time it wasn't looking good. Glenda had belted Spurs into the lead with a superb long-range goal. He was a great player Hoddle. Pity he looked such a fuckin' girl. His shirt outside his super-short shorts and his oh so lovely long legs making it look like he had a baby doll pyjama top and cami-knickers on. He couldn't half play football though.

The reception for Clem when he ran out towards the Kop for the start of the second half is something I'll never forget. I don't have to; it's there in glorious video (and now DVD) colour. That video footage shows amazing pictures of Kopites with their arms above their heads clapping that player like he was still one of our own. If you look at the footage it looks like thousands of seagulls in synchronicity. Wow, that's a big word! That reception even outstripped the one we gave Clem at Wembley a couple of months earlier. Clem gave us Kopites a double clenched fist salute as if to say, "Thanks lads, that was fuckin' brilliant. I know you still love me."

And so we did but we also loved Brucie. Yeah, he was fuckin' nuts but he was ours, one of us and he was a great goalkeeper. Meanwhile, the game at Portman Road was goalless. If things stayed this way it would indeed go to the last game. The Middlesbrough scenario just didn't bear thinking about. An amazing second-half turnaround in both games meant that I didn't have to.

It's very often an unexpected goalscorer who turns up trumps in these situations. Mark Lawrenson was that man! Sammy's corner was met by a thumping header from Lawro, who I swear was about six feet above the bar, and flew past Clem. Game on! Come on, let's make sure. Get another goal!

LIV-ER-POOL, LIV-ER-POOL, LIV-ER-POOL!

Four minutes later. Souness flicks the ball overhead into the Spurs penalty-area. Defenders in confusion. Kenny steps in. Slides the ball past Clem!

FUCKIN' GO 'EAD! GET IN! WHAT A FUCKIN' GOAL! GO 'EAD KENNY LAD! AN' NOW YER GONNA BELIEVE US, WE'RE GONNA WIN THE LEAGUE. KENNY DALGLISH IS COOLER THAN THE FONZ! LIV-ER-POOL, LIV-ER-POOL, LIV-ER-POOL!

Okay, I'm no John Motson but I'm not 'alf passionate aren't I?

I think this was the loudest I heard the Kop since St. Etienne. Three minutes from the end Ronnie nearly broke the net as he lashed in the goal that meant we had definitely won the title. The news that came through from Portman Road was good but didn't matter; we'd done it ourselves, in our way, the way it should be done. For the record though, Peter Davenport (good Birkenhead lad that he is) had rattled in a hat-trick in only his fifth appearance for Forest to give them a 3-1 win.

Unbeknown to most people the "old lady", the League Championship trophy had been delivered to Anfield before the match and kept hidden away. It would have been presumptuous and not the Liverpool way for it be known it was there to be presented if we won. Once it was known the trophy was there though it was party time! Of the eight League titles, including this one, I'd seen us win I rate this, alongside the 1975-76 title, as the ones that gave me the most satisfaction. In both seasons we'd had to come from behind to win it. The 1978-79 title was won by, in my opinion, a better team but then I think that was our greatest ever League Championship winning side and our best title, but the 1981-82 season gave me the most satisfaction. Does that make sense? Does anything I ever write in these books make sense? Probably not but I hope you enjoy them.

Middle of the Kop

Middle of the Kop

Middle of the Kop